COMPANION WORKBOOK FOR BUSINESS ORGANIZATIONS: PRACTICAL APPLICATIONS

Christopher Gulinello

Northern Kentucky University, Chase College of Law

Business Organizations: Practical Applications, Workbook

Gulinello, Christopher

Published by:

Vandeplas Publishing, LLC – April 2016

801 International Parkway, 5th Floor
Lake Mary, FL. 32746
USA

www.vandeplaspublishing.com

ISBN 978-1-60042-283-6

Dedications

To my family, here and in Taiwan.

To all the students at NKU-Chase who suffered through early drafts of this book.

CONTENTS

CHAPTER 1

INTRODUCTION TO THIS WORKBOOK

This workbook is a companion to the introductory treatise, BUSINESS ORGANIZATIONS: PRACTICAL APPLICATIONS, which we will refer to as the "Text." The two books together comprise the materials for a comprehensive survey course on business organization law for law students.

The exercises in this workbook are designed to guide you through specific doctrines, concepts, or skills that are important in the practice of business organization law. Naturally, this book does not claim to provide you all the knowledge or skills you will need to practice in the area, but you will find that it gives you a very strong foundation.

I hope you find the approach of this workbook to be an interesting and effective change of pace from typical law-school casebooks. Each exercise in the workbook sends you to relevant readings in the Text and the statutes, to promote active reading of these resources. Some exercises are very simple, but they are important introductions to critical concepts or doctrines. They will provide you the context you need to develop a deeper understanding of the law of business organizations.

Some exercises require to you to carefully read and analyze long, complicated statutes, clauses, contracts, or various other documents. These exercises are different from the typical case-briefing exercise that is the mainstay of many law-school classes. You would probably not be surprised to hear that lawyers spend a great amount of time reading and analyzing long, complicated statutes and documents. You need to start honing these skills in law school.

There are only a few cases in this workbook – just twelve cases to be exact. The exercises for four cases require you to read both the facts of the cases and the judicial opinions. These exercises do not ask you to brief the cases. Instead, they ask you specific questions. This format allows you to read each case with a specific purpose in mind. The exercises for the remaining eight cases only provide the facts of each case. These exercises require you to do your own analysis based on the law you have gleaned from your readings.

The following is a list of resources you will use throughout this workbook. All of these resources (except for the Text) are available on the internet somewhere. In addition, there are many good (and thick) statutory supplements for other business organizations casebooks that contain all of these resources (except the Text, of course).

> **Text:** BUSINESS ORGANIZATIONS: PRACTICAL APPLICATIONS, by Christopher Gulinello – available from Vandeplas Publishing.
>
> **RMBCA:** The Revised Model Business Corporation Act – prepared by the Committee on Corporate Laws of the Section of Business Law, American Bar Association.

RULLCA: The Revised Uniform Limited Liability Company Act – 2006 version of the Uniform Limited Liability Company Act, prepared by the National Conference of Commissioners on Uniform State Laws (now called the Uniform Law Commission).

RUPA: The Revised Uniform Partnership Act – 1997 version of the Uniform Partnership Act, prepared by the National Conference of Commissioners on Uniform State Laws (now called the Uniform Law Commission).

and to a lesser extent:

DGCL: The Delaware General Corporation Law – found in Title 8, Chapter 1 of the Delaware Code.

DLLCA: The Delaware Limited Liability Company Act – found in Title 6, Chapter 18 of the Delaware Code.

Finally, one word of caution: The agreements, clauses, provisions, and other documents in this workbook and the Text are not model documents. Indeed, some of them are flawed. The intent was to expose you to what you might see in practice, not to provide you with the best examples of those documents.

WORKBOOK

CHAPTER 2

IMPORTANT TERMS AND CONCEPTS

CHAPTER 2 – EXERCISES:

---

(1) TEST YOURSELF:

Read Chapter 2 in the Text. Make sure you know and understand the following terms and concepts:

Corporation

Limited liability company

Partnership

Incorporated business organizations

Unincorporated business organizations

Transactions within the firm vs. across markets

Closely-held company

Public company

Private company

Corporate trio

RMBCA

ULLCA and RULLCA

UPA and RUPA

The role of common law on business organizations

The role of Delaware law on business organizations

The role of federal law on business organizations

Internal affairs doctrine

Debt financing

Equity financing

Limited liability

Legal personality

Centralized management

Freely transferable ownership interests

Agency costs

Dispersed ownership

Default rules

Mandatory rules

---

(2) **<u>THE BENEFITS OF FORMING AN LLC OR CORPORATION:</u>**

Refer to the following sections in the Text to help you answer the questions below:

Text §§2-101 et seq., 2-108(a)

Billy is the owner of Billy's Hardware Store. Supplier has sold one dozen snow shovels to the hardware store for $200 on 30-days credit.

One year later, Supplier has not been paid and Billy's Hardware Store has closed down. Supplier tries to recover the $200 directly from Billy himself?

Is Billy personally responsible for the $200 debt?

(a) Assume Billy is the sole owner of Billy's Hardware Store and he did NOT organize the business as a corporation or an LLC.

(b) Assume Billy and Mandy are the co-owners of Billy's Hardware Store and they did NOT organize the business as a corporation or an LLC.

(c) Assume Billy's Hardware Store was incorporated.

(d) Assume Billy's Hardware Store was organized as an LLC.

---

(3) **<u>ECONOMIC AND FINANCIAL CONCEPTS AND TERMS:</u>**

Refer to the following sections in the Text to help you answer the questions below:

Text §2-200 et seq.

Please state the economic concept(s) illustrated by each of the following examples:

(A) Your professor announces that she will be grading the final exam on a curve. She says that if everyone receives the same grade, she will be forced to give everyone an A.

You come up with a brilliant plan: If everyone gets a zero, everyone will get an A, and no one will have to study.

There are 50 students in the class. Why is your professor confident that the students will study, as usual, and that she will not have to give an A to every student?

(B) You have hired a contractor to build an addition to your house. As you are negotiating the contract price, the question comes up about who will acquire the relevant permits. You are, of course, willing to pay for the permit fees, but who will fill out the applications and file them?

(C) Employee works the midnight to 8 a.m. shift at a 24-hour convenience store. He is the only person in the store from midnight to 8 a.m., except for the occasional customer. The employer is concerned that the employee will take cash from the customers for himself without ringing up the sale on the register. The employer is also concerned that employee will stand around every night, doing nothing, instead of taking advantage of down-time to mop the floor, stock the shelves and straighten the magazines.

The employer hangs a sign in front of the register that reads: "Save your receipt and earn points, which you can apply to future purchases." The employer also hires an assistant manager to make sure the employee has stocked the shelves, mopped the floor, and straightened the magazines during his shift.

(D) You want to buy a used car that you found at a local used-car dealer. You are concerned that the car was one of the many cars submerged underwater in the recent hurricane. You are afraid that there is damage to the car's electrical system that will not fully manifest itself until later.

You could pay for a commercial service that provides you with the history of the car. You also consider paying less for the car so that you have money for repairs if the electrical system fails.

(E) You want to begin saving for your retirement by investing in the stock market. You have $20,000 to invest. You invest in ten different companies in ten different industries.

(F) In a local condominium community, the seasonal insurance policy for the community swimming pool ends on Labor Day. There is interest among many of the residents to keep the pool open for another 14 days. They decide to raise money for the extra 14 days of insurance.

They post the following announcement on the clubhouse bulletin board and on the community's website:

> "Let's raise money to pay for the insurance to keep the pool open for two more weeks after Labor Day. If only one-third of our residents contributes $10 each, we will be able to keep the pool open. Contact Bob W."

Despite the widespread interest in keeping the pool open for two more weeks, the community is not able to raise enough money. What is a likely explanation?

(G) You are investing a significant amount of money in your law school education. Why? Why don't people handle their own legal matters? What economic concept explains why people need attorneys?

---

(4) CONCEPTUAL PROBLEM – AGENCY COSTS:

Refer to the following sections in the Text to help you answer the questions below:

> Text §§2-104, 2-109(a), 2-109(b), 2-109(e)

Compare the following three different business organizations. How do the agency problems and costs differ?

> **Company A** is a corporation whose shares are publicly traded on the New York Stock Exchange. Company A has approximately 50,000 shareholders. It also has a shareholder who owns 51% of the stock. The remaining shares are held by the public, with no one shareholder holding any significant number of shares.
>
> **Company B**'s shares are traded on Nasdaq. Company B has approximately 65,000 shareholders. It does not have a single shareholder or shareholder group that owns a significant number of shares.
>
> **Company C** is a small business with three owners and four employees besides the owners. The three owners are very active in the daily

operations of the company. Each owner has the authority to bind the company to contracts with third parties.

---

(5) <u>CONFLICTS OF LAW:</u>

Refer to the following sections in the Text to help you answer the questions below:

Text §2-106(f)

ABC Inc. is incorporated in Northern Kentucky. Over the past decade, its business has shifted to southern Ohio. In addition, for the past four years, its board meetings and shareholders meetings have taken place in Ohio.

One of the shareholders is suing the board for breaching its fiduciary duties to the corporation with respect to a board decision that occurred last year. The shareholder sues in Ohio. Because all the directors live in Ohio, Ohio courts would have personal jurisdiction over them.

Should the Ohio court apply Ohio law or Kentucky law with respect to the fiduciary duty claim?

---

(6) <u>FREE TRANSFERABILITY OF OWNERSHIP INTERESTS:</u>

Refer to the following sections in the Text to help you answer the questions below:

Text §2-108(d), 2-300 et seq.

Janice, Joan, and Jane are friends who are opening a pet food business together. They plan to set up a business organization. Would they prefer the default rule governing their business organization to allow free transferability of ownership interests? Why or why not?

---

(7) <u>FINANCE:</u>

Refer to the following sections in the Text to help you answer the questions below:

Text §2-107 et seq.

XYZ Corp. wants to raise capital to upgrade its machinery. They need $50 million. What are some methods for XYZ Corp. to raise capital?

---

(8) MANDATORY RULES:

Refer to the following sections in the Text to help you answer the questions below:

Text §2-300 et seq.

Imagine the law of your jurisdiction absolutely prohibits corporations from entering into transactions with their directors or executive officers. Is this a good law?

WORKBOOK

CHAPTER 3

ENTITY SELECTION AND FORMATION

CHAPTER 3 – EXERCISES:

---

(1) TAXATION:

Refer to the following sections in the Text to help you answer the questions below:

> Text §§3A-400 et seq., 3A-500 et seq. (the chart in 3A-503 should be particularly helpful).

Jane is starting a business with her friend Lucy that will manufacture and sell products for pregnant women.

She wants to set up a business entity, but she is not sure which entity is best for her situation. You advise her to get tax advice from a professional. She agrees. She will let you know what her tax professional recommends.

Because you want to be prepared for the conversation with the tax professional, you want to run the numbers yourself to get a better idea of how Jane's taxes would be different under Subchapter C, Subchapter K, and Subchapter S.

Determine Jane's tax under each of Subchapter C, Subchapter S, and Subchapter K.

Please assume the following:

> Jane's individual income tax rate is 20%.
>
> The corporate income tax rate for a C-corp is 22%.
>
> C-corp distributions to shareholders are taxed at 15%.
>
> Jane and Lucy expect the business to have revenues of $200,000 next year. They expect expenses to be $40,000, excluding salaries to owners and any FICA expenses related to owners' salaries.
>
> Salaries for Jane and Lucy will be $35,000 each. These are reasonable salaries for their positions.
>
> Jane will own 50% of the business and will be entitled to 50% of the profits.
>
> Jane and Lucy have agreed to distribute all of the profits to the owners as dividends each year (this is separate from the $35,000 they will each receive as salary).

Would the company qualify for S-corp status? What information do you need?

If the S-corp is the most favorable tax regime, but the best entity for management purposes is the LLC, would they need to choose between the S-corp and the LLC?

---

(2) TAXATION REDUX:

Refer to the following sections in the Text to help you answer the questions below:

Text §§3A-403(a), 3A-404

The following provision comes from a shareholders agreement. What is its purpose?

> To provide the Shareholders with sufficient cash flow to pay state and federal income taxes on the income of the Corporation that is taxable to the Shareholders, the Corporation shall pay cash dividends to its Shareholders during each taxable year in an amount equal to at least 40% of the income of the Corporation that is taxable to the shareholders, as determined for federal income tax purposes.

Why might the following provision jeopardize a corporation's S-corp status?

> To provide the Shareholders with sufficient cash flow to pay state and federal income taxes on income of the Corporation that is taxable to the Shareholders, the Corporation shall pay cash dividends to each Shareholder during each taxable year of the Corporation. The amount of the dividend each shareholder will receive shall equal the amount of the Shareholder's must pay in income taxes on the income of the Corporation that is taxable to her as a Shareholder.

---

(3) PROMISE TO BUY SHARES:

Refer to the following provisions to answer the questions below:

RMBCA §6.20

For further help, please refer to the following sections in the Text:

Text §§3B-301, 3B-302

On **January 1**, Jack, Jenny, and Geraldine entered into an agreement to form a corporation. Each of them agreed to invest $10,000 and receive 1/3 of the firm's issued and outstanding shares.

The parties had an attorney form the corporation, but on **March 1**, when it came time for the corporation to issue shares, Geraldine backed out.

The corporation sues Geraldine for $10,000. Geraldine asserts that the corporation has no standing to sue her because it was not a party to the agreement.

Is Geraldine correct?

---

(4) <u>ULTRA VIRES:</u>

Refer to the following provisions to answer the questions below:

RMBCA §3.04

For further help, please refer to the following sections in the Text:

Text §3B-206 in the Text.

ABC Inc.'s articles of incorporation have the following provision:

> The purpose of the corporation is to provide cleaning and janitorial services.

The company's board of directors passed a resolution to open and run a grocery store. The board entered into the following transaction:

> **A five-year lease for an appropriate space for a grocery store.** The lessor was not aware the purpose stated in the company's articles of incorporation. ABC Inc. signed the lease on February 1. The term of the lease begins in three months, on May 1.

Sam, a shareholder in ABC Inc. did not receive news of the board's decision until after it had entered into the lease. He found out on February 15. Sam thought about whether he should take any action. On April 20, Sam filed a shareholder lawsuit against the corporation.

Sam is asking the court to enjoin the lease and declare it void.

What is the likelihood that the court will grant Sam's requests? Is there any other information you want to know?

---

(5) FORMATION:

Refer to the following provisions to answer the questions below:

> RMBCA §§2.02, RULLCA §201

For further help, please refer to the following sections in the Text:

> Text §§3B-100 et seq., 3B-200 et seq., 3B-300 et seq., 3C-100, 3C-200, 3C-300

Your client has asked you to set up a business for her in the state where your law school is located. Here are the details:

Possible Names:

> Acme Enterprises
>
> Coca-Cola Communications
>
> Good Communications

The company will have three owners, each owner will receive one third of the ownership interests.

Set up an LLC or a corporation (your choice).

The company's purpose is to sell smart phones and smart phone accessories.

Must have pass-through taxation.

Registered Office: 100 Bluegrass Lane, Boone Township

Registered Agent: Burt Lancer

Principal place of business: 100 Bluegrass Lane, Boone Township

Your address: 1200 River Road, Old Port

Please draft the articles of incorporation/organization, as you think they should be drafted, for your client's review. Use the forms on the secretary of state website.

Please also be prepared to explain to your client what steps are required to set up the business with the Secretary of State and, once set up, what formalities it must go through to complete the organization.

---

(6) PROMOTER TRANSACTIONS:

Refer to the following sections in the Text to help you answer the questions below:

Text §3B-400 et seq., 3C-700

Your client is a promoter of a business. She is planning to enter into a lease on behalf of the corporation before it is formed. Your firm's most junior associate has drafted the following contract provisions and a board resolution to try to protect your client.

Please read the draft contract clauses. Prepare to explain to your client the level of protection each clause provides and the likelihood the lessor will agree to it.

Read the draft board resolution and explain what level of protection it provides the client.

Provision 1:

If such incorporation is completed by the Closing Date, all terms of the Lease shall be construed to have been made between Seller and the resultant corporation.

Provision 2:

This lease agreement (the "Lease") is entered into this __ day of February, 20___ by and between [Name of promoter] (the "Lessee") and LMN Properties LLC (the "Lessor").

WHEREAS, the Lessee proposes to form a corporation under the laws of the State of __________ to be called ABC Inc. (the "Company) for the purpose of operating a retail clothing store.

WHEREAS, the Lessee wishes to secure on behalf of the Company the right to lease the Premises.

THEREFORE, in consideration of the recitals of this agreement and for one dollar to the Lessor paid by the Lessee the receipt of which is acknowledged, the Lessor agrees to give and does give and grant to the Lessee an option until [date], of leasing the Premises from the Lessor.

Provision 3:

This Lease is deemed made between Lessor and [Name of promoter], individually and on behalf of the corporation to be formed.

Provision 4:

It is expressly understood and agreed between the parties that [Name of promoter], executes this contract on behalf of ABC Inc., a corporation to be formed under the laws of the state of ________, and not on her own behalf.

[Name of promoter] does not warrant or make any representation that the corporation will be formed and will assume no personal liability under this agreement. Lessor agrees to look solely to ABC Inc. as the lessee under this Lease Agreement.

Draft board resolution:

WHEREAS, [Name of promoter], shareholder, director and officer of the Corporation, has entered into a contract on behalf of the corporation before it was formed on [date] for [describe contract] (the "Lease"); and

WHEREAS, the board of directors has full knowledge of the extent of the Lease and deems it to be beneficial to the corporation;

RESOLVED, the board of directors fully approves and hereby adopts the Lease; and

RESOLVED FURTHER, the president and secretary are hereby authorized to do all acts necessary to carry out the terms of the Lease.

---

(7) <u>IS THERE A PARTNERSHIP?</u>

Refer to the following provisions to answer the questions below:

RUPA §202

For further help, please refer to the following sections in the Text:

Text §3D-200 et seq.

A) Two law professors agree to create and operate a law blog together. They agree to sell advertising on the blog, use the proceeds to pay for the expenses, and share whatever remains.

B) Two siblings own a townhouse together and rent it out. The older sister takes care of almost all of the management of the townhouse. The two split the net proceeds of the rental 60/40, with 60% going to the older sister.

C) XYZ Corp. rented a storefront to ABC LLC. The terms of the lease require ABC to pay minimum monthly rental of $400 plus a 25% share of the annual profits.

D) Company A was experiencing financial difficulties. It needed a loan but did not have good credit or sufficient collateral. Firm X agreed to "lend" securities to Company A to use as collateral to obtain a loan from a bank. The arrangement provided that:

> Company A would return the securities to Firm X after a certain period of time.
>
> While Company A was using of the securities, Firm X would receive 20% of Company A's profits, with an agreed minimum payment of $1,000,000 and a maximum of $2,000,000.
>
> Company A was required to provide Firm X with monthly, detailed reports regarding the operations and finances of the company.
>
> Company A was forbidden from taking on any indebtedness of more than 90 days or $10,000, without the permission of Firm X.
>
> Company A was required to submit all new business proposals to Firm X for approval. Firm X only had the power to veto any transaction they considered "highly speculative or injurious."

---

(8) LIABILITY OF PARTNERS IN AN LLP:

Refer to the following sections in the Text to help you answer the questions below:

Text §3D-400 et seq.

Marvin is a partner in an LLP. The LLP is a public accounting firm. The LLP is involved in the following four disputes:

(1) A paper supplier claims the LLP has breached a contract.

(2) A client claims one of Marvin's partners has committed malpractice.

(3) A client claims a junior accountant working under Marvin committed malpractice.

(4) A client claims Marvin has committed malpractice.

Jurisdiction A has the following liability rules for partners in LLPs:

> A partner of a limited liability partnership is not liable or accountable, directly or indirectly, including by way of indemnification, contribution, or otherwise, for any debts, obligations, or liabilities of or chargeable to the partnership or another partner, whether arising in tort, contract, or otherwise, which are incurred, created, or assumed by the partnership while the partnership is a limited liability partnership solely by reason of being a partner in the partnership or acting or omitting to act in such capacity or rendering professional services or otherwise participating, as an employee, consultant, contractor, or otherwise, in the conduct of the business or activities of the partnership.
>
> This section does not affect:
>
> (1) The liability of a partner of a limited liability partnership for debts and obligations of the partnership that arise from any negligent or wrongful act or omission of the partner or of another partner, employee, or agent of the partnership if the partner is negligent in appointing, directly supervising, or cooperating with the other partner, employee, or agent; or

(2) The liability of the partnership for all its debts and obligations or the availability of the entire assets of the partnership to satisfy its debts and obligations.

What is the potential liability for Marvin under the law of Jurisdiction A?

Is Jurisdictions A's approach different from RUPA's approach? RUPA §306(c)

---

(9) INVESTING SOMETHING OTHER THAN CASH

Refer to the following provisions to answer the questions below:

RMBCA §6.21, RULLCA §402

For further help, please refer to the following sections in the Text:

Text §3A-600 et seq.

Alice, Betty and Carol are forming a business entity together.

Alice will contribute $100,000 in **cash**.

Betty will contribute her **financial expertise** for the next year.

Carol will contribute a **plot of land** she acquired years ago for $80,000, but which is now worth somewhere between $130,000 and $150,000.

Are the prospective shareholders of a corporation allowed to invest something other than cash in exchange for stock?

Are the prospective members of an LLC allowed to invest something other than cash in exchange for membership interests?

Does the fact pattern raise any other issues?

---

(10) USING A NEW NAME AND CROSSING THE BORDER:

Refer to the following sections in the Text to help you answer the questions below:

Text §§3B-304, 3B-305

You helped Alice organize an LLC called "Alice Foods LLC" under the laws of State X. Alice Foods LLC produces a vegetarian substitute for chicken thighs, that it calls "Cluck Thighs."

Alice tells you that she wants the LLC to open a restaurant in the State of X that specializes in dishes made with Cluck Thighs. She wants to call the restaurant "No Harm, No Fowl."

She also says she wants her company to start producing Cluck Thighs across the river in State Y because rent is much cheaper there.

Does Alice Foods LLC need to go through any formalities to accomplish the proposed courses of action?

---

(11) THE DEEP-POCKET PARTNER:

Refer to the following provisions to answer the questions below:

RUPA §307(d)

For further help, please refer to the following sections in the Text:

Text §3D-200

Your client claims the general partnership of XYZ owes her $100,000 for breach of contract, but refuses to pay. Based on the information you have, XYZ is a very profitable business with millions of dollars of assets.

XYZ has one high-profile partner who is a multi-billionaire.[1] Your client suggests that you bring a lawsuit against the high-profile partner for the entire $100,000.

What is your opinion on the client's suggested course of action?

---

[1] Not a very realistic fact pattern, you say? Yes, maybe, but please suspend your disbelief.

(12) BANK LOAN:

Refer to the following provisions to answer the questions below:

RMBCA §6.22, RULLCA §304(a), RUPA §§306, 307

For further help, please refer to the following sections in the Text:

Text §3A-200, 3D-202, 3D-403

Bank Z lends money to small businesses. Its form loan agreement requires the owners of any business entity that borrows money to co-sign the loan agreement in their own names.

Why would Bank Z require corporate shareholders and LLC members to co-sign the loan agreement in their own names?

Why would Bank Z require the partners of a general partnership to co-sign the loan agreement in their own names?

Why would Bank Z require the partners of a limited liability partnership to co-sign the loan agreement in their own names?

WORKBOOK

CHAPTER 4

RAISING CAPITAL

CHAPTER 4 – EXERCISES:

---

(1) AUTHORIZED SHARES:

Refer to the following provisions to answer the questions below:

RMBCA §§6.01, 6.21

For further help, please refer to the following sections in the Text:

Text §§4A-204(a), 4A-204(b), 4A-205(a)

XYZ Corp. has 10,000 shares of stock authorized in is articles of incorporation, of which 5,000 are issued and outstanding. The articles do not specify what type of stock the authorized stock is.

The board of directors passes a resolution to issue and sell 1,000 shares of common stock for $10 per share.

Does the board need shareholder approval?

Would your answer change if the board wanted to issue and sell 8,000 common shares? Why or why not?

Would your answer change if the board wanted to issue and sell 1,000 shares of stock with a dividend preference? Why or why not?

---

(2) THE RESIDUAL CLAIM:

Refer to the following sections in the Text to help you answer the questions below:

Text §§4A-203, 4A-204(a)

ABC Inc. has 100,000 shares authorized in is articles of incorporation, of which 10,000 are issued and outstanding. The company has no preferred stock.

The board passes a resolution to distribute $100,000 to the shareholders in the form of a cash dividend.

Carla owns 500 shares of ABC Inc. common stock. How much will she receive of the $100,000 distribution?

---

(3) AUTHORIZING PREFERRED STOCK:

Refer to the following sections in the Text to help you answer the questions below:

Text §4A-205 et seq.

Also refer to the following provisions:

RMBCA §§6.02

Be prepared to explain the function and significance of the following provision in General Electric's certificate of incorporation?

> The Board of Directors is authorized, subject to limitations prescribed by law and the provisions of this subsection . . . , to provide for the issuance of the preferred shares in series, and by filing a certificate pursuant to the Business Corporation Law, to establish the number of shares to be included in each such series, and to fix the designation, relative rights, preferences and limitations of the shares of each such series. . . .

---

(4) TERMS OF PREFERRED STOCK:

Refer to the following sections in the Text to help you answer the questions below:

Text §4A-204(b)

Also refer to the following provisions:

RMBCA §§6.01(c)-(f)

Explain the purpose and function of each of the following terms of the preferred stock of AmTrust Financial Services Inc. Make sure you use the proper terminology.

Term 1:

"The Series A Preferred Stock will rank senior to our common stock and any other junior stock (as defined herein) with respect to the payment of dividends and distributions of assets upon liquidation, dissolution or winding-up . . .."

Term 2:

"Holders of Series A Preferred Stock will be entitled to receive only when, as and if declared by the Board of Directors of AmTrust or a duly authorized committee of the Board, out of lawfully available funds for the payment of dividends, ... cash dividends from the original issue date, quarterly on the 15th day of March, June, September and December of each year, commencing on September 15, 2013."

Term 3:

"So long as any Series A Preferred Stock remain outstanding for any dividend period, unless the full dividends for the latest completed dividend period on all outstanding Series A Preferred Stock . . . have been declared and paid (or declared and a sum sufficient for the payment thereof has been set aside) . . . no dividend shall be paid or declared on our common stock, or any other junior stock . . . ."

Term 4:

"[I]f our Board of Directors, or a duly authorized committee of the Board, does not declare a dividend on the Series A Preferred Stock payable in respect of any dividend period before the related dividend payment date, such dividend . . . . will not be payable and we will have no obligation to pay a dividend for that dividend period on the dividend payment date or at any future time or to pay interest with respect to such dividends . . .."

Term 5:

"Whenever dividends on any Series A Preferred Stock shall have not been declared and paid for the equivalent of six or more dividend periods, whether or not for consecutive dividend periods (a "nonpayment event"), the holders of the Series A Preferred Stock, voting together as a single class with holders of any and all other series of voting preferred stock (as defined below) then outstanding, will be entitled to vote for the election of a total of two additional members of the Board of Directors of AmTrust . . .."

Term 6:

"The Series A Preferred Stock is not redeemable prior to June 10, 2018. On and after that date, the Series A Preferred Stock will be redeemable at our option, in whole or in part, upon not less than 30 days nor more than 60 days notice, at a redemption price equal to $25 per share plus declared and unpaid dividends . . .."

Term 7:

"Holders will not have the right to convert Series A Preferred Stock into, or exchange Series A Preferred Stock for, any other securities or property of AmTrust."

---

(5) ISSUING DEBT SECURITIES:

Refer to the following sections in the Text to help you answer the questions below:

Text §4A-300 et seq.

Your client is a corporation. It wants to issue debt securities, but the articles of incorporation do not authorize the issuance of debt securities – they are completely silent on the matter.

Does the corporation need to amend the articles to issue the debt securities?

---

(6) TERMS OF DEBT SECURITIES:

Refer to the following sections in the Text to help you answer the questions below:

Text §4A-302

Please read the following summary description of debt securities issued by Walgreens and answer the questions below:

> $1,300,000,000
> WALGREENS
> 4.875% Notes due 2013
>
> Interest on the notes will be paid semi-annually in arrears on February 1 and August 1 of each year, beginning on February 1, 2009. The notes will mature on August 1, 2013. We may redeem the notes, at any time in whole or from time to time in part, at the redemption price described in this prospectus supplement. If a change of control triggering event as described in this prospectus supplement occurs, unless we have exercised

> our option to redeem the notes, we will be required to offer to repurchase the notes at a purchase price equal to 101% of the principal amount of the notes plus accrued and unpaid interest to the date of purchase.
>
> The notes will be our unsecured senior debt obligations and will rank equally with all of our other unsecured senior indebtedness from time to time outstanding. The notes will not be convertible or exchangeable. . . .

Questions:

1. **Is the debt secured or unsecured?**
2. **When will the securities mature?**
3. **When will the company make interest payments? When will it repay the principal?**
4. **What is the ranking of the debt security with respect to other debt securities that the company has issued in the past (or may issue in the future)?**
5. **Does the company have a right redeem the securities before maturity?**
6. **Why are these securities called "notes," rather than "bonds" or "debentures?"**

---

(7) <u>RAISING CAPITAL – SALE OF EQUITY INTERESTS:</u>

Refer to the following sections in the Text to help you answer the questions below:

Text §4A-400 et seq.

Your client is a private corporation formed under the laws of the state of _______. The company needs to raise capital. It proposes posting a notice on an internet message board seeking investors.

Your client's founder envisions that she and her management team would run the company and that the investors they find would only be involved in voting on major, fundamental transactions.

What is your advice to your client?

Does it matter whether the company is a corporation, an LLC, or a partnership? Why or why not?

---

(8) DIFFERENT CLASSES OF SHARES:

Refer to the following sections in the Text to help you answer the questions below:

Text §4A-204(e)

Alpha Corp. is your client. It is incorporated in ____ and has pass-through tax status under federal tax laws.

Alpha Corp. proposes issuing a new class of stock that has a preferred right to dividends.

What crucial piece of advice do you need to give your client?

---

(9) ALLOCATION OF PROFITS AND LOSSES:

Refer to the following sections in the Text to help you answer the questions below:

Text §§4B-202(a), 4A-203

Also refer to the following provisions

RULLCA §404(a)

Albert and Victoria are investors in an LLC. They are the only two members.

Albert contributed $100,000 in exchange for his membership interest.

Victoria contributed $1,000 in exchange for her membership interest.

The company made $100,000 in profits last year.

How much of the profits will be allocated to each member, assuming the operating agreement is silent on the matter?

If this were a corporation, would the default rules create a different result?

---

(10) <u>CONSIDERATION FOR EQUITY INTERESTS:</u>

Refer to the following provisions to answer the questions below:

RMBCA §6.21(b), RULLCA §402, RUPA §202

For further help, please refer to the following sections in the Text:

Text §4A-205(b)

Four friends are planning to form a business entity together:

Alicia will invest $150,000 cash in exchange for equity interests.

Bertha will license her trademark to the business in exchange for equity interests.

Camilla will invest $100,000 cash in exchange for equity interests, but she does not have the cash now. She will get the equity interests immediately, and will pay the money 6 months later.

Dylan will agree to be the CEO for the company in exchange for equity interests.

In addition, the law firm that is taking care of the formation and the relevant agreements has agreed to accept equity interests as payment.

Does the law permit the business entity to issue equity interests for each of the different forms of consideration above?

---

(11) <u>CAPITAL ACCOUNTS:</u>

Refer to the following sections in the Text to help you answer the questions below:

Text §§4B-202 et seq., 4B-203, 4B-204, 4A-204(e)

Angel and Brett are the only two members of the LLC. In the operating agreement, they agree to **share profits equally**.

They also agree to **share losses** as follows: Angel – 30%; Brett – 70%.

Would this type of arrangement be conducive to pass through taxation? Explain.

Please fill in their capital account balances after each transaction.

Angel invests $12,000 and Brett invests $14,000 in exchange for membership interests:

Angel's capital: Brett's capital:

The company suffered a loss in the first year of $5,000:

Angel's capital: Brett's capital:

The company made a profit of $16,000 in the second year:

Angel's capital: Brett's capital:

Angel and Brett each receive a $1,000 distribution from company:

Angel's capital: Brett's capital:

---

(12) DOES ANYONE OWE MONEY?

Refer to the following provisions to answer the questions below:

RUPA §401(b)

For further help, please refer to the following sections in the Text:

Text §4C-202 et seq.

Alice and Bob decided to open a food truck together. They did not form an LLC, a corporation, or any other business entity that requires a filing with the secretary of state.

Alice put $50,000 into the business and Bob put in $10,000. Based on their investments, their capital accounts would be as follows:

Alice's Capital:

20,000

Bob's Capital:

10,000

In the first year, their business lost $26,000.

After the first year, how would their capital accounts change?

If the parties decide to settle up after their first year, and walk away from the business, what monetary obligations would they have toward each other?

---

(13) HOW MUCH IS THE COMPANY WORTH:

Refer to the following sections in the Text to help you answer the questions below:

Text §§4D-100, 4D-200, 4D-300, 4D-500

ABC Inc. manufactures and sells henways. The shareholders are considering an offer to purchase all of their shares in the company. They want to know if the offer is a good one, but they have no idea what the market value is for their company.

You have the following information from the shareholders' financial advisors:

The book value of the company's **assets** is: 9,500,000

The market value of the company's **assets** is about: 10,000,000

The total **liabilities** of the company are: 7,500,000

The company should realize **profits** each year for the next 5 years as follows:

Year 1: 1,250,000

Year 2: 1,600,000

Year 3:	1,800,000
Year 4:	1,300,000
Year 5:	1,000,000

At the end of the 5 years, the company will only have **liquidation value** – projected to be $2,400,000.

An investor in an equally risky investment would want a **25% return** on investment.

How much is the company worth?

WORKBOOK

CHAPTER 5

GOVERNANCE MECHANICS: DECISION-MAKING IN BUSINESS ORGANIZATIONS

CHAPTER 5 – EXERCISES:

SHAREHOLDER VOTING

---

(1) CONCEPTUAL PROBLEM:

Read the following sections in the Text:

Text §5A-100 et seq.

In a corporation, who would make the make the decisions listed below? The executive officers? The other employees/agents? The board of directors? The shareholders?

A decision to buy a ream of paper.

A decision to borrow a significant amount of money to finance the construction of a large retail outlet.

A decision to merge the corporation into another corporation.

---

(2) LEARNING THE STATUTE:

SHAREHOLDER VOTING IN GENERAL:

Refer to the following provisions to answer the questions below:

RMBCA §§7.01, 7.02(a), 7.04(a), 7.05(a),(b)&(c), 7.06(a)&(b), 7.07(a)&(b), 7.25(a)&(c), 7.27(a)

For further help, please refer to the following sections in the Text:

Text §§5A-101, 5A-102 et seq., 5A-105 et seq., 5A-201 et seq., 5A-205, 5A-210

How often must a corporation hold a shareholders meeting?

Who can call for a special shareholders meeting?

Must the notice of the <u>annual</u> shareholders meeting specify the purpose of the meeting?

Must the notice of the special shareholders meeting specify the purpose of the meeting?

Can a shareholder waive late or defective notice? How?

Can the shareholders decide on a matter without actually holding a meeting?

What is the quorum for shareholders meetings?

Can we provide for a greater or smaller quorum?

How many votes are required to approve an action?

Can we provide for a greater or lower approval requirement?

Election and removal of directors:

Refer to the following provisions to answer the questions below:

RMBCA §§7.28(a),(b)&(c), 8.04, 8.08(a),(b)&(c), 8.10(a),(b)&(c)

For further help, please refer to the following sections in the Text:

Text §§5A-103, 5A-104, 5A-202 et seq., 5A-204, 5A-502(b)

How are directors elected?

Can we give the shareholders of a certain class of shares the right to elect a certain number of directors?

How can directors be removed? What special provisions protect the representation of minority shareholders?

How do we fill a vacancy on the board?

Amending the articles and bylaws:

Refer to the following provisions to answer the questions below:

RMBCA §§10.03(a)&(b), 10.05, 10.06, 10.20, 10.21(a)

For further help, please refer to the following sections in the Text:

Text §§5A-206 et seq., 5A-207 et seq.

How can the corporation amend its articles of incorporation?

Can the board amend the articles without shareholder approval?

Can the shareholders amend the articles without a board approval?

How can the corporation amend its bylaws?

Do the board and the shareholders each have a right to amend the bylaws without approval of the other?

If so, could the board nullify a shareholder bylaw amendment?

---

(3) STRAIGHT AND CUMULATIVE VOTING:

Refer to the following sections in the Text to help you answer the questions below:

Text §§5A-202 et seq., 5A-203

Also refer to the following provisions:

RMBCA §7.28

(A) XYZ Inc. has a board of directors comprised of 7 members. XYZ Inc. has 1,000 shares of common stock issued and outstanding. Alice owns 200 shares and Betty owns 301 shares. Charlie owns the remaining 499 shares.

Alice and Betty enter into a shareholders agreement where they agree to pool their votes to **vote for seven specific nominees** for board seats: themselves (two nominees), their spouses (two nominees), one common friend, who is also a trusted financial advisor (one nominee); and their children (two nominees) [each has only one child].

If the election is a straight-voting process, how many of their nominees will Alice and Betty be able to elect? Please explain.

(B) ABC Inc. has a board of directors consisting of 7 members. ABC Inc. has 1,000 shares of common stock authorized in its articles, 630 of which are issued and outstanding. All 7 of the board seats are up for election this year. Please assume the election process will be **cumulative voting**.

(i) **How many shares would a shareholder or a group of shareholders need to ensure they could elect one member of the board (assuming all other shares will be voted collectively)?**

(ii) **How would your answer change if the board was staggered and only 4 director seats were up for election this year?**

(iii) **How many shares would be needed to ensure election of a majority of the board (cumulative voting, no staggered board)?**

(iv) **Assuming Ms. X holds 250 shares, how will she cast her votes in the following scenario (cumulative voting, no staggered board)?** [Please fill in the table below]

	Nominee X1*	**Nominee X2***	**Nominee X3***	**Nominee X4***	**Nominee X5***		**Nominee A**	**Nominee B**	**Nominee C**	**Nominee D**	**Nominee E**
Ms. X's votes											
Other Shareholder votes											

* Indicates a nominee that Ms. X supports.

---

(4) SHAREHOLDERS MEETINGS:

Refer to the following sections in the Text to help you answer the questions below:

Text §§5A-201 et seq., 5A-210

Please read the two documents below and answer the following questions:

What are these documents and how are they different?

Why are they used? Are they used frequently?

Are they legally valid?

[Title of Document]

The undersigned shareholder of XYZ Inc., an [RMBCA State] corporation, and holder of the number of shares set opposite my name, hereby consents to the following resolution:

RESOLVED, the corporation shall amend its articles of incorporation to increase its authorized capital to ten thousand (10,000) shares.

Dated: ________ 2015

Signature: ________________________

Print name:________________________ Number of XYZ Inc.'s shares owned: ______

[Title of Document]

The undersigned shareholder of XYZ Inc., an [RMBCA State] corporation, and holder of the number of shares set opposite my name, hereby waives any and all notice required by laws, or the Articles of Incorporation or Bylaws of the corporation, and do hereby consent to the holding of an annual meeting of shareholders of the corporation, on May 25, 2015, at 10:00 A.M., or any adjournment or adjournments, at the office of the Corporation, at *5155 Willoughby Lane, Cedar Township.*

Dated: ________ 2015

Signature: ________________________

Print name:________________________ Number of XYZ Inc.'s shares owned: ______

---

(5) **PROXIES:**

Refer to the following sections in the Text to help you answer the questions below:

Text §5A-209 et seq.

Also refer to the following provisions:

RMBCA §7.22

Review the three proxy appointments below and answer these questions:

How do the three appointments of proxy differ from each other?

Do the expiration dates make them irrevocable? If not, how could we make them irrevocable? Give some examples of situations when parties would want irrevocable proxies.

If they had no expiration date, how long would they be effective? Why does the law provide a default expiration date?

Does the shareholder need to expressly state that this proxy revokes all previous proxies?

See next page for the three proxy forms

Appointment of Proxy

The undersigned shareholder (the "Shareholder") of XYZ Inc. (the "Company") hereby appoints Ms. Polly Proxy as proxy, with full power of substitution, for and in the name of the Shareholder to attend all shareholder meetings of the Company and to act, vote, and execute consents with respect to any or all shares of the Company belonging to Shareholder.

This appointment may be revoked by the Shareholder at any time, but if not revoked will continue in effect until December 31, 2015.

Sally Shareholder 2/13/2015

Sally Shareholder

Appointment of Proxy

The undersigned shareholder (the "Shareholder") of XYZ Inc. (the "Company") hereby appoints Ms. Polly Proxy as proxy, with full power of substitution, for and in the name of the Shareholder to attend the annual shareholders meeting of the Company to be held on March 12, 2015 and to act, vote, at such meeting and any adjournment thereof with respect to any or all shares of the Company belonging to Shareholder.

Any previous appointment by the Shareholder for such meeting is hereby revoked.

Sally Shareholder 2/13/2015

Sally Shareholder

Appointment of Proxy

The undersigned shareholder (the "Shareholder") of XYZ Inc. (the "Company") hereby appoints Ms. Polly Proxy as proxy, with full power of substitution, for and in the name of the Shareholder to attend the annual shareholders meeting of the Company to be held on March 12, 2015 and to act, vote, at such meeting and any adjournment thereof with respect to any or all shares of the Company belonging to Shareholder as directed below and in her discretion as to other business matters that may properly come before the meeting or any adjournment thereof:

To vote FOR the following persons to be directors of the Company:

Ursula Ursine
Barry Bovine
Lois Lupine

and to withhold votes for any other nominees.

Any previous appointment by the Shareholder for such meeting is hereby revoked.

Sally Shareholder 2/13/2015

Sally Shareholder

(6) RIGHT TO VOTE AT SHAREHOLDER MEETINGS:

Refer to the following provisions to answer the questions below:

RMBCA §§7.05, 7.07

For further help, please refer to the following sections in the Text:

Text §5A-201 et seq.

On **February 5**, Sally Shareholder sold and transferred her shares in Corporation (by indorsing the share certificate) to Prudence Purchaser.

On **February 6**, Prudence Purchaser submitted the share certificate (properly indorsed by Sally Shareholder) to the corporate secretary of Corporation.

On **February 10**, the corporate secretary promptly removed Sally Shareholder from the shareholder ledger and entered Prudence Purchaser's name. The corporate secretary also issued a new share certificate to Prudence Purchaser in her name.

Earlier, on **January 15**, the board of directors of Corporation had approved a record date of February 1 for the annual shareholders meeting (the **annual meeting to occur on March 1**).

> **Who should receive the notice of the shareholders meeting and who has the right to vote the shares at the meeting - Sally or Prudence?**
>
> **How could you structure the transaction (aside from changing the dates of the transfer) to ensure Prudence had a right to vote the shares at the annual meeting?**

---

(7) ACCESS TO CORPORATE BOOKS AND RECORDS:

Refer to the following provisions to answer the questions below:

RMBCA §§16.01, 16.02, 16.03, 16.20

For further help, please refer to the following sections in the Text:

Text §5A-211

Read the following fact pattern and provide the information your supervisor wants (at the end of the fact pattern).

Ms. Client comes to your law firm for advice. She is a shareholder of XYZ Corp. and she suspects the board of directors has lied to the shareholders in connection with a merger with ABC Inc. in 2014.

She wants access to some corporate books and records to help her discover the truth. She would also like to nominate herself for a board seat and needs to communicate with the other shareholders to solicit proxies.

Ms. Client is not listed as a shareholder in the company's stockholder ledger because she placed her shares in a voting trust a few years ago.

She wants access to the following records:

1) The minutes of the board meeting of June 12, 2014 discussing and approving the merger with ABC Inc.
2) The minutes of the shareholder meeting of July 15, 2014 approving the merger with ABC Inc.
3) The XYZ bylaws;
4) A list of the shareholders of XYZ Inc.; and
5) The most recent financial statements of XYZ Inc.

Your supervisor asks you to research whether Ms. Client will have right to access the documents and obtain photocopies or electronic copies of them.

---

(8) SHAREHOLDER VOTING ARRANGEMENTS:

Refer to the following provisions to answer the questions below:

RMBCA §§7.30, 7.31

For further help, please refer to the following sections in the Text:

Text §§5A-208 et seq., 5A-209 et seq.

Please read the contract below and answer these questions:

What kind of shareholder agreement is it?

Why did the parties make a proxy part of the contract?

Will the proxy be irrevocable?

What purpose does clause 4, "Legend," serve?

Does the contract envision filing the document with the corporation? Does law require the parties to file the agreement with the corporation?

Is clause 6 necessary?

What is the duration of the agreement? Why do you think it has that duration?

This _____________ agreement ("Agreement") is made this day, June 12, 2015, by and between, __________, residing at ___________ ("Seller") and ______________, residing at ___________ ("Purchaser").

WHEREAS, Seller is the sole shareholder of the Class A Common Stock of Linton Corp., a corporation duly organized and existing under the laws of the State of __ having its principal place of business at 1530 Willoughby St., Queen City, ___ ("Corporation").

WHEREAS, Seller and Purchaser have entered into a stock purchase agreement dated June 12, 2015 whereby Seller has agreed to sell to Purchaser, and Purchaser has agreed to purchase from Seller, Twenty Five Percent (25%) of Seller's Class A Common Stock of the Corporation ("Stock Purchase Agreement").

WHEREAS, Seller and Purchaser desire, upon completion of the transfer contemplated by the Stock Purchase Agreement, to vote all the Class A Common Stock of the Corporation as one voting bloc and, to that end, have made this Agreement a condition precedent to the closing of the sale under the Stock Purchase Agreement.

NOW, THEREFORE, the parties agree as follows:

1. **Voting:** The Parties hereby agree that for all matters that come to the shareholder of the Corporation, Seller will have the exclusive right to vote all shares of the Corporation's Class A Common Stock that is now owned or may hereafter be acquired by Purchaser, and to execute all consents in lieu of meetings, in the sole discretion of Seller. Seller agrees to vote all of the Corporation's Class A Common Stock subject to this agreement (including any Stock which Seller owns individually), and to execute all consents of Shareholders in lieu of meetings, in the same manner.

2. **Proxies.** Purchaser agrees to execute and deliver to Seller a proxy in the form of Schedule A attached to this Agreement and agrees that such proxy shall irrevocably appoint Seller as Purchaser's proxy to vote Purchaser's Class A Common Stock in accordance with the terms of this Agreement. Purchaser acknowledges that such proxy is coupled with an interest.

3. **Rights and Obligations Upon Transfer.** All subsequent transferees of Class A Common Stock from the Purchaser will also be bound by the terms of this Agreement. The Purchaser shall not sell, assign, transfer, pledge, hypothecate, mortgage or dispose of, by gift or otherwise, any shares of the Corporation's Class A Common Stock unless the person or other entity acquiring such stock shall first agree in writing, delivered to

all parties to this Agreement, to be bound by all the terms of this Agreement with respect to such stock, to the same extent as the Purchaser. The parties to this Agreement agree that any sale or transfer made contrary to the provisions of this section shall be null and void.

4. **Legend.** Upon the execution of this Agreement, and during the term, each certificate evidencing Class A Common Stock held by a Shareholder shall conspicuously bear the following legend: THE SHARES REPRESENTED BY THIS CERTIFICATE ARE SUBJECT TO A SHAREHOLDERS VOTING AGREEMENT AND PROXY APPOINTMENT BETWEEN ________ AND DATED _______. A COPY OF THE AGREEMENT IS ON FILE AT THE OFFICE OF THIS CORPORATION.

5. **Filings.** Seller shall cause signed copies of this Agreement to be filed with the Corporation.

6. **Injunctive Relief.** The parties recognize and agree that the agreements contained herein are reasonable and necessary to protect the rights and interests of all of them, that any breach of this Agreement will result in irreparable injury and harm to the non-breaching parties, that the ascertainment of damages in the event of any breach of any covenant or agreement contained in this Agreement would be difficult if not impossible, and that the non-breaching parties will be without an adequate remedy at law in the event of such a breach. Therefore, in addition to, and without limiting any other remedy or right provided by law or at equity, the parties agree and consent that any party shall be entitled to: (i) specific enforcement of the provisions of this Agreement against any breaching party, or (ii) temporary, preliminary and permanent injunctions to prevent a breach of, or a contemplated breach of, this Agreement by any party, or to otherwise enforce any of the provisions contained in this Agreement against any party. Each party further agrees that, in any action by any other party or parties hereto to enforce this Agreement by specific enforcement, or temporary, preliminary or permanent injunctions or orders, such party or parties will not assert that such other parties have an adequate remedy at law.

7. **Term & Termination.** This Agreement will have a term of 10 years. Otherwise, this agreement will terminate by mutual agreement of the Seller and Purchaser or upon the death of Seller.

8. **Governing Law.** This Agreement shall be governed by and construed in accordance with the laws of the State of ___. Wherever possible, each provision of this Agreement shall be interpreted in such manner as to be effective and valid under applicable law, but if any provision hereof shall be prohibited by or invalid under any such law, such provision shall be ineffective to the extent of such prohibition or invalidity, without invalidating or nullifying the remainder of such provision or any other provisions of this Agreement.

9. **Entire Agreement; Amendment; Waiver.** This Agreement and the agreements expressly referenced herein constitute the entire agreement between the parties with respect to the subject matter, and supersedes all prior written agreements and all contemporaneous oral agreements or understandings between the parties and may not be subsequently changed or terminated orally. No amendment, termination or waiver of this Agreement will be valid unless in writing and signed by all parties. A waiver on one

occasion shall not constitute a waiver on any future occasion.

IN WITNESS WHEREOF, Seller and Purchaser have executed this Agreement as of the date and year first written above.

[Name of Seller]
Signature: ____________________.

[Name of Purchaser]
Signature: ____________________.

Schedule A

IRREVOCABLE PROXY

I, ___________, the undersigned, being the owner of shares of Class A Common Stock of Linton Corp., a corporation duly organized and existing under the laws of the State of __ ("Corporation"), do hereby constitute and appoint ***[Name of Seller]*** as my true and lawful attorney, to vote as my proxy all my shares in the Corporation, with full power of substitution for the period set forth below, with respect to any matter submitted to a vote of the shareholders of the Corporation at any and all meetings, regular or special, or any adjournments that may be held during such period, and to execute any actions by written consent of Shareholders in lieu of any meetings, giving and granting to my said attorneys all of the powers the undersigned would possess if personally present.

This proxy shall continue in effect for a period of ___________ years from the date specified below.

I hereby revoke all previous proxies, if any.

This proxy is irrevocable and coupled with an interest.

___________*[date]*.

[Name of Shareholder]
Signature: ____________________

---

(9) MORE SHAREHOLDER VOTING ARRANGEMENTS:

Refer to the following provisions to answer the questions below:

RMBCA §§7.30, 7.31, 7.32

For further help, please refer to the following sections in the Text:

Text §§5A-208 et seq., 5A-213 et seq., and Chapter 3, §3A-404

Clarissa Client has presented you with a draft Shareholders Agreement that was prepared by one of her fellow shareholders. She asks you to review it.

Are the provisions legally enforceable?

Any red flags about S-corp status?

This agreement is made on ________, 20___ by and among __________________ (the "Corporation") and the undersigned shareholders of the Corporation (the "Shareholders" collectively, or the "Shareholder" individually)

The Corporation and each of the Shareholders agrees as follows:

(1) The corporation shall have three directors. Each Shareholder, so long as he or she owns shares in the Corporation, will have the right to serve as a director of the Corporation or to designate a person to serve as director. The Shareholder or any such person named by the Shareholder must be reasonably capable of performing the duties of a director.

(2) Each Shareholder, so long as he or she owns shares in the Corporation, will have the right, but will not be required, to serve as an officer of the Corporation. The compensation paid to each Shareholder during each calendar year for his or her services as an officer of the Corporation will be equal to the compensation paid to each other Shareholder of the corporation for services as an officer. From time to time, the Board of Directors shall determine the titles and duties of each Shareholder employed by the Corporation.

(3) The Corporation shall pay each Shareholder a dividend in an amount equal to her individual income tax obligations for undistributed earnings of the Corporation because of the Corporation's S-Corp status.

(4) The Shareholders agree to vote their shares in such a way as to give effect to the terms of this agreement.

IN WITNESS WHEREOF, the parties have executed this Agreement on the date indicated above.

X________________________________ X________________________________

[Shareholder's name] *[Shareholder's name]*

X________________________________ X________________________________

[Shareholder's name] *[Shareholder's name]*

[Corporation's name]

By: ____________________

[name and title of person signing on behalf of the corporation]

(10) <u>AMENDING THE ARTICLES OF INCORPORATION:</u>

Refer to the following provisions to answer the questions below:

RMBCA §§10.01 – 10.06, 13.02

For further help, please refer to the following sections in the Text:

Text §§5A-207 et seq.

Please read the board minutes and the articles of incorporation below. Answer the following questions:

(A) Will the shareholders have a right to vote on the board resolution to register as a foreign corporation in Indiana? Explain.

(B) Will the shareholders have a right to vote on the board resolution to change the company's name? Explain.

(C) Which classes of shares have a right to vote on the board resolution to change Article 3, Section 1 (regarding authorized capital for each of the three classes of stock)? Explain. Hint: Think of this amendment as three separate issues for shareholder vote.

(D) Which classes of shares have a right to vote on the board resolution to change Article 3, Section 2, Part A (regarding the preferred dividend)? Explain.

(E) Which classes of shares have a right to vote on the board resolution to add Article 5 (regarding the exculpation of directors)? Explain.

Documents begin on next page

XYZ Corp.
Minutes of the Board of Directors Meeting of March 3, 2015

The board of directors of XYZ Corp. (the "Company") held a meeting on March 3, 2015 at 12:00 p.m. The following directors were in attendance and constituted a quorum of the board:

Liza Little
Peter Smith
Mary Jones
John White
Nancy Black
Lois Lupine
Ellen Equine

The meeting was called to order and it was moved, seconded, and carried that Liza Little act as chair of the meeting and John Smith act as secretary.

Minutes of the meeting of the board of directors meeting of January 10, 2015 were approved.

The following resolutions were adopted by the Company's board of directors:

RESOLVED, the Company shall register as a foreign corporation with the Secretary of State of the State of Indiana and the officers of the Company are directed and authorized to do all that is reasonably necessary to complete and maintain such registration for as long as the Company deems necessary.

RESOLVED, the Company amends its articles of incorporation to change its name XYZ Inc.

RESOLVED, the board of directors recommends the shareholders approve the following amendments to the Company's Articles of Incorporation:

Article 3, Section 1 shall be amended to read, in its entirety:

> The total number of shares the Corporation is authorized to issue is: Twenty Thousand (20,000) shares of Class A Common Stock with a par value of One Dollar ($1.00) per share; Ten Thousand (10,000) shares of Class B (Non-Voting) Common Stock, which shall have no par value; and Ten Thousand (10,000) shares of Preferred Stock with a par value of One Hundred Dollars ($100.00) per share.

Article 3, Section 2, Part A shall be amended to read, in its entirety:

> A. The holders of the Preferred Stock will be entitled to receive cumulative preferred dividends in the amount of Three Dollars ($3.00) per share annually before any dividends shall be payable

on any other class of stock. Dividends on the Preferred Stock shall be cumulative (regardless of whether they were declared or whether the Company was legally allowed to pay any dividends). Accumulated and unpaid dividends on the Preferred Stock will not bear interest.

New Article 5 shall be added as follows:

ARTICLE 5 - Exculpation:

A director of this Corporation shall not be liable to the Corporation or its shareholders for monetary damages for breach of fiduciary duty as a director, except to the extent such exemption from liability or limitation thereof is not permitted under the law of the state of incorporation.

XYZ Corp.
Articles of Incorporation

Pursuant to the Business Corporation Act of the State of __, the undersigned submits these Articles of Incorporation:

ARTICLE 1 - Name:

The name of the corporation is XYZ Corp.

ARTICLE 2 - Registered Office and Agent:

The street address of the corporation's initial registered office is 212 45th Avenue, River Banks City, ___ and its registered agent at that office is Mr. Morris J. McCleedy.

ARTICLE 3 - Capital Stock:

Section 1 - Authorized Capital:

The total number of shares the Corporation is authorized to issue is: Ten Thousand (10,000) shares of Class A Common Stock with a par value of One Dollar ($1.00) per share; Five Thousand (5,000) shares of Class B (Non-Voting) Common Stock, which shall have no par value; and Five Thousand (5,000) shares of Preferred Stock with a par value of One Hundred Dollars ($100.00) per share.

Section 2 - Dividends:

A. The holders of the Preferred Stock will be entitled to receive cumulative preferred dividends in the amount of Four Dollars ($4.00) per share annually before any dividends shall be payable on any other class of stock. Dividends on the Preferred Stock shall be cumulative (regardless of whether they were declared or whether the Company was legally allowed to pay any dividends). Accumulated and unpaid dividends on the Preferred Stock will not bear interest.

B. When and if declared by the Board of Directors, dividends are payable to the holders of Classes A and B of the Common Stock in equal amounts per share as if both Classes of the Common Stock were one Class. Dividends payable to the Common Stock are payable out of the unreserved earned surplus remaining after the payment of the dividends on the Preferred Stock. No dividends are payable on Classes A and B of the Common Stock if there are any accrued dividends on the Preferred Stock, up to and including the current quarterly dividend period for such Preferred Stock, which have not been paid, or which have been declared and a sum set aside for repayment. The holders of the Preferred Stock shall not participate in any dividend distributed to holders of Classes A and B of the Common Stock.

Section 3 - Redemption of Preferred Stock:

A. The Corporation may, at the option of the Board of Directors, redeem all or any part of the outstanding Preferred Stock. Such redemption may take place at any time, as determined by resolution of the Board of Directors in accordance with relevant law.

B. The redemption price shall be One Hundred Dollars ($100.00) per share plus accrued dividends. The notice of redemption shall contain the date and price of redemption, the manner in which redemption is to be effected, and the effect of such redemption on the rights of stockholders who fail to present their shares for redemption.

C. If notice of redemption shall have been given as provided above, and if, on or before the redemption date stated in the notice, the funds necessary for such redemption shall have been set aside, then from and after the designated redemption date, all rights with respect to such Preferred Stock, including, but not limited to, the right to receive dividends and to vote at corporate meetings, shall cease, except for the right to receive payment for the shares called for redemption without interest.

Section 4 - Liquidation:

A. In the event of any liquidation, dissolution, or winding up of the Corporation, whether voluntary or involuntary, the holders of the Preferred Stock are entitled to be paid out of the assets of the Corporation legally available for distribution to its shareholders an amount equal to $100 per share plus all accumulated and unpaid dividends (including a prorated quarterly dividend from the last Dividend Payment Date to the date of such payment) Such payment shall be made before any payment, distribution, or setting aside for payment of any amount will be made in respect to the holder of the Common Stock.

B. If upon any liquidation, dissolution or winding up of the Company, whether voluntary or involuntary, if the assets of the corporation available for distribution to its shareholders exceed the amount payable to the holders of the Preferred Stock, the remaining assets shall be distributed to the holders of Classes A and B of the Common Stock in equal amounts per share as if both Classes of the Common Stock were one Class.

C. A consolidation or merger of the Corporation with or into any other corporation or corporations in which the stockholders of the Corporation will receive capital stock of the acquiring or surviving corporation exclusively and no other consideration (except for cash in lieu of fractional shares) or of the direct or indirect parent corporation of the acquiring corporation , will not be deemed to be a liquidation, dissolution, or winding up of the Company.

Section 5 - Voting Rights:

A. Each holder of the Class A Common Stock shall be entitled to one vote for each share of stock standing in his name on the books of the Corporation. At each election of directors, each holder of the Class A Common Stock shall have as many votes as the number of shares of Class A Common Stock owned by him multiplied by the number of directors to be elected by the holders of the Common Stock. These votes may be divided among the total number of directors to be elected by the holders of Common Stock, or distributed among any lesser number, in such proportion as the holder may desire.

B. The holders of the Class B Common Stock shall have no voting rights except as required by law.

C. The holders of the Preferred Stock shall have no voting rights except as required by law, *provided, however*, whenever the dividends on the Preferred Stock, at the time of any annual meeting, shall be in arrears to the amount of Eight Dollars ($8.00) of annual dividends, at such annual meeting and at all any meeting thereafter called for the election of directors, until such time as the dividends on the Preferred Stock are no longer in arrears, the holders of the Preferred Stock shall be entitled to elect a majority of the directors. Such directors shall serve until the next annual meeting. At elections for such directors, each holder of Preferred Stock shall have as many votes as the number of shares of Preferred Stock owned by him multiplied by the number of directors to be elected by the holders of the Preferred Stock. These votes may be divided among the total number of directors to be elected by the holders of Preferred Stock, or distributed among any lesser number of such directors, in such proportion as the holder may desire.

ARTICLE 4 - Board of Directors:

Section 1 - Election of Directors:

The Directors shall be elected at the annual meeting of shareholders. Each Director shall hold office until next succeeding annual meeting of shareholders and until his successor is elected, or until his earlier resignation, removal from office, or death.

Section 2 - Number of Directors:

A. The number of Directors shall be not less than seven (7), otherwise the number of directors may be fixed or changed at a meeting of the shareholders called for the purpose of electing Directors at which a quorum is present, by the affirmative vote of the holders of a majority of the shares represented at the meeting and entitled to vote on such proposal.

B. In addition to the authority of the shareholders to fix or change the number of Directors, the number of Directors so fixed may be increased or decreased by not more than two (2) between shareholders' meetings by the Board of Directors at a meeting or by action without a meeting, and the number of Directors as so changed shall be the number of Directors until further changed in accordance with this Section, provided that no such decrease in the number of Directors shall result in the removal of any incumbent Director or reduction in the term of any incumbent Director. In the event that the Directors increase the number of Directors, the Directors who are then in office may fill any vacancy created thereby.

---

(11) AMENDING THE BYLAWS:

Refer to the following provisions to answer the questions below:

RMBCA §§10.20, 10.21, 10.22

For further help, please refer to the following sections in the Text:

Text §5A-206 et seq.

Please read through the bylaws provided below. Try to get a feel for how bylaws are drafted. Although the sample bylaws are simple, bylaws are generally not much more complicated than the sample.

Please answer the following questions:

Is Article 2, Section 7 legally permissible? (see RMBCA §7.04(b))

Who has a right to amend the bylaws – shareholders, directors, both?

May a shareholder propose any of the following amendments to the bylaws and require the corporation to allow shareholders to vote on the proposal? (Before forming your final legal opinion, is there any other document you would like to review?):

(A) Shareholders meetings must be within the state of incorporation.

(B) The directors shall not manufacture products that promote the use or sale of tobacco products.

(C) Notice of shareholder meetings shall be no fewer than twenty (20) days and no more than thirty (30) days prior to the date of such meeting.

(D) The corporation must hire more women and minorities to develop a more diverse workforce.

If the shareholder proposing the above amendments wants to prevent the directors from reversing them, what language would you suggest she draft into her proposal?

Bylaws of
Goo Corp.

Article 1. Corporate Offices.

Section 1. Principal office. The corporation shall maintain its principal office within the corporation's state of incorporation in a location the board may determine from time to time. The board will have discretion to establish offices at other locations as the corporation's business may require.

Section 2. Registered office. The corporation shall maintain a registered office in its state of incorporation. The registered office need not be the same as its principal office.

Article 2. Shareholders' meetings.

Section 1. Annual meeting. The corporation shall hold its annual meeting of shareholders on the third Wednesday in May each year or on a convenient date within sixty (60) days following the third Wednesday in May as the board may from time to time determine.

Section 2. Special meetings. Special meetings of the shareholders for any purpose permitted by law may be called by the board of directors, the president of the corporation, or by the president of the corporation at the request of the holders of at least one-third of the outstanding shares of the corporation entitled to vote at the meeting.

Section 3. Location. Meetings of the shareholders will be held at the corporation's principal office or at any other location designated in the notice of the meeting.

Section 4. Notice. The corporation shall provide written notice of the time, place, and purposes of any annual or special meeting of shareholders no fewer than ten (10) days and no more than sixty (60) days prior to the date of such meeting. The notice for any meeting at which directors will be elected must include the names of the persons the board intends to nominate for election. In the case of an annual meeting of stockholders, the shareholders may act upon matters that may properly come before the meeting, regardless of whether such matters were stated in the notice. In the case of a special shareholders meeting, the shareholder may only act upon matters that are stated in the notice for such meeting.

A shareholder may waive notice of any meeting before or after the meeting by a writing signed by the shareholder and delivered to the secretary of the corporation for inclusion in the minutes of the meeting. In addition, a shareholder's attendance at any meeting will constitute a waiver of notice, unless the shareholder, at the beginning of the meeting, expressly objects to the transaction of any business because of the lack of notice.

Section 5. Quorum and voting. Except as otherwise required by applicable law, a majority of the outstanding shares of the corporation entitled to vote, represented in person or by proxy, shall constitute a quorum at a meeting of the shareholders. Except as otherwise required by applicable law, the affirmative vote of the holders of a majority of the shares entitled vote and present (in person or by proxy) at a meeting at which there is a quorum is required for approval of any resolution by the shareholders, except in the case of the election of directors, which requires a plurality.

For the election of directors only, a shareholder may cumulate her votes; provided, however, the shareholder states her intention to cumulate her votes after the nomination of candidates and before the commencement of voting for directors. Once a shareholder has properly stated her intention to cumulate votes for the election of directors, all shareholders will be entitled to cumulate their votes.

The shareholders present in person or by proxy at such meeting may continue to do business until adjournment even though the withdrawal of shareholders from the meeting results in less than a quorum remaining.

Section 6. Proxies. At any meeting of the shareholders, a shareholder may vote in person or by written proxy executed in accordance with applicable law and filed with the secretary of the corporation at the beginning of the meeting or prior to the meeting.

Section 7. Action without meeting. Any action the law allows shareholders to take at a meeting may be taken without a meeting if one or more written consents, specifying the action taken, are signed by the holders of at least eighty percent (80%) of the shares entitled to vote at the meeting.

Article 3. Directors

Section 1. Powers. The business and affairs of the corporation shall be managed by, or under the direction of, the board of directors.

Section 2. Number. The number of directors shall be no fewer than five (5) and no more than seven (7) as fixed or changed, within the specified limits, from time to time by the vote of the shareholders or by a vote of the directors.

Section 3. Election and term of office. The directors are elected by the shareholders and hold office until their successors have been elected at next annual meeting, and qualified, or until her earlier removal, resignation, death, or incapacity.

Section 4. Removal of directors. The shareholders may remove a director, with or without cause, at any time at a special meeting of shareholders called for that purpose. The board of directors may remove a director only for cause.

Section 5. Vacancies on the board. A vacancy on the board occurs upon the death resignation, or removal of a director, or upon the increase of the authorized number of directors. The remaining board members or the shareholders may vote to fill the vacancy. The director who fills the vacancy holds office until the next annual shareholders' meeting and until her successor has been duly elected and qualified.

Section 6. Regular meetings. The board of directors shall hold its regular meeting immediately following the annual meeting of shareholders. The board of directors may, by resolution, provide for additional regular meetings of the board.

Section 7. Special meetings. The president of the corporation or the chairman of the board may call special meetings of the directors for any purpose or purposes permitted by law. The person who calls a special meeting may fix the time and place for meeting.

Section 8. Notice. Notice of regular meetings of the board of directors is not necessary. Notice of special meetings must be provided to directors at least seven (7) days, but no more than thirty (30) days, prior to the special meeting.

A director may waive notice of any meeting before or after the meeting by a writing signed by the director and delivered to the secretary of the corporation for inclusion in the minutes of the meeting. In addition, a director's attendance at a meeting will constitute a waiver of notice, unless the director, at the beginning of the meeting, expressly objects to the transaction of any business because of the lack of notice.

Section 9. Quorum and voting. Except as otherwise required by applicable law, a majority of the directors constitutes a quorum at any meeting of the directors. A director may participate in a meeting of directors, and will be considered present for quorum purposes, by means of teleconference any other communication device by which all directors participating in the meeting can simultaneously hear one another.

Each director is entitled to one vote upon each matter voted on at a meeting of the directors. Except as otherwise required by applicable law, the affirmative vote of a majority of the directors that are present at a meeting at which there is a quorum is required for approval of any resolution by the directors.

Section 10. Proxies. Directors may not attend a meeting or vote by proxy.

Section 11. Action without meeting. Any action the law allows directors to take at a meeting may be taken without a meeting if one or more written consents, specifying the action taken, are signed by all the directors.

Section 12. Committees. The board of directors may create committees composed of one or more directors. Each committee will have the powers granted to it by the board of directors to the extent permitted by the relevant law. A majority of the members of any committee of the board of directors will constitute a quorum for all committee action.

Section 13. Compensation for directors. The board of directors may authorize the payment to all directors of a fixed sum for attendance at each meeting and the reimbursement of all expenses of each director related to the director's attendance at any meeting of directors.

Article 4. Officers.

Section 1. Officers. The board of directors may appoint a President, a Treasurer, and a Secretary. The board of directors may appoint other officers from time to time as it sees fit. Officers of the corporation will serve at the pleasure of the board of directors, and will have the authority and duties specified by the board of directors. The board of directors will determine the salary and benefits of officers.

Article 5. Miscellaneous.

Section 1. Share certificates. Shareholders of the corporation are entitled to receive one or more certificates representing shares owned by such shareholders. Share certificates shall be in the form specified from time to time by the board of directors.

Section 2. Dividends and distributions. The board of directors may from time to time declare, and the corporation may pay, dividends on outstanding shares of the corporation, subject to limitations provided by law and the articles of incorporation of the corporation.

Section 3. Fiscal year. The fiscal year of the corporation shall be the period designated by the board of directors.

Section 4. Amendment. These bylaws may be amended from time to time in the manner permitted by applicable law.

CHAPTER 5 – EXERCISES:

BOARD VOTING

---

(12) LEARNING THE STATUTE:

The board of directors and its committees:

Refer to the following provisions to answer the questions below:

RMBCA §§3.02, 8.01, 8.02, 8.03, 8.25

For further help, please refer to the following sections in the Text:

Text §§5A-401, 5A-402, 5A-404, 5A-501 et seq., 5A-507 et seq.

What are the powers of the board? Generally? Specific examples?

May the board cause the corporation to make a donation to a charity? Must the donation serve some corporate purpose or benefit the corporation in some way?

Must directors meet certain qualifications?

What are the minimum and maximum numbers of directors a board may have?

May the board establish committees?

Board voting in general:

Refer to the following provisions to answer the questions below:

RMBCA §§8.20, 8.21, 8.22, 8.23, 8.24

For further help, please refer to the following sections in the Text:

Text §§5A-406 et seq., 5A-407 et seq., 5A-503

May the board (or board committee) meet by conference call? Instant messaging?

May the board (or board committee) take action without meeting?

Is notice required for board meetings (or board committee meetings)? Must the notice state a purpose?

May a director waive notice? How?

What is the quorum for a board meeting (or board committee meeting)?

What is the approval requirement?

Removal of directors and filling board vacancies:

Refer to the following provisions to answer the questions below:

RMBCA §§8.08, 8.09, 8.10

For further help, please refer to the following sections in the Text:

Text §§5A-502(b), 5A-502(c), 5A-204

Can the board remove a director without shareholder action?

Can the board fill a vacancy on the board without shareholder approval?

---

(13) BOARD COMMITTEES:

Refer to the following provisions to answer the questions below:

RMBCA §8.25

For further help, please refer to the following sections in the Text:

Text §5A-507 et seq.

Please read the provision from the bylaws of Microsoft Inc., below.

Be prepared to explain the general purpose of the provision.

How closely does this bylaw provision track the relevant RMBCA provision?

Could the Microsoft board establish a board committee under the RMBCA without this bylaw provision?

What types of board committees might you expect Microsoft to have? What would each of these committees do?

. . .

2.12 Committees

The Board of Directors, by resolution adopted by a majority of the full Board, may designate from among its members one or more committees, each of which:

Shall have two (2) or more members;

a. Shall be governed by the same rules regarding meetings, action without meetings, notice, and waiver of notice, and quorum and voting requirements as applied to the Board; and

b. To the extent provided in such resolution, shall have and may exercise all the authority of the Board, except no such committee shall have the authority to:

    i. Authorize or approve a distribution except according to a general formula or method prescribed by the Board;

    ii. Approve or propose to shareholders action which the WBCA requires to be approved by shareholders;

    iii. Fill vacancies on the Board or on any of its committees;

    iv. Amend the Articles of Incorporation;

    v. Adopt, amend, or repeal the Bylaws;

    vi. Approve a plan of merger not requiring shareholder approval; or

    vii. Authorize or approve the issuance or sale or contract for sale of shares, or determine the designation and relative rights, preferences, and limitations on a class or series of shares, except that the Board may authorize a committee, or a senior executive officer of the Corporation, to do so within limits specifically prescribed by the Board.

---

(14) STAGGERED/CLASSIFIED BOARD:

Refer to the following sections in the Text to help you answer the questions below:

Text §5A-203

Delaware Law provides:

> The directors of any corporation organized under this chapter may, by the certificate of incorporation or by an initial bylaw, or by a bylaw adopted by a vote of the stockholders, be divided into 1, 2 or 3 classes; the term of office of those of the first class to expire at the first annual meeting held after such classification becomes effective; of the second class 1 year thereafter; of the third class 2 years thereafter; and at each annual election held after such classification becomes effective, directors shall be chosen for a full term, as the case may be, to succeed those whose terms expire. . . . (Delaware General Corporation Law §141(d))

Fill in the blanks below:

According to your reading of the statute, if a seven (7) person board is **staggered into the two classes** below, how would each class of directors be elected?

<u>**Class 1**</u> (comprising 4 board seats):

Year 1 (*i.e.,* the first year of classification)**:** Elected to the board for a ________-year term.

Year 2: ____________________

Year 3: ____________________

<u>**Class 2**</u> (comprising 3 board seats):

Year 1 (*i.e.,* the first year of classification)**:** Elected to the board for a ________-year term.

Year 2: ____________________

Year 3: ____________________

---

(15) <u>BOARD COMPOSITION:</u>

Refer to the following sections in the Text to help you answer the questions below:

Text §5A-506

Microsoft Corporation has the following provision in its Corporate Governance Guidelines:

> **CEO, Chairman, and Lead Independent Director.** The Board selects the Company's CEO and Chairman in the manner that it determines to be in the best interests of the Company's shareholders. The Board does not have a policy as to whether the Chairman should be an independent director, an affiliated director, or a member of management. When the Chairman is an affiliated director or a member of Company management, or when the independent directors determine that it is in the best interests of the Company, the independent directors will annually appoint from among themselves a Lead Independent Director. The Lead Independent Director coordinates the activities of the independent directors, coordinates with the CEO and corporate secretary to set the agenda for Board meetings, chairs executive sessions of the independent directors, and performs the other duties either specified in these guidelines or assigned from time to time by the Board.

Please explain the background and purpose of this provision.

---

(16) <u>BOARD SIZE:</u>

Refer to the following provisions to answer the questions below:

RMBCA §8.03, 8.10, 8.25, 10.20

For further help, please refer to the following sections in the Text:

Text §§5A-502(a), 5A-502(b)

Read the minutes of the board meeting provided below and answer these questions:

Does the law allow the board to take these actions? Explain your answer by citing to specific provisions of the RMBCA.

Why might a board take these actions?

[Excerpt from bylaws of Goo Corp.]

Article 2 - The Board of Directors

Section 1- Board Size: The number of directors constituting the board shall be seven (7).

Goo Corp.
Minutes of the Board of Directors Meeting of May 5, 2015

The board of directors of XYZ Corp. (the "Company") held a meeting on May 5, 2015 at 12:00 p.m. The following directors were in attendance and constituted a quorum of the board:

Penelope Piscine
Barry Bovine
Lois Lupine
Ellen Equine
Oliver Ovine
Mary Murine
Veronica Vulpine

The meeting was called to order and it was moved, seconded, and carried that Lois Lupine act as chair of the meeting and Barry Bovine act as secretary.

The following resolutions were adopted by the Company's board of directors:

WHEREAS, the Company is seeking to purchase real property on which to build an office building for its headquarters;

WHEREAS, Little Leopard Inc. owns a plot of land suitable for the Company's needs;

WHEREAS, each of the directors of the Company has shareholdings in Little Leopard Inc.;

RESOLVED, the board amends Article 2, Section 1 of the Company's bylaws to read as follows:

"The number of directors constituting the board shall be nine (9)."

RESOLVED, the following persons are immediately appointed to the board of directors to fill the two (2) vacancies on the board, created by the increase in the size of the board, to serve until their successors are qualified and elected at the next annual meeting of shareholders:

Lisa Lapine
Carl Caprine

RESOLVED, the board creates a special committee of the board of directors that shall, to the extent permitted by law, exercise the powers and act with full authority of the board of directors for the limited purpose of considering and deciding upon the purchase of real property from Little Leopard Inc.

RESOLVED, the board appoints the following directors to the special committee:

Lisa Lapine
Carl Caprine

These resolutions are effectively immediately.

CHAPTER 5 – EXERCISES:

THE AUTHORITY OF OFFICERS AND EMPLOYEES

---

(17) AN AGENT'S AUTHORITY:

Refer to the following sections in the Text to help you answer the questions below:

Text §§5A-700 et seq.

XYZ Inc. was seeking to sell its maple syrup bottling operations (the "Business").

Employee was a vice president and the treasurer/comptroller of XYZ Inc.

Employee approached **Broker** and promised that XYZ would pay Broker a large commission if Broker found an offer for the Business that the XYZ board accepted.

Employee told the Broker that the board of XYZ had authorized him to enter into a contract with a broker. In fact, the XYZ board had not expressly authorized Employee to do so. Furthermore, the XYZ board had authorized another agent to negotiate with brokers and Employee was aware of this fact.

Broker knew that Employee was a vice president and the treasurer/comptroller of XYZ Inc. Employee and Broker had dealings in the past when Broker had worked with XYZ on other deals. During those deals, Employee had provided documents and information to the Broker on behalf of XYZ, but has not acted to bind XYZ in any way.

Broker solicited a very good offer from a buyer. Broker submitted the offer to Employee, who presented it to XYZ's board. XYZ's board accepted the offer without knowing of Broker's involvement in soliciting the offer.

Broker has demanded that XYZ pay her commission. The XYZ board refuses to pay.

Explore whether XYZ will be liable for the Broker's commission under the following theories:

Express authority

Implied authority

Apparent authority

---

(18) <u>CORPORATE OFFICERS:</u>

Refer to the following provisions to answer the questions below:

RMBCA §8.40, 8.41

For further help, please refer to the following sections in the Text:

Text §5A-801

Match the following corporate offices to their respective bylaw descriptions. You may use a corporate office more than once.

[Do not look it up on the internet]

Chairman of the board	**Chief financial officer**	**Vice presidents**
Chief executive officer	**Secretary**	**Assistant secretary**
President	**Treasurer**	**Assistant treasurer**

(A) ____________________

The ________ shall be an executive officer of the Corporation and may also be the Chief Executive Officer, as determined by the Board of Directors. Subject to the direction of the Board of Directors and the Chief Executive Officer, the ________ shall have supervision of the business of the Corporation and its other officers and agents. He may sign, with any other officer thereunto duly authorized, certificates of stock of the Corporation the issuance of which shall have been duly authorized (the signature to which may be a facsimile signature), and may sign and execute in the name of the Corporation, deeds, mortgages, bonds, contracts, agreements or other instruments duly authorized by the Board of Directors except in cases where the signing and execution thereof shall be expressly delegated by the Board of Directors to some other officer or agent. From time to time, he shall report to the Board of Directors all matters within his knowledge which the interests of the Corporation may require to be brought to its attention. He shall also perform such other duties as are given to him by these By laws, or from time to time may be assigned to him by the Chief Executive Officer or the Board of Directors. (from the bylaws of Humana Inc.)

(B) ____________________

The ________ shall perform such duties and exercise such authority as shall from time to time may be assigned to them by the Board of Directors, the Chairman of the Board, the Chief Executive Officer or the President, and, in the order of their seniority, or in any other order as the Board of Directors may from time to time determine, shall, in the absence of the President, have all the powers of and be subject to all restrictions upon the President. (from the bylaws of Humana Inc.)

(C) ____________________

The ________ shall
(a) Record all the proceedings of the meetings of the stockholders, the Board of Directors, and any committees in a book or books to be kept for that purpose;
(b) Cause all notices to be duly given in accordance with the provisions of these By laws and as required by statute;
(c) Whenever any committee shall be appointed in pursuance of a resolution of the Board of Directors, furnish the chairman of such committee with a copy of such resolution;
(d) Be custodian of the records and of the seal of the Corporation, and cause such seal to be affixed to all certificates representing stock of the Corporation prior to the issuance thereof and to all instruments the execution of which on behalf of the Corporation under its seal shall have been duly authorized;
(e) See that the lists, books, reports, statements, certificates and other documents and records required by statute are properly kept and filed;
(f) Have charge of the stock and transfer books of the Corporation, and exhibit such stock book at all reasonable times to such persons as are entitled by statute to have access thereto;
(g) Sign (unless the Treasurer or an Assistant Secretary or an Assistant Treasurer shall sign) certificates representing stock of the Corporation the issuance of which shall have been duly authorized (the signature to which may be a facsimile signature); and
(h) In general, perform all duties incident to the office of the ________ and such other duties as are given to him by these By laws or as from time to time may be assigned to him by the Board of Directors, the Chairman of the Board, the Chief Executive Officer or the President. (from the bylaws of Humana Inc.)

(D) ____________________

The Board of Directors may elect from among its members an officer designated as the ________, but the appointment of a ________ shall not be required. If a ________ shall be elected, then the ________ shall have such other duties and authority as may be prescribed by the Board of Directors from time to time. In general the ________ shall perform all duties incident to the position of ________ or as may be prescribed by the Board of Directors or these Bylaws from time to time.
The ________ shall be a director who is independent from the Corporation. For purposes of this Bylaw, "independent" has the meaning set forth in the New York

Stock Exchange ("NYSE") listing standards, unless the Corporation's common stock ceases to be listed on the NYSE and is listed on another exchange, in which case such exchange's definition of independence shall apply. If the Board of Directors determines that a ________who was independent at the time he or she was selected is no longer independent, the Board of Directors shall select a new ________ who satisfies the requirements of this Bylaw within 60 days of such determination. Compliance with this Bylaw shall be excused if no director who qualifies as independent is elected by the Stockholders or if no director who is independent is willing to serve as ________. (from the bylaws of Bank of America Corporation)

____

(E) ____________________

The ________s in the order determined by the Board shall, in the absence or disability of the Treasurer, perform the duties and exercise the powers of the Treasurer and shall perform such other duties and exercise such other powers as may be assigned by the Board, the Chief Executive Officer, if one, the President, or the Treasurer. (from the bylaws of Wal-mart Stores, Inc.)

____

(F) ____________________

Subject to these Bylaws and the direction of the Board, the ________ shall have the responsibility and the power necessary for the general management, oversight, supervision and control of the business and affairs of the Corporation, and to ensure that all orders and resolutions of the Board are carried into effect. If the Board has elected a Chief Executive Officer of the Corporation, (1) the Chief Executive Officer shall have all of the powers granted by these Bylaws to the ________ and (2) the ________ shall, subject to the powers of supervision and control conferred upon the Chief Executive Officer, have such duties and powers as assigned to him or her by the Board or the Chief Executive Officer. (from the bylaws of Wal-mart Stores, Inc.)

____

(G) ____________________

The ________ shall have general charge and supervision of the financial affairs of the Corporation, including budgetary and accounting methods, and shall approve payment, or designate others serving under him or her to approve for payment, all vouchers for distribution of funds and shall perform such other duties as may be assigned to him or her by the Board, the Chief Executive Officer, if one, or the President. (from the bylaws of Wal-mart Stores, Inc.)

____

(19) CERTIFICATES OF AUTHORITY:

Refer to the following sections in the Text to help you answer the questions below:

Text §5A-802 et seq.

Please read the four certificates below:

What are the differences between the various forms?

Which form provides the third party with the greatest security?

Under what circumstances (i.e., for what type of transaction) would a third party be justified in asking for the certificate that provides her the greatest security?

What kind of authority does each of these certificates create?

If you were the corporate secretary, would you have reservations about the language in Certificate C stating: ". . . *constitutes a legally binding obligation of the Company?*"

(A)

CERTIFICATE OF INCUMBENCY

The undersigned, ________, does hereby certify:

(1) she is the Secretary of ___________ (the "Company") and has the authority to execute this certificate on behalf of the Company; and

(2) the following named person is authorized to execute [the transaction documents] on behalf of the Company:

[name of authorized agent]

x____________________ Date:

______________, Corporate Secretary, _______ Company, Inc.

More certificates on next page

(B)

CERTIFICATE OF INCUMBENCY

The undersigned, ________ , does hereby certify:

(1) she is the Secretary of ___________ (the "Company") and has the authority to execute this certificate on behalf of the Company; and

(2) the following named person holds the office in the company indicated next to her name:

[name of person – title and office in the company]

x____________________ Date:

_____________, Corporate Secretary, _______ Company, Inc.

(C)

CERTIFICATE OF INCUMBENCY

The undersigned, ________, does hereby certify:

(1) she is the duly elected, qualified, and incumbent Secretary of ___________ (the "Company") and has the authority to execute this certificate on behalf of the Company; and

(2) pursuant to the Company's bylaws and certain resolutions adopted by the Company's board of directors, the following named person was given authority to execute [the transaction documents] on behalf of the Company and the execution of the [transaction documents] by the named person constitutes a legally binding obligation of the Company:

[name of authorized agent]

x____________________ Date:

_____________, Corporate Secretary, _______ Company, Inc.

One more certificate on next page

(D)

SECRETARY'S CERTIFICATE

The undersigned, ________, does hereby certify:

(1) she is the Secretary of ___________ (the "Company") and has the authority to execute this certificate on behalf of the Company;

(2) the attached resolution is a true and accurate copy of the resolution adopted by the Company's board of directors on [May 25, 2015] at a duly held meeting at which a quorum of directors was present; and

(3) the resolution has not been rescinded or modified as of the date of this certificate.

x____________________ Date:

______________, Corporate Secretary, _______ Company, Inc.

RESOLUTION OF THE BOARD OF DIRECTORS
OF [___ COMPANY, INC.]

"RESOLVED, that the board approves [description of transaction] (the "Transaction") and authorizes ____________ to execute all instruments on behalf of the corporation necessary to effectuate the Transaction."

CHAPTER 5 – EXERCISES:

PARTNERSHIP VOTING AND PARTNER AUTHORITY

---

(20) CONCEPTUAL PROBLEM:

Read the following sections in the Text:

Text §5B-100 et seq.

In a general partnership, who would make the decisions listed below? The employees/agents (including a partner acting as agent)? The partners by a majority voting standard? The partners by a greater-than-majority voting standard?

A decision to buy a ream of paper?

A decision to borrow a significant amount of money to finance the construction of a large retail outlet.

A decision to merge the partnership with another entity.

---

(21) LEARNING THE STATUTE:

Partnership voting:

Refer to the following provisions to answer the questions below:

RUPA §§401(f),(i),(j), 902(b), 905(a)&(c)

For further help, please refer to the following sections in the Text:

Text §§5B-103, 5B-201 et seq.

When will partners vote on ordinary business matters?

What is the approval requirement for ordinary business matters?

How are partners' votes weighted? Pro rata based on capital contribution or per capita?

What types of matters are ordinary matters?

What is the approval requirement for extraordinary business matters?

What types of matters are extraordinary matters?

Must the partners decide matters by formal meetings?

Partner authority:

Refer to the following provisions to answer the questions below:

RUPA §§301, 102, 308

For further help, please refer to the following sections in the Text:

Text §§5B-104, 5B-203(a), 5B-203(b), 5B-203(c)

If a partner does not have express or implied authority, under what circumstances will she be able to bind the partnership?

Under what circumstances will the partner never be able to bind the partnership without actual authority?

Is it possible for a person who is not a partner to bind the partnership by misrepresenting to third parties that she is a partner?

---

(22) PARTNERSHIP VOTING & AUTHORITY:

Refer to the following provisions to answer the questions below:

RUPA §§401(f),(i),(j), 301, 102, 308

For further help, please refer to the following sections in the Text:

Text §§5B-103, 5B-104, 5B-201 et seq., 5B-203(a), 5B-203(b), 5B-203(c)

Harry, Helen, Mary, and Martin are partners in a general partnership. The partnership operates a large grocery store.

Harry has contributed 30% of the partnership's capital and **H**elen has contributed 38%. According to the partnership agreement, Harry is allocated 30% of the partnership profits and Helen is allocated 38%.

Mary has contributed 10% of the partnership's capital and **M**artin has contributed 22%. According to the partnership agreement, Mary is allocated 10% of the partnership profits and Martin is allocated 22%.

Harry and **H**elen do not want the grocery store to buy produce from Fruit & Veg Inc. because they believe the quality of its produce is not very good.

In contrast, **M**ary and **M**artin want to buy produce from Fruit & Veg Inc. because its prices are low.

The partners vote on the disagreement:

> **H**arry and Helen vote against buying produce from Fruit & Veg
>
> **M**ary and Martin vote in favor of buying produce from Fruit & Veg

Hypothetical A:

A few days after the partners' vote, **M**artin places an order on behalf of the partnership for 10 cases of apples from Fruit & Veg. Fruit & Veg accepts the order, unaware of the partners' vote.

> **Is the partnership bound by the order? What other facts do you need to know in order to form your legal opinion?**

Hypothetical B:

Immediately after the partners' vote, **H**arry calls Fruit & Veg and informs them that the partnership has put Fruit & Veg on its "blacklist" and that no partner has the authority to place orders with Fruit & Veg on behalf of the partnership.

However, a few days later, **M**artin places an order with Fruit & Veg for 10 cases of apples on behalf of the partnership. Fruit & Veg accepts the order despite the warning from Harry.

> **Is the partnership bound by the order? Would it make a difference if the partnership had been buying produce from Fruit & Veg on a regular basis for the past 10 years?**

---

(23) THE PARTNERSHIP AGREEMENT & PARTNERSHIP VOTING:

Refer to the following provisions to answer the questions below:

> RUPA §§401(f),(i),(j), 902(b), 905(a)&(c)

For further help, please refer to the following sections in the Text:

> Text §§5B-103, 5B-104, 5B-201 et seq., 5B-203(a), 5B-203(b), 5B-203(c)

Please review the three partnership agreements, below.

How does each of these agreements change the default management and voting rules of the RUPA?

Are there any provisions that closely track the language of the law?

Do they require a formal meeting of partners to make decisions?

PARTNERSHIP AGREEMENT 1:

. . .

Article 1 - Definitions:

. . .

"Partnership Interest" means the percentage of the Partnership owned by a Partner as set forth in Schedule ___ , as amended from time to time.

. . .

Article 6 – Management:

6.1. Partner voting in general: Except as otherwise provided in this Agreement, matters related to the business, management, and internal governance of the Partnership shall be decided by a simple majority of the Partnership Interests. Each Partner shall have a weighted vote equal to her respective Partnership Interest.

6.2. Partner voting on certain matters: No Partner shall, without the written consent of three-fourths of the Partners on a *per capita* basis, do any of the following:

Assign the Partnership property in trust for creditors or on an assignee's promise to pay the debts of the Partnership;

Dispose of the goodwill of the business;

Do any other act which would make it impossible to carry on the ordinary business of the Partnership;

Confess a judgment against the Partnership;

Submit a Partnership claim or liability to arbitration or reference;

Make, execute or deliver for the Partnership any bond, mortgage, deed of trust, guarantee, indemnity bond, surety bond or accommodation paper or accommodation endorsement;

Borrow money in the Partnership name or use Partnership property as collateral on either a recourse or a non-recourse basis;

Assign, transfer, pledge, compromise or release any claim of or debt owing to the Partnership except upon payment in full;

Convey any Partnership real property;

Pledge or transfer in any manner its interest in the Partnership except to another Partner, or as otherwise provided in this Agreement;

Bind the Partnership in making contracts and incurring obligations in the name and on the credit of the Partnership; or

Admit or purport to admit a new Partner to the Partnership.

6.3. Written Consents and Approvals Required: Whenever the consent or approval of any Partner is required or permitted under this Agreement, such consent or approval must be evidenced in a writing signed by such Partner.. . .

Partnership Agreement 2:

. . .

Article 6 – Management:

6.1. Partner Meetings: The partnership shall convene a meeting of Partners at the request of a majority of the Partners. Such request must be in writing, signed by the partners calling the meeting, and specify the date and purpose(s) of the meeting.

6.2. Voting at Meetings: At any meeting of Partners, each Partner will have one vote. Except as otherwise provided in this agreement, a quorum will exist if a majority of Partners are present in person. Voting by proxy is not permitted.

Except as otherwise provided in this agreement, a majority of the votes cast in a meeting where a quorum is present may determine any other issue at a Partnership meeting.

6.3. Two-thirds Vote Required for Certain Actions: The affirmative vote of two-thirds of the Partners is required for each of the following actions:

1. A determination that a Partner is under permanent disability;
2. Expulsion of a Partner from the firm;
3. Mandating a Partner to retire;
4. Granting a Partner a temporary withdrawal from the firm;
5. Termination and liquidation of the firm;
6. Amendment of this Agreement, except as otherwise provided in 6.4 below.
7. Incurrence by the firm of any obligation in the principal amount of more than $________;
8. Compromise of any amount owed to the Partnership (including amounts of unbilled time or work in process) of more than $_____; or
9. Relocation of the Partnership's principal place of business or opening any additional offices.

6.4. Unanimous Approval Required for Certain Actions: A quorum of two-thirds of the Partners and the affirmative vote of all Partners in attendance is required for each of the following actions:

1. Admission as a Partner of a person not presently a Partner; or
2. Amendment of this Agreement with respect to the participation in profits and losses of the Partnership;

6.5. Partner Authority: Each Partner is authorized to take the following actions on behalf of the Partnership, without a prior vote by the partnership to permit the Partner to carry on the practice of law:

1. Accept clients on behalf of the Partnership and perform legal services for any Partnership client that will not create a conflict with any other Partnership client; provide, however, Partnership approval shall be required for any contingent fee arrangements and pro bono matters;
2. Authorize the Partnership to incur expenses and make routine advances with respect to the legal representation of a client up to $______;
3. Render legal opinions as to any legal matter within the expertise and knowledge of the Partner, and
4. Any action incidental to the Partner's practice of law.

6.6. Managing Partner: In December of each year, the Partnership shall select a Managing Partner for the following year. The Managing Partner will manage and control the day-to-day administrative affairs of the Partnership. The Managing Partner shall receive compensation for his services as Managing Partner in the amount of $______ per month. The Managing Partner shall use reasonable efforts to implement or cause to be implemented all decisions approved by the Partnership and to conduct or cause to be conducted the ordinary and usual business and affairs of the Partnership in accordance with this Agreement.

. . .

Partnership Agreement 3:

. . .

Article 6 – Management:

6.1. Authority of the Managing Partner: Except as otherwise provided in this Agreement, the right and authority to manage and control of the business and affairs of the Partnership shall be vested exclusively in the Managing Partner. The Managing Partner shall have the full discretionary power and authority to take any and all action she deems necessary, appropriate, incidental, or convenient in performing her duties as Managing Partner, provided, however, the Managing Partner shall not take any of the following actions without first obtaining the prior written approval of all the Partners:

(i) Knowingly do any act in contravention of this Agreement;

(ii) Knowingly do any act that would make it impossible to carry on the ordinary business of the Partnership, except as otherwise provided in this Agreement;

(iii) Cause the Partnership to incur any indebtedness or other contractual obligation obligating the Partnership to pay an aggregate amount (exclusive of interest) of more than $______;

(iv) Cause the Partnership to incur any indebtedness or other contractual obligation that, taken with all other existing indebtedness or contractual obligations (other than anticipated obligations to pay for routine services and supplies), will require the Partnership to pay more than $_____ in any fiscal year;

(v) Confess a judgment against the Partnership;

(vi) Possess Partnership property, or assign rights in specific Partnership property, for other than a Partnership purpose;

(vii) Cause or permit the Partnership to acquire any equity securities in any Partner or any of its Affiliates;

(viii) Sell or otherwise dispose of all or substantially all of any other Partnership property, except for liquidating sales of Partnership property in connection with the dissolution of the Partnership;

(ix) Dispose of the goodwill of the Partnership;

(x) Submit a Partnership claim or liability to arbitration or reference; or

(xi) Assign any Partnership property in trust for creditors or on the assignee's promise to pay the debts of the Partnership.

6.2. Authority of Other Partners: Notwithstanding the ability of any Partner to bind the Partnership in accordance with relevant provisions of partnership law, each Partner promises not to take any action that would have the effect of binding the Partnership in any manner whatsoever without the consent of the Managing Partner.

. . .

---

(24) AUTHORITY TO TRANSFER PARTNERSHIP PROPERTY:

Transfer of real property – UPA approach:

Refer to the following provisions to answer the questions below:

UPA §§8, 10

For further help, please refer to the following sections in the Text:

Text §§5B-203(d), 5B-203(e)

What is the legal effect of the purported transfer of partnership real property in each of the following circumstances?

(A) Title to real property is held in the name of the partnership. A partner executes conveyance in the partnership name.

(B) Title to real property is held in the name of the partnership. A partner executes conveyance in her own name.

(C) Title to real property is held in the name of one partner (or more than one partner), although the real property is partnership property. The partner(s) named on the title executes conveyance in her own name.

(D) Title to real property is held in the name of one partner (or more than one partner), although the real property is partnership property. A partner not named on the title executes conveyance in her own name.

(E) Title to real property is held in the name of all of the partners and all of them execute the conveyance.

Transfer of property – RUPA approach:

Refer to the following provisions to answer the questions below:

RUPA §302, 303

For further help, please refer to the following sections in the Text:

Text §§5B-203(d), 5B-203(e)

Assuming the partnership has not filed a statement of partnership authority, what is the legal effect of the purported transfer of partnership real property in each of the following circumstances?

(A) Title to real/personal property is held in the name of the partnership. A partner executes conveyance in the partnership name.

(B) Title to real/personal property is held in the name of the partnership. A partner executes conveyance in her own name.

(C) Title to real/personal property is held in the name of one partner (or more than one partner), although the real property is partnership property. The partner(s) named on the title executes conveyance in her own name.

(D) Title to real/personal property is held in the name of one partner (or more than one partner), although the real property is partnership property. A partner not named on the title executes conveyance in her own name.

(E) Title to real/personal property is held in the name of all of the partners and all of them execute the conveyance.

In general, how would a statement of partnership authority change your answers?

CHAPTER 5 – EXERCISES:

LLC VOTING AND AUTHORITY

---

(25) <u>CONCEPTUAL PROBLEM:</u>

Read the following sections in the Text:

Text §5C-100 et seq.

In a <u>member-managed</u> LLC, who would make the decisions listed below? The employees/agents (including a member acting as agent)? The members by a majority voting standard? The members by a greater-than-majority voting standard?

A decision to buy a ream of paper?

A decision to borrow a significant amount of money to finance the construction of a large retail outlet.

A decision to merge the LLC with another entity.

In a <u>manager-managed</u> LLC, who would make the decisions listed below? The employees/agents (including a manager acting as agent)? The managers by a majority voting standard? The members by a majority voting standard? The members by a greater-than-majority voting standard?

A decision to buy a ream of paper?

A decision to borrow a significant amount of money to finance the construction of a large retail outlet.

A decision to merge the LLC with another entity.

---

(26) <u>LEARNING THE STATUTE:</u>

In a member-managed LLC and a manager-managed LLC:

Refer to the following provisions to answer the questions below:

RULLCA §407

For further help, please refer to the following sections in the Text:

Text §§5C-103 et seq., 5C-201(a), 5C-201(b), 5C-201(c), 5C-201(e)

How often must an LLC hold a members' meeting?

May the members decide on a matter without actually holding a meeting? If so, does the law require unanimous consent?

Who can call for a members meeting or for a vote of the members if there will be no actual meeting?

How far in advance of the members meetings should the LLC provide notice of the meeting to the members?

Does the notice need to specify the purpose of the meeting?

How many votes are required to approve an action? Is voting based on the proportion of a member's investment in the LLC or per capita?

In a manager-managed LLC:

Refer to the following provisions to answer the questions below:

RULLCA §407

For further help, please refer to the following sections in the Text:

Text §§5C-103(b), 5C-201(d)

How many managers are required?

How are managers appointed or elected?

How are managers removed?

---

(27) <u>MEMBER VOTING & AUTHORITY:</u>

Refer to the following provisions to answer the questions below:

RULLCA §407

For further help, please refer to the following sections in the Text:

Text §§5C-201(b), 5C-201(c)

Harry, Helen, Mary and Martin are members in a member-managed LLC. The LLC operates a large grocery store.

> **H**arry has contributed 30% of the LLC's capital and **H**elen has contributed 38%. According to the LLC operating agreement, Harry is allocated 30% of the LLC profits and Helen is allocated 38%.
>
> **M**ary has contributed 10% of the partnership's capital and **M**artin has contributed 22%. According to the LLC operating agreement, Mary is allocated 10% of the LLC profits and Martin is allocated 22%.

Harry and **H**elen do not want the grocery store to buy produce from Fruit & Veg Inc. because they believe the quality of its produce is not very good.

In contrast, **M**ary and **M**artin want to buy produce from Fruit & Veg Inc. because its prices are low.

The members vote on the disagreement:

> **H**arry and Helen vote against buying produce from Fruit & Veg
>
> **M**ary and Martin vote in favor of buying produce from Fruit & Veg

Hypothetical A:

A few days after the members' vote, **M**artin places an order on behalf of the LLC for 10 cases of apples from Fruit & Veg. Fruit & Veg accepts the order, unaware of the members' vote.

> **Is the LLC bound by the order? What other facts do you need to know in order to form your legal opinion?**

Hypothetical B:

Immediately after the members' vote, **H**arry calls Fruit & Veg and informs them that the LLC has put Fruit & Veg on its "blacklist" and that no member has the authority to place orders with Fruit & Veg on behalf of the LLC.

However, a few days later, **M**artin places an order with Fruit & Veg for 10 cases of apples on behalf of the LLC. Fruit & Veg accepts the order despite the warning from Harry.

> **Is the LLC bound by the order? Would it make a difference if the LLC had been buying produce from Fruit & Veg on a regular basis for the past 10 years?**

---

(28) EXTRAORDINARY TRANSACTIONS:

Refer to the following provisions to answer the questions below:

RULLCA, generally & DLLCA, generally

For further help, please refer to the following sections in the Text:

Text §5C-201(c)

Please complete this chart comparing the RULLCA and DLLCA approaches to extraordinary transactions. Fill in whether the law requires approval by managers or members and what standard of approval is required (majority, supermajority, unanimous)?

	RULLCA approach	**DLLCA approach**
Merger of the LLC into another entity	Member-managed LLC: Manager-managed LLC:	Member-managed LLC: Manager-managed LLC:
Sale of substantially all the LLC's assets	Member-managed LLC: Manager-managed LLC:	Member-managed LLC: Manager-managed LLC:
Dissolution of the LLC	Member-managed LLC: Manager-managed LLC:	Member-managed LLC: Manager-managed LLC:
Amending the articles of organization	Member-managed LLC: Manager-managed LLC:	Member-managed LLC: Manager-managed LLC:

Amending the operating agreement	Member-managed LLC: Manager-managed LLC:	Member-managed LLC: Manager-managed LLC:
Admission of new members	Member-managed LLC: Manager-managed LLC:	Member-managed LLC: Manager-managed LLC:
Distributions to members	Member-managed LLC: Manager-managed LLC:	Member-managed LLC: Manager-managed LLC:
Compromising an obligation to make a contribution to the LLC.	Member-managed LLC: Manager-managed LLC:	Member-managed LLC: Manager-managed LLC:
Ratifying self-dealing transactions	Member-managed LLC: Manager-managed LLC:	Member-managed LLC: Manager-managed LLC:

---

(29) DRAFTING THE OPERATING AGREEMENT:

Attorneys often use a "checklist" as a guide for interviewing a client to determine her needs and gather the information required to draft the operating agreement.

As an exercise, please "reverse engineer" the process.

Below, please find the relevant parts of

(1) a "checklist;" and

(2) an operating agreements.

Explain how the client answered the questions on the checklist. Please assume that the attorney drafted the agreement according to the information she gathered when she interviewed the client using the checklist.

<u>LLC Operating Agreement Checklist:</u>

. . .

Will the LLC be member-managed or manager-managed?

If member-managed:

> Will all members have the authority to bind the LLC?
>
> What are the relative voting rights of members? Per capita, based on investment interest, based on different classes of membership interest, etc.
>
> What actions will require member approval? What approval standard?
>
> What are the voting processes? Formal meetings? Proxies? Notice? Consent without meetings? Who has the right to call a meeting?
>
> Will the members have an annual meeting?

If manager-managed:

> How many managers?
>
> How will the manager(s) be chosen?
>
> How long will manager(s) serve? How will the manager(s) be removed before expiration of their term?
>
> If there are multiple managers, how will the managers make decisions? Formal meetings? Regularly scheduled meetings? Proxies? Notice? Consent without meetings? Who has the right to call a meeting?
>
> What actions will require member approval? What approval standard?
>
> What are the voting processes for members? Formal meetings? Proxies? Notice? Consent without meetings? Who has the right to call a meeting?
>
> Will the members have an annual meeting? . . .

GOO ENTERPRISES, LLC
OPERATING AGREEMENT

This Operating Agreement ("Agreement") is entered into this 12th day of October, 2015 by the persons signing this Agreement (each a "Member" and, collectively, the "Members").

Whereas, the Members desire to form a limited liability company;

Now, therefore, the Members agree to the following terms and conditions:

ARTICLE I:
DEFINITIONS

The following terms, as used in this Agreement, have the indicated definitions:

. . .

"**Membership Interest**" has the meaning assigned to it in Section 3.3
. . .

ARTICLE II:
FORMATION, PURPOSES, DURATION

Section 2.1. Name: The Company will be named Goo Enterprises, LLC.

Section 2.2. Formation: The Members shall cause Articles of Organization of the Company to be filed with the Secretary of State of [name of the state of organization] on or before November 12, 2015.

Section 2.3. Purposes: The Members are forming the Company to manufacture and sell semiconductors. The Company may also conduct or promote any lawful business or purpose permitted by the law of [name of the state of organization].

Section 2.4. Duration: The existence of the Company will begin on the date the Secretary of State of [name of the state of organization] files the Articles of Organization and will continue perpetually until the Company is dissolved pursuant to relevant law or the terms of this Agreement.

ARTICLE III:
CAPITAL CONTRIBUTIONS, MEMBERSHIP INTERESTS, AND CAPITAL ACCOUNTS

Section 3.1. Initial Contributions: The Members shall make initial contributions of capital to the Company in the amounts enumerated in Exhibit A, attached to this Agreement. The Members shall make their respective initial contributions within thirty (30) days of receipt of the notice from the Secretary of State of [name of the state of organization] that the Articles of Organization have been duly filed.

Section 3.2. Additional Contributions: The Members shall not be required to make any additional capital contributions or loans to the Company. If two-thirds of Membership Interests determine that additional capital contributions from the Members is appropriate, a Member may, but shall not be required, to contribute additional capital to the Company.

Section 3.3.Membership Interests: The Membership Interest of a Member at any time shall be determined according to the following formula:

(the total amount of all of the Member's capital contributions, less her withdrawals of capital, if any) ***divided by*** (the total amount of all Members' capital contributions, less their total withdrawals of capital, if any)

Section 3.4. Loan Guaranties by Members: . . .

ARTICLE IV:
ALLOCATION OF PROFITS AND LOSSES

. . .

ARTICLE V:
MEMBER'S SALARIES AND WITHDRAWALS FROM CAPITAL ACCOUNTS

. . .

ARTICLE VI:
MANAGEMENT

Section 6.1. General: The Company shall be managed by its Members. Each member shall have an equal voice in the management of the Company except as otherwise provided in this Agreement.

Section 6.2. Powers of Members: Each Member shall have the right, power and authority to do or cause to be done any acts furthering the business and affairs of the Company, subject to the restrictions in Section 6.3 and 6.4.

Section 6.3. Action Requiring the Vote of a Majority of Membership Interests: If a disagreement arises with respect to any action or transaction, other than those transactions listed is Section 6.4 requiring the consent of all the Members, the Members shall vote to resolve the disagreement. An affirmative vote of the Majority of Membership Interests will resolve the disagreement.

Section 6.4. Actions Requiring the Consent of All Members: Notwithstanding any other provision of this agreement, each of the following transactions requires the written consent of all Members of the Company:

(a) The execution of a promissory note on behalf of the Company;

(b) A promise on behalf of the Company to guaranty the obligation(s) of any person or entity;

(c) A transaction between the Company and any of its Members;

(d) The execution on behalf of the Company of any mortgage, security agreement, bond, or lease;

(e) The purchase or promise to purchase, or the sale or promise to sell, on behalf of the Company any property other than property bought or sold in the regular course of the Company's business;

(f) The dissolution of the Company;

(g) The merger or consolidation of the Company, regardless of whether the Company is the surviving entity or the target entity;

(h) The sale, transfer, contribution, exchange, mortgage, pledge, encumbrance, lease, or other disposition of all or substantially all of the Company's assets;

(i) The admission of new Members, either through the issuance of new Membership Interests by the Company or through the Transfer of Membership Interests by a person who is already a Member pursuant to Article VIII below;

(j) Distributions to Members; or

(k) The amendment of this Agreement.

Section 6.5. Processes for Approval, Consent, Voting, and Ratification: When applicable law or this Agreement requires the consent, approval, ratification, vote or similar action of the Members of the Company, such consent, approval, ratification, vote or action may be accomplished with or without a formal meeting of the Members.

Section 6.6. Member Meetings: The Members shall cause the Company to hold one regular meeting of Members each year, the date of which shall be determined by a Majority of the Membership Interests. Each Member will have the right to call a special meeting of the Members. When the Company holds a formal meeting, a Member will have the right to attend the meeting and vote by written proxy or written consent.

ARTICLE VII:
BOOKS AND RECORDS

. . .

ARTICLE VIII:
ASSIGNMENT AND TRANSFER OF MEMBERSHIP INTERESTS

. . .

ARTICLE IX:
DISSOLUTION AND LIQUIDATION

. . . .

Exhibit A
Initial Member Contributions

(30) THE APPOINTMENT OF MANAGERS:

Refer to the following provisions to answer the questions below:

RULLCA §407; DLLCA §18-402

For further help, please refer to the following sections in the Text:

Text §5C-201(d)

You are drafting an LLC operating agreement. The LLC will be manager-managed. There will only be three members - A, B, and C. Each of them will be managers.

Your client is C. C will contribute 56% of the initial LLC capital.

How would draft for the appointment/election and removal of managers? [The purpose of this exercise for you to think of a way to draft it, not to actually draft it.]

Which default rules, DLLCA or RULLCA, are most likely best for your client if the operating agreement is silent on appointment/election and removal of managers?

(31) CLASS VOTING:

Refer to the following provisions to answer the questions below:

DLLCA §§18-302(d), 18-302(a), 18-209(b)

For further help, please refer to the following sections in the Text:

Text §5C-201(f)

Imagine you have set up an LLC under Delaware law for your client with four classes of membership interests: Classes A, B, C, and D. Each of the four founding members holds one of the classes.

Each class has 100 "units." Each unit represents one vote.

The members discuss merging their LLC into another LLC. The matter comes to a vote and the votes are cast in the following manner.

Class A: 100 units voted ***in favor*** of the merger

Class B: 100 units voted ***in favor*** of the merger

Class C: 100 units voted ***in favor*** of the merger

Class D: 100 units voted ***against*** the merger

Would the members need to have a formal meeting?

Does the merger pass? Is this the result you expected? Is it the result your client expected? Please feel free to speculate on the various possible expectations of your client?

WORKBOOK

CHAPTER 6

FIDUCIARY DUTIES

CHAPTER 6 – EXERCISES:

---

(1) CONCEPTUAL PROBLEMS:

Please read §6A-100 et seq. in the Text.

(A) **Why should the law treat duty of loyalty issues differently from duty of care issues?** [Please read §§6A-202(a), 6A-204(g) in the Text.]

(B) **What is the purpose of having a higher standard of conduct with a more lax standard of liability for the duty of care?** [Please read §6A-204(b) in the Text.]

(C) **What is the business judgment rule? How does it protect officers and directors from liability for their decisions? Generally, how can a shareholder overcome the business judgment rule?** [Please read §6A-104 in the Text.]

(D) **Is it good to protect directors from legal liability for their bad decisions?** [Please read §6A-204(g) in the Text.]

---

(2) EXCULPATION:

Refer to the following provisions to answer the questions below:

RMBCA §2.02(b)(4)

For further help, please refer to the following sections in the Text:

Text §§6A-106, 6A-202(j), 6A-204(d), 6A-205(h), 6A-209 et seq.

Please read the clause below and answer the following questions:

Where would you find this clause?

What is the significance of the clause?

Does the clause protect officers? Could we draft the clause to protect officers?

Would the clause protect directors against an injunction?

Would the clause protect a director if . . .

(a) She embezzled from the corporation?

(b) She and the other directors participated in a reckless decision-making process?

(c) She took a kickback from one of the corporation's suppliers?

(d) She intentionally tried to cause harm to the corporation?

(e) She sold land to the corporation for an exorbitant price?

(f) She took a business opportunity that the corporation wanted.

(g) She and the other directors failed to prevent the employees from stealing from the corporation?

The liability of the Corporation's directors to the Corporation or its stockholders for damages for breach of duty as a director shall be eliminated to the fullest extent permitted by the [Business Corporation Law of the State of ________], as it exists on the date hereof or as it may hereafter be amended. No amendment to or repeal of this article shall apply to or have any effect on the liability or alleged liability of any director of the Corporation for or with respect to any acts or omissions of such director occurring prior to such amendment or repeal.

---

(3) CONFLICTED TRANSACTIONS:

Refer to the following provisions to answer the questions below:

RMBCA §§8.60-8.63

For further help, please refer to the following sections in the Text:

Text §6A-202 et seq.

Read RMBCA §§8.60-8.63 and compare it with the Duty of Loyalty – Conflicted Transaction Flowchart (and its alternate) at §6A-202(k) in the Text.

Is the RMBCA's approach consistent with the flowchart? Where does it differ?

---

(4) <u>CORPORATE OPPORTUNITY:</u>

Refer to the following provisions to answer the questions below:

RMBCA §8.70

For further help, please refer to the following sections in the Text:

Text §6A-203 et seq.

Read RMBCA §8.70 and compare it with the Duty of Loyalty – Corporate Opportunity Flowchart at §6A-203(d) in the Text.

Is the RMBCA's approach consistent with the flowchart? Where does it differ?

---

(5) <u>CORPORATE OPPORTUNITY – FACT PATTERN:</u>

Refer to the following sections in the Text to help you answer the questions below:

Text §6A-203 et seq.

(A) Singer was hired as general manager of GA Inc. GA did tooling and machining – i.e., providing custom machined parts for engines, factory equipment and the like. GA hired Singer because of his excellent reputation in the industry.[2]

Under Singer's management, GA became very profitable. In fact, it was operating at full capacity and could not take any new orders.

A customer called Singer at GA's offices and said: "Singer, I have not seen you in a while. How are things as the general manager GA? My company has a large job and I trust your skill and expertise to handle it right."

Singer explained that because GA was working at full capacity, it could not accept the order, but he could personally act as a broker to find several machine shops to handle the work.

The customer agreed. Singer outsourced the work to several machine shops and earned broker's fees for himself.

---

[2] Fact pattern based on *General Automotive Mfg. v. Singer*, 120 N.W.2d 659 (Wis. 1963)

When the board of directors of GA discovered that Singer had acted as broker for the customer, it sued Singer for breaching his fiduciary duties.

What are the board's prospects of success?

(B) Change the facts above: Singer is not the general manager. He is a director on the board of GA. The customer ran into him at a bar and was not aware that he was on the board of GA when he asked Singer to help him.

Do these fact changes make a difference?

---

(6) DECISION-MAKING:

Refer to the following sections in the Text to help you answer the questions below:

Text §§6A-105, 6A-204 et seq., 6A-206 et seq., 6A-207

Also refer to the following provisions:

RMBCA §§8.30, 8.31

The board of XYZ Corp. is deliberating whether to undertake Project A or Project B.

The board spent a significant amount of time gathering information and discussing it. The board also solicited the advice of three experts. All three experts recommended the corporation undertake Project A, not Project B.

The board spent considerable time discussing the recommendations of the experts and the merits of each project. In the end, the board approved Project B, despite the experts' recommendations of Project A.

Project B turns out to be a complete failure for the corporation. The corporation loses millions of dollars on Project B.

A shareholder sues the board of directors for breaching its fiduciary duty. What is your analysis of the prospects of success of the shareholder's claim?

---

(7) DISCLOSURE IN CONFLICTED TRANSACTIONS:

Refer to the following sections in the Text to help you answer the questions below:

Text §6A-202(d)

Also refer to the following provisions:

RMBCA §§8.60(7), 8.62

The board of Goo Inc. is deliberating the purchase of a plot of land, on which it plans to build a manufacturing plant. There are five directors on the board. Director X owns the plot of land that Goo Inc. in planning to purchase.

(A) When the board meets to discuss the purchase, director X shows up for the meeting.

You are advising the board. May director X attend the meeting? May she vote on the transaction?

(B) Director X knows the following about the land:

- There is an abandoned, unstable mineshaft under the surface;
- She is willing to accept a price as low as $500,000, even though she is asking for $750,000;
- The land is reputed to be haunted;
- There is a very similar plot of land in the nearby vicinity that is selling for half the price;
- She urgently needs the money to pay off her debts;

What information must director X disclose to the board to ensure the board vote is a valid ratification of the conflicted transaction?

If she does not make the required disclosures and the board approves the purchase of the land, what are the ramifications for her?

If it were an arm's length transaction, what information would she need to disclose?

(C) Assume that director X is NOT the owner of the land. Instead, Lando Inc. owns the land. Director X is also sits on the board of Lando Inc. Assume the information about the land applies *mutatis mutandis* to Lando Inc. and that director X knows all of the information.

What must director X disclose to the board of Goo Inc.?

---

(8) LOANS TO DIRECTORS:

Refer to the following sections in the Text to help you answer the questions below:

Text §6A-202(g)

XYZ Inc. is a private company. It is welcoming a new director to the board. The new director is well-known and well respected in the industry. The new director does not like to travel. She would like to move closer to the corporation's principal place of business.

The board of directors agrees to reimburse her for all moving expenses up to $20,000. It also agrees to give her a loan of $600,000 with a favorable interest rate to help her purchase a home in the area.

You are advising the board.

Are there any procedures the board should consider?

If XYZ Inc. were a public corporation, might your advice be different?

---

(9) SHAREHOLDER RATIFICATION:

Refer to the following sections in the Text to help you answer the questions below:

Text §§6A-202(k) (alternate flowchart), 6A-211(a)-(d)

Alpha Corp. is the controlling shareholder of Zeta Inc., owning 51% of Zeta's common stock. Alpha Corp. plans to merge Zeta Inc. into Alpha and cash out Zeta's minority shareholders.

Zeta's board approved the merger with Alpha. All of Zeta's directors are employees of Alpha. Zeta's board submits the merger to Zeta's shareholders for approval of Zeta's minority shareholders.

The merger receives approval of "a majority of the minority."

Several months later, a former Zeta minority shareholder sues Alpha for breach of fiduciary duties? Alpha asks the court to apply the business judgment rule and dismiss the case.

What are the chances the judge will dismiss the case?

If the court does not dismiss the case, what is the next step in the trial?

---

(10) OOPS:

Refer to the following sections in the Text to help you answer the questions below:

Text §§6A-204 et seq., 6A-205 et seq.

Also refer to the following provisions:

RMBCA §§8.30, 8.31

During a very busy year, XYZ Corp. forgot to renew its fire insurance. Unfortunately, the company's warehouse burned down soon after the policy lapsed.

A shareholder sues the board for the loss of the warehouse, which was not covered by insurance.

What are the shareholder's prospects of success?

---

(11) RISK:

Refer to the following sections in the Text to help you answer the questions below:

Text §6A-204 et seq.

Also refer to the following provisions:

RMBCA §§8.30, 8.31

The board of directors of LMNO Inc. is considering investing $500 million in "Project Zed." The board recognizes that Project Zed is very risky. Indeed, according to the board's own assessment, there is a 60% chance that the project will fail and the corporation will lose its entire $500 million.

The board decides to go through with Project Zed after much research and deliberation. Unfortunately, the investment is a spectacular failure. LMNO loses its entire $500 million.

A shareholder sues the board for breach of its fiduciary duties.

What are the prospects of success for the shareholder's lawsuit?

---

(12) BOARD RATIFICATION:

Refer to the following sections in the Text to help you answer the questions below:

Text §§6A-202 et seq., 6A-204 et seq., 6A-206 et seq., 6A-207

The board of directors of **Alpha Corp.** approved the purchase the assets of **Beta Corp**. for $30,000,000. Alpha subsequently paid the purchase price and acquired the assets.

The Alpha board consisted of seven (7) directors.

Four of the Alpha board members ("**The Four**") were the sole shareholders of Beta Corp (each owning 25% of Beta's outstanding shares).

The other three directors of Alpha ("**The Three**") had no shareholdings in Beta, nor did they have any other employment or financial relationship with Beta or with The Four.

Susan is a shareholder of Alpha. Susan felt that Alpha paid an excessively high price for Beta's assets. She brought a shareholder derivative lawsuit again all the directors on Alpha's board.

Susan's derivative suit survived the board's request for dismissal. The following additional facts come out during discovery:

> Alpha's total assets immediately prior to the purchase of Beta's assets were valued at $60,000,000.
>
> Before Alpha entered into the transaction with Beta, The Four disclosed their financial interests in Beta to The Three. The Four also provided The Three with all information they had about the condition of Beta's assets, any latent defects in the assets, and Beta's projections about the ability of its assets to produce income.

The Three met among themselves, outside the presence of The Four. They voted to approve the transaction after twenty minutes of review and discussion of the information provided to them by The Four.

The Four are also the executive officers of Alpha and they control who is nominated for board positions. The Three have employment and income aside from the compensation they receive for serving on Alpha's board. Indeed, the compensation they receive for serving on Alpha's board is an insignificant percentage of each of their annual incomes.

All seven of the directors on Alpha's board have served on the same board for 12 years. They have grown to be friends. They visit each other's houses for social occasions. The directors all have children that attend the same school. They are all active on the school's board of advisors.

There is conflicting evidence about whether the price Alpha paid for Beta's assets was excessive. There is also conflicting evidence with respect to whether Alpha actually needed Beta's assets.

The articles of incorporation of Alpha contain the following provision:

> "No director or officer of the corporation shall be liable to the corporation for any breach of her fiduciary duties."

(A) Discuss Susan's prospects of success against <u>The Four</u> for breach of their fiduciary duties.

(B) Discuss Susan's prospects of success against <u>The Three</u> for breach of their fiduciary duties.

---

(13) TO WHOM DO DIRECTORS OWE FIDUCIARY DUTIES?

Refer to the following sections in the Text to help you answer the questions below:

Text §6A-210 et seq.

Read the three following provisions from various corporate law statutes (Ohio, Connecticut, Iowa) and answer the following questions:

What is the significance of these provisions?

What are the major differences between these three provisions?

OHIO:

> [A] director, in in determining what the director reasonably believes to be in the best interests of the corporation, shall consider the interests of the corporation's shareholders and, in the director's discretion, may consider any of the following:
>
> (1) The interests of the corporation's employees, suppliers, creditors, and customers;
>
> (2) The economy of the state and nation;
>
> (3) Community and societal considerations;
>
> (4) The long-term as well as short-term interests of the corporation and its shareholders, including the possibility that these interests may be best served by the continued independence of the corporation.

CONNECTICUT:

> (a) A director shall discharge his duties as a director, including his duties as a member of a committee: (1) In good faith; (2) with the care an ordinarily prudent person in a like position would exercise under similar circumstances; and (3) in a manner he reasonably believes to be in the best interests of the corporation. . . .
>
> (d) For purposes of sections **33-817, 33-830, 33-831, 33-841 and 33-844**,* a director of a corporation which has **a class of voting stock registered pursuant to Section 12 of the Securities Exchange Act of 1934**,** . . . may consider, in determining what he reasonably believes to be in the best interests of the corporation, (1) the long-term as well as the short-term interests of the corporation, (2) the interests of the shareholders, long-term as well as short-term, including the possibility that those interests may be best served by the continued independence of the corporation, (3) the interests of the corporation's employees, customers, creditors and suppliers, and (4) community and societal considerations including those of any community in which any office or other facility of the corporation is located. A director may also in his discretion consider any other factors he reasonably considers appropriate in determining what he reasonably believes to be in the best interests of the corporation.

*NB 1: These sections in Connecticut's statutes address various types of corporate mergers, acquisitions, and takeovers.

**NB 2: Registration under Section 12 of the Securities Exchange Act of 1934 means the class of stock is publicly traded.

IOWA:

1. A director, in determining what is in the best interest of the corporation when considering a tender offer or proposal of acquisition, merger, consolidation, or similar proposal, may consider any or all of the following community interest factors, in addition to consideration of the effects of any action on shareholders:

a. The effects of the action on the corporation's employees, suppliers, creditors, and customers.

b. The effects of the action on the communities in which the corporation operates.

c. The long-term as well as short-term interests of the corporation and its shareholders, including the possibility that these interests may be best served by the continued independence of the corporation.

2. If on the basis of the community interest factors described in subsection 1, the board of directors determines that a proposal or offer to acquire or merge the corporation is not in the best interests of the corporation, it may reject the proposal or offer. If the board of directors determines to reject any such proposal or offer, the board of directors has no obligation to facilitate, to remove any barriers to, or to refrain from impeding, the proposal or offer. Consideration of any or all of the community interest factors is not a violation of the business judgment rule or of any duty of the director to the shareholders, or a group of shareholders, even if the director reasonably determines that a community interest factor or factors outweigh the financial or other benefits to the corporation or a shareholder or group of shareholders.

---

(14) THE DUTY OF LOYALTY – CORPORATE OPPORTUNITY:

Refer to the following sections in the Text to help you answer the questions below:

Text §6A-203 et seq.

Please read the facts of ***Broz v. Cellular Information Systems, Inc.***,[3] below, and answer the following questions:

[3] 673 A.2d 148 (Del. 1996).

Should Broz be liable for taking a corporate opportunity?

Broz asked several members of the board if he could take the opportunity and they all agreed. Would this count as board ratification? Why or why not?

Who had the burden of proof in the case, Broz or the plaintiff?

. . . Robert F. Broz ("Broz") is the President and sole stockholder of RFB Cellular, Inc. ("RFBC"), a Delaware corporation engaged in the business of providing cellular telephone service in the Midwestern United States. At the time of the conduct at issue in this appeal, Broz was also a member of the board of directors of plaintiff below-appellee, Cellular Information Systems, Inc. ("CIS"). CIS is a publicly held Delaware corporation and a competitor of RFBC.

The conduct before the Court involves the purchase by Broz of a cellular telephone service license for the benefit of RFBC.[1] The license in question, known as the Michigan-2 Rural Service Area Cellular License ("Michigan-2"), is issued by the Federal Communications Commission ("FCC") and entitles its holder to provide cellular telephone service to a portion of northern Michigan. CIS brought an action against Broz and RFBC for equitable relief, contending that the purchase of this license by Broz constituted a usurpation of a corporate opportunity properly belonging to CIS, irrespective of whether or not CIS was interested in the Michigan-2 opportunity at the time it was offered to Broz. . . .

---

1. The Court recognizes that the actual purchase of the Michigan-2 license was consummated by RFBC as a corporate entity, rather than by Broz acting as an individual for his own benefit. Broz is, however, the sole party in interest in RFBC and all actions taken by RFBC, including the acquisition of Michigan-2, are accomplished at the behest of Broz. Therefore, insofar as the purchase of Michigan-2 is concerned, the Court will not distinguish between the actions of Broz and those of RFBC in analyzing Broz' alleged breach of fiduciary duty.

Broz has been the President and sole stockholder of RFBC since 1992. RFBC owns and operates an FCC license area, known as the Michigan-4 Rural Service Area Cellular License ("Michigan-4"). The license entitles RFBC to provide cellular telephone service to a portion of rural Michigan. Although Broz' efforts have been devoted primarily to the business operations of RFBC, he also served as an outside director of CIS at the time of the events at issue in this case. CIS was at all times fully aware of Broz' relationship with RFBC and the obligations incumbent upon him by virtue of that relationship.

In April of 1994, Mackinac Cellular Corp. ("Mackinac") sought to divest itself of Michigan-2, the license area immediately adjacent to Michigan-4. To this end,

Mackinac contacted Daniels & Associates ("Daniels") and arranged for the brokerage firm to seek potential purchasers for Michigan-2. In compiling a list of prospects, Daniels included RFBC as a likely candidate. In May of 1994, David Rhodes, a representative of Daniels, contacted Broz and broached the subject of RFBC's possible acquisition of Michigan-2. Broz later signed a confidentiality agreement at the request of Mackinac, and received the offering materials pertaining to Michigan-2.

Michigan-2 was not, however, offered to CIS. Apparently, Daniels did not consider CIS to be a viable purchaser for Michigan-2 in light of CIS' recent financial difficulties. The record shows that, at the time Michigan-2 was offered to Broz, CIS had recently emerged from lengthy and contentious Chapter 11 proceedings. Pursuant to the Chapter 11 Plan of Reorganization, CIS entered into a loan agreement that substantially impaired the company's ability to undertake new acquisitions or to incur new debt. In fact, CIS would have been unable to purchase Michigan-2 without the approval of its creditors.

The CIS reorganization resulted from the failure of CIS' rather ambitious plans for expansion. From 1989 onward, CIS had embarked on a series of cellular license acquisitions. In 1992, however, CIS' financing failed, necessitating the liquidation of the company's holdings and reduction of the company's total indebtedness. During the period from early 1992 until the time of CIS' emergence from bankruptcy in 1994, CIS divested itself of some fifteen separate cellular license systems. CIS contracted to sell four additional license areas on May 27, 1994, leaving CIS with only five remaining license areas, all of which were outside of the Midwest.

On June 13, 1994, following a meeting of the CIS board, Broz spoke with CIS' Chief Executive Officer, Richard Treibick ("Treibick"), concerning his interest in acquiring Michigan-2. Treibick communicated to Broz that CIS was not interested in Michigan-2. Treibick further stated that he had been made aware of the Michigan-2 opportunity prior to the conversation with Broz, and that any offer to acquire Michigan-2 was rejected. After the commencement of the PriCellular tender offer, in August of 1994, Broz contacted another CIS director, Peter Schiff ("Schiff"), to discuss the possible acquisition of Michigan-2 by RFBC. Schiff, like Treibick, indicated that CIS had neither the wherewithal nor the inclination to purchase Michigan-2. In late September of 1994, Broz also contacted Stanley Bloch ("Bloch"), a director and counsel for CIS, to request that Bloch represent RFBC in its dealings with Mackinac. Bloch agreed to represent RFBC, and, like Schiff and Treibick, expressed his belief that CIS was not at all interested in the transaction. Ultimately, all the CIS directors testified at trial that, had Broz inquired at that time, they each would have expressed the opinion that CIS was not interested in Michigan-2. . . .

. . . Mackinac did not consider CIS a viable candidate for the acquisition of Michigan-2. Accordingly, Mackinac did not offer the property to CIS. . . .

. . . The record shows that CIS was in a precarious financial position at the time Mackinac presented the Michigan-2 opportunity to Broz. Having recently emerged from lengthy and contentious bankruptcy proceedings . . .. Further, the loan agreement entered into by CIS and its creditors severely limited the discretion of CIS as to the acquisition of new assets and substantially restricted the ability of CIS to incur new debt.

. . . At the time the opportunity was presented, CIS was actively engaged in the process of divesting its cellular license holdings. CIS' articulated business plan did not involve any new acquisitions. Further, as indicated by the testimony of the entire CIS board, the Michigan-2 license would not have been of interest to CIS even absent CIS' financial difficulties and CIS' then current desire to liquidate its cellular license holdings. . . .

---

(15) THE DUTY OF CARE:

Refer to the following sections in the Text to help you answer the questions below:

Text §§6A-204 et seq., 6A-209 et seq.

Smith v. Van Gorkom[4] is one of those cases that you must know if you want to consider yourself literate in corporate law.

Please read the facts of ***Smith v. Van Gorkom***, below, and answer the following questions:

What is the liability standard for the duty of care?

Although the court's opinion was not expressly organized as such, the case is about (1) whether the board was grossly negligent in its decision-making process, and (2) assuming the board was grossly negligent, whether it proved the transaction was fair. Which facts are relevant to the gross negligence issue and which facts are relevant to the fairness issue?

The defendants claimed that the lawyer told them they would be sued by the shareholders if they did not approve the deal. Assuming the lawyer gave this advice, was this good advice? What advice

[4] 488 A.2d 858 (Del. 1985)

would you give about a possible shareholder lawsuit for not approving the deal?

The Trans Union shareholders voted in favor of the transaction, with overwhelming support. What affect should the shareholder vote have on the lawsuit?

What was the legislative aftermath of this case?

<u>Background to help you understand the transaction in the case:</u>

The board of directors of Trans Union was considering a merger. In the merger, Trans Union would be merged into Marmon (actually a subsidiary of Marmon). Trans Union would become part of Marmon and the Trans Union shareholders would be bought out at $55 per share.

The parties contemplated that the merger would be a leveraged buy-out ("LBO"). An LBO sounds complicated, but when people purchase homes, they almost always use an LBO-like structure.

In an LBO, the buyer – Marmon in this case – puts up a little money of its own and borrows the remainder. It is very similar to a mortgage loan, except in the LBO, the buyer usually borrows from the market by issuing bonds to investors, not from a bank. The buyer is hoping that the cash flow from its new company – Trans Union in this case – will be enough to pay the interest and principal on the bonds.

Think of an LBO as analogous to borrowing money to buy a house you hope to keep as an investment property. You put up a little cash of your own and borrow the rest. You "cash out" the current owner, take over ownership of the house, rent it out to a tenant, and hope the rent income covers the monthly mortgage payments.

<u>The facts of the case:</u>

. . .

I.

The nature of this case requires a detailed factual statement. The following facts are essentially uncontradicted: [Trans Union was unable to take advantage a favorable tax laws because it did not have enough taxable income. Trans Union acquired several companies in order to increase Trans Union's taxable income]. . . .

-B-

On August 27, 1980, Van Gorkom [the Chief Executive Officer of Trans Union] met with Senior Management of Trans Union. Van Gorkom reported on his . . . desire to find a solution to the tax credit problem more permanent than a continued program of acquisitions. Various alternatives were suggested and discussed preliminarily, including the sale of Trans Union to a company with a large amount of taxable income.

Donald Romans, Chief Financial Officer of Trans Union, stated that his department had done a "very brief bit of work on the possibility of a leveraged buy-out." . . . As Romans stated, this analysis "was very first and rough cut at seeing whether a cash flow would support what might be considered a high price for this type of transaction."

On September 5, at another Senior Management meeting which Van Gorkom attended, Romans again brought up the idea of a leveraged buy-out as a "possible strategic alternative" to the Company's acquisition program. Romans and Bruce S. Chelberg, President and Chief Operating Officer of Trans Union, had been working on the matter in preparation for the meeting. According to Romans: They did not "come up" with a price for the Company. They merely "ran the numbers" at $50 a share and at $60 a share with the "rough form" of their cash figures at the time. Their "figures indicated that $50 would be very easy to do but $60 would be very difficult to do under those figures." This work did not purport to establish a fair price for either the Company or 100% of the stock. It was intended to determine the cash flow needed to service the debt that would "probably" be incurred in a leveraged buy-out, based on "rough calculations" without "any benefit of experts to identify what the limits were to that, and so forth." These computations were not considered extensive and no conclusion was reached.

At this meeting, Van Gorkom stated that he would be willing to take $55 per share for his own 75,000 shares. . . . Van Gorkom, a certified public accountant and lawyer, had been an officer of Trans Union for 24 years, its Chief Executive Officer for more than 17 years, and Chairman of its Board for 2 years. It is noteworthy in this connection that he was then approaching 65 years of age and mandatory retirement. . . .

Van Gorkom decided to meet with Jay A. Pritzker, a well-known corporate takeover specialist and a social acquaintance. . . . Van Gorkom assembled a proposed per share price for sale of the Company and a financing structure by which to accomplish the sale. Van Gorkom did so without consulting either his Board or any members of Senior Management except one: Carl Peterson, Trans Union's Controller. Telling Peterson that he wanted no other person on his staff to know what he was doing, but without telling him why, Van Gorkom directed Peterson to calculate the feasibility of a leveraged buy-out at an assumed price per share of $55. Apart from the Company's historic stock market price, and

Van Gorkom's long association with Trans Union, the record is devoid of any competent evidence that $55 represented the per share intrinsic value of the Company. . . .

Van Gorkom arranged a meeting with Pritzker at the latter's home on Saturday, September 13, 1980. Van Gorkom prefaced his presentation by stating to Pritzker: "Now as far as you are concerned, I can, I think, show how you can pay a substantial premium over the present stock price and pay off most of the loan in the first five years. . . . If you could pay $55 for this Company, here is a way in which I think it can be financed."

Van Gorkom then reviewed with Pritzker his calculations based upon his proposed price of $55 per share. Although Pritzker mentioned $50 as a more attractive figure, no other price was mentioned. However, Van Gorkom stated that to be sure that $55 was the best price obtainable, Trans Union should be free to accept any better offer. Pritzker demurred, stating that his organization would serve as a "stalking horse" for an "auction contest" only if Trans Union would permit Pritzker to buy 1,750,000 shares of Trans Union stock at market price which Pritzker could then sell to any higher bidder. After further discussion on this point, Pritzker told Van Gorkom that he would give him a more definite reaction soon.

On Monday, September 15, Pritzker advised Van Gorkom that he was interested in the $55 cash-out merger proposal and requested more information on Trans Union. Van Gorkom agreed to meet privately with Pritzker . . .. The meetings took place on September 16 and 17. Van Gorkom was "astounded that events were moving with such amazing rapidity."

On Thursday, September 18, Van Gorkom met again with Pritzker. At that time, Van Gorkom knew that Pritzker intended to make a cash-out merger offer at Van Gorkom's proposed $55 per share. Pritzker instructed his attorney, a merger and acquisition specialist, to begin drafting merger documents. There was no further discussion of the $55 price. However, the number of shares of Trans Union's treasury stock to be offered to Pritzker was negotiated down to one million shares; the price was set at $38 – 75 cents above the per share price at the close of the market on September 19. At this point, Pritzker insisted that the Trans Union Board act on his merger proposal within the next three days, stating to Van Gorkom: "We have to have a decision by no later than Sunday [evening, September 21] before the opening of the English stock exchange on Monday morning." Pritzker's lawyer was then instructed to draft the merger documents, to be reviewed by Van Gorkom's lawyer, "sometimes with discussion and sometimes not, in the haste to get it finished." . . .

On Friday, September 19, Van Gorkom called a special meeting of the Trans Union Board for noon the following day. He also called a meeting of the Company's Senior Management to convene at 11:00 a.m., prior to the meeting of the Board. No one, except Chelberg and Peterson, was told the purpose of the meetings. . . .

. . . Van Gorkom disclosed the offer and described its terms, but he furnished no copies of the proposed Merger Agreement. Romans announced that his department had done a second study which showed that, for a leveraged buy-out, the price range for Trans Union stock was between $55 and $65 per share. Van Gorkom neither saw the study nor asked Romans to make it available for the Board meeting. . . .

Ten directors served on the Trans Union Board, five inside (defendants Bonser, O'Boyle, Browder, Chelberg, and Van Gorkom) and five outside (defendants Wallis, Johnson, Lanterman, Morgan and Reneker). All directors were present at the meeting, except O'Boyle who was ill. Of the outside directors, four were corporate chief executive officers and one was the former Dean of the University of Chicago Business School. None was an investment banker or trained financial analyst. All members of the Board were well informed about the Company and its operations as a going concern. They were familiar with the current financial condition of the Company, as well as operating and earnings projections reported in the recent Five Year Forecast. The Board generally received regular and detailed reports and was kept abreast of the accumulated investment tax credit and accelerated depreciation problem.

Van Gorkom began the Special Meeting of the Board with a twenty-minute oral presentation. Copies of the proposed Merger Agreement were delivered too late for study before or during the meeting. . . . Van Gorkom did not disclose to the Board, however, the methodology by which he alone had arrived at the $55 figure, or the fact that he first proposed the $55 price in his negotiations with Pritzker.

Van Gorkom outlined the terms of the Pritzker offer as follows: Pritzker would pay $55 in cash for all outstanding shares of Trans Union stock upon completion of which Trans Union would be merged into New T Company, a subsidiary wholly-owned by Pritzker and formed to implement the merger; for a period of 90 days, Trans Union could receive, but could not actively solicit, competing offers; the offer had to be acted on by the next evening, Sunday, September 21; Trans Union could only furnish to competing bidders published information, and not proprietary information; the offer was subject to Pritzker obtaining the necessary financing by October 10, 1980; if the financing contingency were met or waived by Pritzker, Trans Union was required to sell to Pritzker one million newly-issued shares of Trans Union at $38 per share.

Van Gorkom took the position that putting Trans Union "up for auction" through a 90-day market test would validate a decision by the Board that $55 was a fair price. He told the Board that the "free market will have an opportunity to judge whether $55 is a fair price." Van Gorkom framed the decision before the Board not as whether $55 per share was the highest price that could be obtained, but as whether the $55 price was a fair price that the stockholders should be given the opportunity to accept or reject.

Attorney Brennan advised the members of the Board that they might be sued if they failed to accept the offer and that a fairness opinion was not required as a matter of law.

Romans attended the meeting as chief financial officer of the Company. He told the Board . . . his studies did not indicate either a fair price for the stock or a valuation of the Company; that he did not see his role as directly addressing the fairness issue; and that he and his people "were trying to search for ways to justify a price in connection with such a [leveraged buy-out] transaction, rather than to say what the shares are worth." Romans testified:

I told the Board that the study ran the numbers at 50 and 60, and then the subsequent study at 55 and 65, and that was not the same thing as saying that I have a valuation of the company at X dollars. But it was a way-a first step towards reaching that conclusion.

Romans told the Board that, in his opinion, $55 was "in the range of a fair price," but "at the beginning of the range." . . .

The Board meeting of September 20 lasted about two hours. Based solely upon Van Gorkom's oral presentation, Chelberg's supporting representations, Romans' oral statement, Brennan's legal advice, and their knowledge of the market history of the Company's stock, the directors approved the proposed Merger Agreement. . . .

The Merger Agreement was executed by Van Gorkom during the evening of September 20 at a formal social event that he hosted for the opening of the Chicago Lyric Opera. Neither he nor any other director read the agreement prior to its signing and delivery to Pritzker.

On Monday, September 22, the Company issued a press release announcing that Trans Union had entered into a "definitive" Merger Agreement with an affiliate of the Marmon Group, Inc., a Pritzker holding company. Within 10 days of the public announcement, dissent among Senior Management over the merger had become widespread. Faced with threatened resignations of key officers, Van Gorkom met with Pritzker who agreed to several modifications of the Agreement. Pritzker was willing to do so provided that Van Gorkom could persuade the dissidents to remain on the Company payroll for at least six months after consummation of the merger.

Van Gorkom reconvened the Board on October 8 and secured the directors' approval of the proposed amendments-sight unseen. The Board also authorized the employment of Salomon Brothers, its investment banker, to solicit other offers for Trans Union during the proposed "market test" period.

The next day, October 9, Trans Union issued a press release announcing: (1) that Pritzker had obtained "the financing commitments necessary to consummate" the merger with Trans Union; (2) that Pritzker had acquired one million shares of Trans Union common stock at $38 per share; (3) that Trans Union was now permitted to actively seek other offers and had retained Salomon Brothers for that purpose; and (4) that if a more favorable offer were not received before February 1, 1981, Trans Union's shareholders would thereafter meet to vote on the Pritzker proposal.

It was not until the following day, October 10, that the actual amendments to the Merger Agreement were prepared by Pritzker and delivered to Van Gorkom for execution. As will be seen, the amendments were considerably at variance with Van Gorkom's representations of the amendments to the Board on October 8; and the amendments placed serious constraints on Trans Union's ability to negotiate a better deal and withdraw from the Pritzker agreement. Nevertheless, Van Gorkom proceeded to execute what became the October 10 amendments to the Merger Agreement without conferring further with the Board members and apparently without comprehending the actual implications of the amendments.

Salomon Brothers' efforts over a three-month period from October 21 to January 21 produced only one serious suitor for Trans Union-General Electric Credit Corporation ("GE Credit"), a subsidiary of the General Electric Company. However, GE Credit was unwilling to make an offer for Trans Union unless Trans Union first rescinded its Merger Agreement with Pritzker. When Pritzker refused, GE Credit terminated further discussions with Trans Union in early January.

In the meantime, in early December, the investment firm of Kohlberg, Kravis, Roberts & Co. ("KKR"), the only other concern to make a firm offer for Trans Union, withdrew its offer under circumstances hereinafter detailed.

. . . On January 21, Management's Proxy Statement for the February 10 shareholder meeting was mailed to Trans Union's stockholders. On January 26, Trans Union's Board met and, after a lengthy meeting, voted to proceed with the Pritzker merger. The Board also approved for mailing, "on or about January 27," a Supplement to its Proxy Statement. The Supplement purportedly set forth all information relevant to the Pritzker Merger Agreement, which had not been divulged in the first Proxy Statement.

On February 10, the stockholders of Trans Union approved the Pritzker merger proposal. Of the outstanding shares, 69.9% were voted in favor of the merger; 7.25% were voted against the merger; and 22.85% were not voted.

. . . the Board based its September 20 decision to approve the cash-out merger primarily on Van Gorkom's representations. None of the directors, other than Van Gorkom and Chelberg, had any prior knowledge that the purpose of the meeting was to propose a cash-out merger of Trans Union. No members of Senior Management were present, other than Chelberg, Romans and Peterson; and the latter two had only learned of the proposed sale an hour earlier. Both general counsel Moore and former general counsel Browder attended the meeting, but were equally uninformed as to the purpose of the meeting and the documents to be acted upon.

Without any documents before them concerning the proposed transaction, the members of the Board were required to rely entirely upon Van Gorkom's 20-minute oral presentation of the proposal. No written summary of the terms of the merger was presented; the directors were given no documentation to support the adequacy of $55 price per share for sale of the Company; and the Board had before it nothing more than Van Gorkom's statement of his understanding of the substance of an agreement which he admittedly had never read, nor which any member of the Board had ever seen.

. . . [T]here was no call by the Board, either on September 20 or thereafter, for any valuation study or documentation of the $55 price per share as a measure of the fair value of the Company in a cash-out context. It is undisputed that the major asset of Trans Union was its cash flow. Yet, at no time did the Board call for a valuation study taking into account that highly significant element of the Company's assets. . . .

. . . The Board rested on Romans' elicited response that the $55 figure was within a "fair price range" within the context of a leveraged buy-out. No director sought any further information from Romans. No director asked him why he put $55 at the bottom of his range. No director asked Romans for any details as to his study, the reason why it had been undertaken or its depth. No director asked to see the study; and no director asked Romans whether Trans Union's finance department could do a fairness study within the remaining 36A-hour period available under the Pritzker offer.

. . . None of the directors, Management or outside, were investment bankers or financial analysts.

. . . There is no evidence: (a) that the Merger Agreement was effectively amended to give the Board freedom to put Trans Union up for auction sale to the highest bidder; or (b) that a public auction was in fact permitted to occur. The minutes of the Board meeting make no reference to any of this. . . .

. . . [T]he Agreement barred Trans Union from actively soliciting such offers and from furnishing to interested parties any information about the Company other than that already in the public domain. Whether the original Agreement of September 20 went so far as to authorize Trans Union to receive competitive proposals is arguable. . . . Van Gorkom, conceding that he never read the Agreement, stated that he was relying upon his understanding that, under corporate law, directors always have an inherent right, as well as a fiduciary duty, to accept a better offer notwithstanding an existing contractual commitment by the Board. . . .

Several defendants testified that Brennan advised them that Delaware law did not require a fairness opinion or an outside valuation . . .

A second claim is that counsel advised the Board it would be subject to lawsuits if it rejected the $55 per share offer. . .

. . . The defendants contend that the stockholders' "overwhelming" vote approving the Pritzker Merger Agreement had the legal effect of curing any failure of the Board to reach an informed business judgment in its approval of the merger. . . .

---

(16) THE FINE LINE BETWEEN DUE CARE AND GOOD FAITH:

Refer to the following sections in the Text to help you answer the questions below:

Text §§6A-204 et seq., 6A-206 et seq., 6A-207

The "**Disney Case**" is another case you must know if you want to consider yourself literate in corporate law.

Please answer the following questions regarding ***In Re Walt Disney Co. Derivative Litigation*** below.

Did the board engage in a careful process in hiring Ovitz?

Did the board engage in a careful process in firing Ovitz without cause?

Should the board have erred on the side of caution by firing Ovitz for cause? If the board fired him for cause and was wrong, Ovitz would have won a judgment for the $130 million. If the board was right, Disney would have saved $130 million. It seems like it was worth the chance.

How did the plaintiffs want the court to define the duty of good faith? Does their definition of good faith look like the standard of liability for another fiduciary duty?

How does the Delaware Supreme Court define and explain the duty of good faith?

Would waste be a good argument for the plaintiffs?

In Re Walt Disney Co. Derivative Litigation
906 A.2d 27 (Del. Sup. Ct. 2006)

. . . In August 1995, Michael Ovitz ("Ovitz") and The Walt Disney Company ("Disney" or the "Company") entered into an employment agreement under which Ovitz would serve as President of Disney for five years. In December 1996, only fourteen months after he commenced employment, Ovitz was terminated without cause, resulting in a severance payout to Ovitz valued at approximately $130 million. . . .

A. *Negotiation Of The Ovitz Employment Agreement*

. . . Ovitz owned 55% of CAA [(a Hollywood talent agency)] and earned approximately $20 to $25 million a year from that company. From the beginning Ovitz made it clear that he would not give up his 55% interest in CAA without "downside protection." Considerable negotiation then ensued over downside protection issues. During the summer of 1995, the parties agreed to a draft version of Ovitz's employment agreement (the "OEA"). . .. As described by the Chancellor, the draft agreement included the following terms:

> Under the proposed OEA, Ovitz would receive a five-year contract with two tranches of options. The first tranche consisted of three million options vesting in equal parts in the third, fourth, and fifth years, and if the value of those options at the end of the five years had not appreciated to $50 million, Disney would make up the difference. The second tranche consisted of two million options that would vest immediately if Disney and Ovitz opted to renew the contract.
>
> The proposed OEA sought to protect both parties in the event that Ovitz's employment ended prematurely, and provided that absent defined causes, neither party could terminate the agreement without penalty. If Ovitz, for example, walked away, for any reason other than those permitted under the OEA, he would forfeit any benefits remaining under the OEA and could be enjoined from working for a competitor. Likewise, if Disney fired Ovitz for any reason other than gross negligence or malfeasance, Ovitz would be entitled to a non-fault payment (Non-Fault

> Termination or "NFT"), which consisted of his remaining salary, $7.5 million a year for unaccrued bonuses, the immediate vesting of his first tranche of options and a $10 million cash out payment for the second tranche of options. . . .

. . . Eisner told Ovitz that: (1) the number of options would be reduced from a single grant of five million to two separate grants, the first being three million options for the first five years and the second consisting of two million more options if the contract was renewed; and (2) Ovitz would join Disney only as President, not as a co-CEO with Eisner. After deliberating, Ovitz accepted those terms . . ..

On August 14, Eisner and Ovitz signed a letter agreement (the "OLA"), which outlined the basic terms of Ovitz's employment, and stated that the agreement (which would ultimately be embodied in a formal contract) was subject to approval by Disney's compensation committee and board of directors. Russell called Sidney Poitier, a Disney director and compensation committee member, to inform Poitier of the OLA and its terms. Poitier believed that hiring Ovitz was a good idea because of Ovitz's reputation and experience. Watson called Ignacio Lozano, another Disney director and compensation committee member, who felt that Ovitz would successfully adapt from a private company environment to Disney's public company culture. Eisner also contacted each of the other board members by phone to inform them of the impending new hire, and to explain his friendship with Ovitz and Ovitz's qualifications.

That same day, a press release made the news of Ovitz's hiring public. The reaction was extremely positive: Disney was applauded for the decision, and Disney's stock price rose 4.4 % in a single day, thereby increasing Disney's market capitalization by over $1 billion.

Once the OLA was signed, Joseph Santaniello, a Vice President and counsel in Disney's legal department, began to embody in a draft OEA the terms that Russell and Goldman had agreed upon and had been memorialized in the OLA. . . .

On September 26, 1995, the Disney compensation committee (which consisted of Messrs. Russell, Watson, Poitier and Lozano) met for one hour to consider, among other agenda items, the proposed terms of the OEA. A term sheet was distributed at the meeting, although a draft of the OEA was not. The topics discussed were historical comparables, such as Eisner's and Wells' option grants, and also the factors that Russell, Watson and Crystal had considered in setting the size of the option grants and the termination provisions of the contract. Watson testified that he provided the compensation committee with the spreadsheet analysis that he had performed in August, and discussed his findings with the committee. Crystal did not attend the meeting, although he was available by telephone to respond to questions if needed, but no one from the committee called. After Russell's and Watson's presentations, Litvack also responded to substantive questions. At trial Poitier and Lozano testified that they believed they had received sufficient information from Russell's and Watson's presentations to exercise their judgment in the best interests of the Company. The committee voted unanimously to approve the OEA terms, subject to "reasonable further negotiations within the framework of the terms and conditions" described in the OEA.

Immediately after the compensation committee meeting, the Disney board met in executive session. The board was told about the reporting structure to which Ovitz had agreed, but the initial negative reaction of Litvack and Bollenbach to the hiring was not recounted. Eisner led the discussion relating to Ovitz, and Watson then explained his analysis, and both Watson and Russell responded to questions from the board. After further deliberation, the board voted unanimously to elect Ovitz as President. . . .

B. *Ovitz's Performance As President of Disney*

. . . When Ovitz took office, the initial reaction was optimistic, and Ovitz did make some positive contributions while serving as President of the Company. By the fall of 1996, however, it had become clear that Ovitz was "a poor fit with his fellow executives." By then the Disney directors were discussing that the disconnect between Ovitz and the Company was likely irreparable and that Ovitz would have to be terminated. . . .

Although the plaintiffs attempted to show that Ovitz acted improperly (*i.e.,* with gross negligence or malfeasance) while in office, the Chancellor found that the trial record did not support those accusations. . . .

. . . Lastly, the Chancellor found that the record did not support, and often contradicted, the appellants' third claim-that Ovitz had violated the Company's policies relating to expenses and to reporting gifts he received while President of Disney.

Nonetheless, Ovitz's relationship with the Disney executives did continue to deteriorate through September 1996. In mid-September, Litvack, with Eisner's approval, told Ovitz that he was not working out at Disney and that he should start looking for a graceful exit from Disney and a new job. Litvack reported this conversation to Eisner, who sent Litvack back to Ovitz to make it clear that Eisner no longer wanted Ovitz at Disney and that Ovitz should seriously consider other opportunities, including one then developing at Sony. Ovitz responded by telling Litvack that he was not leaving and that if Eisner wanted him to leave Disney, Eisner could tell him that to his face.

On September 30, 1996, the Disney board met. During an executive session of that meeting, and in small group discussions where Ovitz was not present,

Eisner told the other board members of the continuing problems with Ovitz's performance. On October 1, Eisner wrote a letter to Russell and Watson detailing Eisner's mounting difficulties with Ovitz, including Eisner's lack of trust of Ovitz and Ovitz's failures to adapt to Disney's culture and to alleviate Eisner's workload. Eisner's goal in writing this letter was to prevent Ovitz from succeeding him at Disney. Because of that purpose, the Chancellor found that the letter contained "a good deal of hyperbole to help Eisner 'unsell' Ovitz as his successor." neither that letter nor its contents were shared with other members of the board.

Those interchanges set the stage for Ovitz's eventual termination as Disney's President.

C. *Ovitz's Termination At Disney*

. . . Eisner met with Ovitz personally on November 13. . .. Eisner left that meeting believing that "Ovitz just would not listen to what he was trying to tell him and instead, Ovitz insisted that he would stay at Disney, going so far as to state that he would chain himself to his desk."

During this period Eisner was also working with Litvack to explore whether they could terminate Ovitz under the OEA for cause. If so, Disney would not owe Ovitz the NFT payment. From the very beginning, Litvack advised Eisner that he did not believe there was cause to terminate Ovitz under the OEA. Litvack's advice never changed.

At the end of November 1996, Eisner again asked Litvack if Disney had cause to fire Ovitz and thereby avoid the costly NFT payment. Litvack proceeded to examine that issue more carefully. He studied the OEA, refreshed himself on the meaning of "gross negligence" and "malfeasance," and reviewed all the facts concerning Ovitz's performance of which he was aware. . . Eisner testified that after Litvack notified Eisner that he did not believe cause existed, Eisner "checked with almost anybody that [he] could find that had a legal degree, and there was just no light in that possibility. It was a total dead end from day one." Although the Chancellor was critical of Litvack and Eisner for lacking sufficient documentation to support his conclusion and the work they did to arrive at that conclusion, the Court found that Eisner and Litvack "did in fact make a concerted effort to determine if Ovitz could be terminated for cause, and that despite these efforts, they were unable to manufacture the desired result."

Litvack also believed that it would be inappropriate, unethical and a bad idea to attempt to coerce Ovitz (by threatening a for-cause termination) into negotiating for a smaller NFT package than the OEA provided. The reason was that when pressed by Ovitz's attorneys, Disney would have to admit that in fact there was no cause, which could subject Disney to a wrongful termination lawsuit. Litvack believed that attempting to avoid legitimate contractual obligations would harm Disney's reputation as an honest business partner and would affect its future business dealings.

The Disney board next met on November 25. By then the board knew Ovitz was going to be fired, yet the only action recorded in the minutes concerning Ovitz was his renomination to a new three-year term on the board. Although that action was somewhat bizarre given the circumstances, Stanley Gold, a Disney director, testified that because Ovitz was present at that meeting, it would have been a "public hanging" not to renominate him. An executive session took place after the board meeting, from which Ovitz was excluded. At that session, Eisner informed the directors who were present that he intended to fire Ovitz by year's end, and that he had asked Gary Wilson, a board member and friend of Ovitz, to speak with Ovitz while Wilson and Ovitz were together on vacation during the upcoming Thanksgiving holiday. . . .

After returning from the Thanksgiving trip, Ovitz met with Eisner on December 3, to discuss his termination. Ovitz asked for several concessions, all of which Eisner ultimately rejected. Eisner told Ovitz that all he would receive was what he had contracted for in the OEA.

On December 10, the Executive Performance Plan Committee met to consider annual bonuses for Disney's most highly compensated executive officers. At that meeting, Russell informed those in attendance that Ovitz was going to be terminated, but without cause. . . .

Ovitz's termination was memorialized in a letter, dated December 12, 1996, that Litvack signed on Eisner's instruction. The board was not shown the letter, nor did it meet to approve its terms. A press release announcing Ovitz's termination was issued that same day. Before the press release was issued, Eisner attempted to contact each of the board members by telephone to notify them that Ovitz had been officially terminated. None of the board members at that time, or at any other time, objected to Ovitz's termination, and most, if not all, of them thought it was the appropriate step for Eisner to take. Although the board did not meet to vote on the termination, the Chancellor found that most, if not all, of the Disney directors trusted Eisner's and Litvack's conclusion that there was no cause to terminate Ovitz, and that Ovitz should be terminated without cause even though that involved making the costly NFT payment.

A December 27, 1996 letter from Litvack to Ovitz, which Ovitz signed, memorialized the termination, accelerated Ovitz's departure date from January 31, 1997 to December 31, 1996, and informed Ovitz that he would receive roughly $38 million in cash and that the first tranche of three million options would vest immediately. By the terms of that letter agreement, Ovitz's tenure as an executive and a director of Disney officially ended on December 27, 1996. Shortly thereafter, Disney paid Ovitz what was owed under the OEA for an

NFT, minus a holdback of $1 million pending final settlement of Ovitz's accounts. One month after Disney paid Ovitz, the plaintiffs filed this action.. . .

IV. *THE CLAIMS AGAINST THE DISNEY DEFENDANTS*

. . . In its Opinion the Court of Chancery defined bad faith as follows:

> Upon long and careful consideration, I am of the opinion that the concept of *intentional dereliction of duty,* a *conscious disregard for one's responsibilities,* is an appropriate (although not the only) standard for determining whether fiduciaries have acted in good faith. Deliberate indifference and inaction *in the face of a duty to act* is, in my mind, conduct that is clearly disloyal to the corporation. It is the epitome of faithless conduct.

The appellants contend that definition is erroneous for two reasons. First they claim that the trial court had adopted a different definition in its 2003 decision denying the motion to dismiss the complaint, and the Court's post-trial (2005) definition materially altered the 2003 definition to appellants' prejudice. Their argument runs as follows: under the Chancellor's 2003 definition of bad faith, the directors must have *"consciously and intentionally disregarded their responsibilities,* adopting a 'we don't care about the risks' attitude concerning a material corporate decision." Under the 2003 formulation, appellants say, "directors violate their duty of good faith if they are making material decisions without adequate information and without adequate deliberation[,]"but under the 2005 post-trial definition, bad faith requires proof of a subjective bad motive or intent. . . .

. . . [A]s a matter of simple logic, at least three different categories of fiduciary behavior are candidates for the "bad faith" pejorative label.

The first category involves so-called "subjective bad faith," that is, fiduciary conduct motivated by an actual intent to do harm. That such conduct constitutes classic, quintessential bad faith is a proposition so well accepted in the liturgy of fiduciary law that it borders on axiomatic. We need not dwell further on this category, because no such conduct is claimed to have occurred, or did occur, in this case.

The second category of conduct, which is at the opposite end of the spectrum, involves lack of due care-that is, fiduciary action taken solely by reason of gross negligence and without any malevolent intent. In this case, appellants assert claims of gross negligence to establish breaches not only of director due care but also of the directors' duty to act in good faith. Although the Chancellor found, and we agree, that the appellants failed to establish gross negligence, to afford guidance we address the issue of whether gross negligence (including a failure to inform one's self of available material facts), without more, can also constitute bad faith. The answer is clearly no.

From a broad philosophical standpoint, that question is more complex than would appear, if only because (as the Chancellor and others have observed) "issues of good faith are (to a certain degree) inseparably and necessarily intertwined with the duties of care and loyalty...." But, in the pragmatic, conduct-regulating legal realm which calls for more precise conceptual line drawing, the answer is that grossly negligent conduct, without more, does not and cannot constitute a breach of the fiduciary duty to act in good faith. The conduct that is the subject of due care may overlap with the conduct that comes within the rubric of good faith in a psychological sense, but from a legal standpoint those duties are and must remain quite distinct. Both our legislative history and our common law jurisprudence distinguish sharply between the duties to exercise due care and to act in good faith, and highly significant consequences flow from that distinction.

To adopt a definition of bad faith that would cause a violation of the duty of care automatically to become an act or omission "not in good faith," would eviscerate the protections accorded to directors by the General Assembly's adoption of Section 102(b)(7). . . .

That leaves the third category of fiduciary conduct, which falls in between the first two categories of (1) conduct motivated by subjective bad intent and (2) conduct resulting from gross negligence. This third category is what the Chancellor's definition of bad faith-intentional dereliction of duty, a conscious disregard for one's responsibilities-is intended to capture. The question is whether such misconduct is properly treated as a non-exculpable . . . violation of the fiduciary duty to act in good faith. In our view it must be, for at least two reasons.

First, the universe of fiduciary misconduct is not limited to either disloyalty in the classic sense (*i.e.,* preferring the adverse self-interest of the fiduciary or of a related person to the interest of the corporation) or gross negligence. Cases have arisen where corporate directors have no conflicting self-interest in a decision, yet engage in misconduct that is more culpable than simple inattention or failure to be informed of all facts material to the decision. To protect the interests of the corporation and its shareholders, fiduciary conduct of this kind, which does not involve disloyalty (as traditionally defined) but is qualitatively more culpable than gross negligence, should be proscribed. A vehicle is needed to address such violations doctrinally, and that doctrinal vehicle is the duty to act in good faith. The Chancellor implicitly so recognized in his Opinion, where he identified different examples of bad faith as follows:

> The good faith required of a corporate fiduciary includes not simply the duties of care and loyalty, in the narrow sense that I have

> discussed them above, but all actions required by a true faithfulness and devotion to the interests of the corporation and its shareholders. A failure to act in good faith may be shown, for instance, where the fiduciary intentionally acts with a purpose other than that of advancing the best interests of the corporation, where the fiduciary acts with the intent to violate applicable positive law, or where the fiduciary intentionally fails to act in the face of a known duty to act, demonstrating a conscious disregard for his duties. There may be other examples of bad faith yet to be proven or alleged, but these three are the most salient. . . .

Those articulated examples of bad faith are not new to our jurisprudence. Indeed, they echo pronouncements our courts have made throughout the decades.

Second, the legislature has also recognized this intermediate category of fiduciary misconduct, which ranks between conduct involving subjective bad faith and gross negligence. Section 102(b)(7)(ii) of the DGCL expressly denies money damage exculpation for "acts or omissions not in good faith or which involve intentional misconduct or a knowing violation of law." By its very terms that provision distinguishes between "intentional misconduct" and a "knowing violation of law" (both examples of subjective bad faith) on the one hand, and "acts ... not in good faith," on the other. Because the statute exculpates directors only for conduct amounting to gross negligence, the statutory denial of exculpation for "acts ... not in good faith" must encompass the intermediate category of misconduct captured by the Chancellor's definition of bad faith.

For these reasons, we uphold the Court of Chancery's definition as a legally appropriate, although not the exclusive, definition of fiduciary bad faith. We need go no further. To engage in an effort to craft (in the Court's words) "a definitive and categorical definition of the universe of acts that would constitute bad faith" would be unwise and is unnecessary to dispose of the issues presented on this appeal. . . .

---

(17) <u>DUTY TO MONITOR:</u>

Refer to the following sections in the Text to help you answer the questions below:

Text §6A-205 et seq.

Caremark and **Stone** are cases that you must know if you want to consider yourself literate in corporate law.

Please answer the following questions regarding ***In Re Caremark International Inc. Derivative Litigation*** and ***Stone v. Ritter*** below.

> **In each case, how does the court articulate the standard of liability for a failure of oversight?**
>
> **Does a board have no duty to act unless it has received some sort of warning sign?**
>
> **In Caremark, does it appear that the board failed to implement an information and reporting system?**

In re Caremark International Inc. Derivative Litigation

698 A.2d 959 (Del. Ch. 1996)

. . . Pending is a motion pursuant to . . . to approve as fair and reasonable a proposed settlement of a consolidated derivative action on behalf of Caremark International, Inc. ("Caremark"). The suit involves claims that the members of Caremark's board of directors (the "Board") breached their fiduciary duty of care to Caremark in connection with alleged violations by Caremark employees of federal and state laws and regulations applicable to health care providers. As a result of the alleged violations, Caremark was subject to an extensive four year investigation by the United States Department of Health and Human Services and the Department of Justice. In 1994 Caremark was charged in an indictment with multiple felonies. It thereafter entered into a number of agreements with the Department of Justice and others. Those agreements included a plea agreement in which Caremark pleaded guilty to a single felony of mail fraud and agreed to pay civil and criminal fines. Subsequently, Caremark agreed to make reimbursements to various private and public parties. In all, the payments that Caremark has been required to make total approximately $250 million.

. . . The parties now propose that it be settled and, after notice to Caremark shareholders, a hearing on the fairness of the proposal was held on August 16, 1996.

A motion of this type requires the court to assess the strengths and weaknesses of the claims asserted in light of the discovery record and to evaluate the fairness and adequacy of the consideration offered to the corporation in exchange for the release of all claims made or arising from the facts alleged. The ultimate issue then is whether the proposed settlement appears to be fair to the corporation and its absent shareholders. . . .

Legally, evaluation of the central claim made entails consideration of the legal standard governing a board of directors' obligation to supervise or monitor corporate performance. For the reasons set forth below I conclude, in light of the discovery record, that there is a very low probability that it would be determined that the directors of Caremark breached any duty to appropriately monitor and supervise the enterprise. Indeed the record tends to show an active consideration by Caremark management and its Board of the Caremark structures and programs that ultimately led to the company's indictment and to the large financial losses incurred in the settlement of those claims. It does not tend to show knowing or intentional violation of law. Neither the fact that the Board, although advised by lawyers and accountants, did not accurately predict the severe consequences to the company that would ultimately follow from the deployment by the company of the strategies and practices that ultimately led to this liability, nor the scale of the liability, gives rise to an inference of breach of any duty imposed by corporation law upon the directors of Caremark.

I. BACKGROUND

. . . Caremark, a Delaware corporation with its headquarters in Northbrook, Illinois, was created in November 1992 . . . and became a publicly held company listed on the New York Stock Exchange. . . . During the relevant period Caremark was involved in two main health care business segments, providing patient care and managed care services. As part of its patient care business, which accounted for the majority of Caremark's revenues, Caremark provided alternative site health care services, including infusion therapy, growth hormone therapy, HIV/AIDS-related treatments and hemophilia therapy. Caremark's managed care services included prescription drug programs and the operation of multi-specialty group practices.

A. Events Prior to the Government Investigation

A substantial part of the revenues generated by Caremark's businesses is derived from third party payments, insurers, and Medicare and Medicaid reimbursement programs. The latter source of payments are subject to the terms of the Anti-Referral Payments Law ("ARPL") which prohibits health care providers from paying any form of remuneration to induce the referral of Medicare or Medicaid patients. . . . Caremark did have a practice of entering into contracts for services (*e.g.,* consultation agreements and research grants) with physicians at least some of whom prescribed or recommended services or products that Caremark provided to Medicare recipients and other patients. Such contracts were not prohibited by the ARPL but they obviously raised a possibility of unlawful "kickbacks."

As early as 1989, [Caremark] issued an internal "Guide to Contractual Relationships" ("Guide") to govern its employees in entering into contracts with physicians and hospitals. The Guide tended to be reviewed annually by lawyers and updated. Each version of the Guide stated as Caremark's . . . policy that no payments would be made in exchange for or to induce patient referrals. But what one might deem a prohibited *quid pro quo* was not always clear. Due to a scarcity of court decisions interpreting the ARPL, however, Caremark repeatedly publicly stated that there was uncertainty concerning Caremark's interpretation of the law.

To clarify the scope of the ARPL, the United States Department of Health and Human Services ("HHS") issued "safe harbor" regulations in July 1991 stating conditions under which financial relationships between health care service providers and patient referral sources, such as physicians, would *not* violate the ARPL. Caremark contends that the narrowly drawn regulations gave limited guidance as to the legality of many of the agreements used by Caremark that did not fall within the safe-harbor. [Caremark], however, amended many of its standard forms of agreement with health care providers and revised the Guide in an apparent attempt to comply with the new regulations.

B. Government Investigation and Related Litigation

In August 1991, the HHS Office of the Inspector General ("OIG") initiated an investigation of [Caremark]. . . . [Caremark] was served with a subpoena requiring the production of documents, including contracts between [Caremark] and physicians (Quality Service Agreements ("QSAs")). Under the QSAs, [Caremark] appears to have paid physicians fees for monitoring patients under [Caremark]'s care, including Medicare and Medicaid recipients. Sometimes apparently those monitoring patients were referring physicians, which raised ARPL concerns.

In March 1992, the Department of Justice ("DOJ") joined the OIG investigation and separate investigations were commenced by several additional federal and state agencies. . . .

C. Caremark's Response to the Investigation

. . . The first action taken by management, as a result of the initiation of the OIG investigation, was an announcement that as of October 1, 1991, [Caremark] would no longer pay management fees to physicians for services to Medicare and Medicaid patients. Despite this decision, Caremark asserts that its management, pursuant to advice, did not believe that such payments were illegal under the existing laws and regulations.

During this period, Caremark's Board took several additional steps consistent with an effort to assure compliance with company policies concerning the ARPL and the contractual forms in the Guide. . . .

Although there is evidence that inside and outside counsel had advised

Caremark's directors that their contracts were in accord with the law, Caremark recognized that some uncertainty respecting the correct interpretation of the law existed. . . .

Throughout the period of the government investigations, Caremark had an internal audit plan designed to assure compliance with business and ethics policies. In addition, Caremark employed Price Waterhouse as its outside auditor. On February 8, 1993, the Ethics Committee of Caremark's Board received and reviewed an outside auditors report by Price Waterhouse which concluded that there were no material weaknesses in Caremark's control structure. Despite the positive findings of Price Waterhouse, however, on April 20, 1993, the Audit & Ethics Committee adopted a new internal audit charter requiring a comprehensive review of compliance policies and the compilation of an employee ethics handbook concerning such policies.

The Board appears to have been informed about this project and other efforts to assure compliance with the law. For example, Caremark's management reported to the Board that Caremark's sales force was receiving an ongoing education regarding the ARPL and the proper use of Caremark's form contracts which had been approved by in-house counsel. On July 27, 1993, the new ethics manual, expressly prohibiting payments in exchange for referrals and requiring employees to report all illegal conduct to a toll free confidential ethics hotline, was approved and allegedly disseminated. The record suggests that Caremark continued these policies in subsequent years, causing employees to be given revised versions of the ethics manual and requiring them to participate in training sessions concerning compliance with the law. . . .

D. Federal Indictments Against Caremark and Officers

On August 4, 1994, a federal grand jury in Minnesota issued a 47 page indictment charging Caremark. . . with violating the ARPL over a lengthy period. . . .

In reaction to the Minnesota Indictment and the subsequent filing of this and other derivative actions in 1994, the Board met and was informed by management that the investigation had resulted in an indictment; Caremark denied any wrongdoing relating to the indictment and believed that the OIG investigation would have a favorable outcome. Management reiterated the grounds for its view that the contracts were in compliance with law.

Subsequently, five stockholder derivative actions were filed in this court and consolidated into this action. The original complaint, dated August 5, 1994, alleged, in relevant part, that Caremark's directors breached their duty of care by failing adequately to supervise the conduct of Caremark employees, or institute corrective measures, thereby exposing Caremark to fines and liability. . . .

After each complaint was filed, defendants filed a motion to dismiss. According to defendants, if a settlement had not been reached in this action, the case would have been dismissed . . . [because] plaintiffs had failed to state a cause of action due to the fact that Caremark's charter eliminates directors' personal liability for money damages, to the extent permitted by law. . . .

II. LEGAL PRINCIPLES

A. Principles Governing Settlements of Derivative Claims

As noted at the outset of this opinion, this Court is now required to exercise an informed judgment whether the proposed settlement is fair and reasonable in the light of all relevant factors. . . .

B. Directors' Duties To Monitor Corporate Operations

The complaint charges the director defendants with breach of their duty of attention or care in connection with the on-going operation of the corporation's business. The claim is that the directors allowed a situation to develop and continue which exposed the corporation to enormous legal liability and that in so doing they violated a duty to be active monitors of corporate performance. The complaint thus does not charge either director self-dealing or the more difficult loyalty-type problems arising from cases of suspect director motivation, such as entrenchment or sale of control contexts. The theory here advanced is possibly the most difficult theory in corporation law upon which a plaintiff might hope to win a judgment. . . .

1. *Potential liability for directoral decisions:* Director liability for a breach of the duty to exercise appropriate attention may, in theory, arise in two distinct contexts. First, such liability may be said to follow *from a board decision* that results in a loss because that decision was ill advised or "negligent". Second, liability to the corporation for a loss may be said to arise from an *unconsidered failure of the board to act* in circumstances in which due attention would, arguably, have prevented the loss. . . . The first class of cases will typically be subject to review under the director-protective business judgment rule, assuming the decision made was the product of *a process* that was *either* deliberately considered in good faith or was otherwise rational. . . . . [C]ompliance with a director's duty of care can never appropriately be judicially determined by reference to *the content of the board decision* that leads to a corporate loss, apart from consideration of the good faith *or* rationality of the process employed. That is, whether a judge or jury considering the matter after the fact, believes a decision substantively wrong, or degrees of wrong extending through "stupid" to "egregious" or "irrational", provides no ground for director liability, so long as the court determines that the process employed was either rational or employed in *a good faith* effort to advance corporate interests. To employ a different rule-one that permitted an "objective" evaluation of the decision-would expose directors to substantive second guessing by ill-equipped judges or juries, which would, in the long-run, be injurious to investor interests. Thus, the business judgment rule is process oriented and informed by a deep respect for all *good faith* board decisions.

. . . Where a director *in fact exercises a good faith effort to be informed and to exercise appropriate judgment,* he or she should be deemed to satisfy fully the duty of attention. If the shareholders thought themselves entitled to some other quality of judgment than such a director produces in the good faith exercise of the powers of office, then the shareholders should have elected other directors. . . .

2. *Liability for failure to monitor:* The second class of cases in which director liability for inattention is theoretically possible entail circumstances in which a loss eventuates not from a decision but, from unconsidered inaction. Most of the decisions that a corporation, acting through its human agents, makes are, of course, not the subject of director attention. Legally, the board itself will be required only to authorize the most significant corporate acts or transactions: mergers, changes in capital structure, fundamental changes in business, appointment and compensation of the CEO, etc. As the facts of this case graphically demonstrate, ordinary business decisions that are made by officers and employees deeper in the interior of the organization can, however, vitally affect the welfare of the corporation and its ability to achieve its various strategic and financial goals. . . .

Modernly this question has been given special importance by an increasing tendency, especially under federal law, to employ the criminal law to assure corporate compliance with external legal requirements, including environmental, financial, employee and product safety as well as assorted other health and safety regulations. In 1991, pursuant to the Sentencing Reform Act of 1984, the United States Sentencing Commission adopted Organizational Sentencing Guidelines which impact importantly on the prospective effect these criminal sanctions might have on business corporations. The Guidelines set forth a uniform sentencing structure for organizations to be sentenced for violation of federal criminal statutes and provide for penalties that equal or often massively exceed those previously imposed on corporations. The Guidelines offer powerful incentives for corporations today to have in place compliance programs to detect violations of law, promptly to report violations to appropriate public officials when discovered, and to take prompt, voluntary remedial efforts.

In 1963, the Delaware Supreme Court in *Graham v. Allis-Chalmers Mfg. Co.,* addressed the question of potential liability of board members for losses experienced by the corporation as a result of the corporation having violated the anti-trust laws of the United States. There was no claim in that case that the directors knew about the behavior of subordinate employees of the corporation that had resulted in the liability. Rather, as in this case, the claim asserted was that the directors *ought to have known* of it and if they had known they would have been under a duty to bring the corporation into compliance with the law and thus save the corporation from the loss. . . . [T]he court stated that "absent cause for suspicion there is no duty upon the directors to install and operate a corporate system of espionage to ferret out wrongdoing which they have no reason to suspect exists." The Court found that there were no grounds for suspicion in that case and, thus, concluded that the directors were blamelessly unaware of the conduct leading to the corporate liability.

How does one generalize this holding today? Can it be said today that, absent some ground giving rise to suspicion of violation of law, that corporate directors have no duty to assure that a corporate information gathering and reporting systems exists which represents a good faith attempt to provide senior management and the Board with information respecting material acts, events or conditions within the corporation, including compliance with applicable statutes and regulations? I certainly do not believe so. I doubt that such a broad generalization of the *Graham* holding would have been accepted by the Supreme Court in 1963. The case can be more narrowly interpreted as standing for the proposition that, absent grounds to suspect deception, neither corporate boards nor senior officers can be charged with wrongdoing simply for assuming the integrity of employees and the honesty of their dealings on the company's behalf.

A broader interpretation of *Graham v. Allis-Chalmers*-that it means that a corporate board has no responsibility to assure that appropriate information and reporting systems are established by management-would not, in any event, be accepted by the Delaware Supreme Court in 1996, in my opinion. In stating the basis for this view, I start with the recognition that in recent years the Delaware Supreme Court has made it clear . . . the seriousness with which the corporation law views the role of the corporate board. Secondly, I note the elementary fact that relevant and timely *information* is an essential predicate for satisfaction of the board's supervisory and monitoring role under Section 141 of the Delaware General Corporation Law. Thirdly, I note the potential impact of the federal organizational sentencing guidelines on any business organization. Any rational person attempting in good faith to meet an organizational governance responsibility would be bound to take into account this development and the enhanced penalties and the opportunities for reduced sanctions that it offers.

In light of these developments, it would, in my opinion, be a mistake to conclude that our Supreme Court's statement in *Graham* concerning "espionage" means that corporate boards may satisfy their obligation to be reasonably informed concerning the corporation, without assuring themselves that information and reporting systems exist in the organization that are reasonably designed to provide to senior management and to the board itself timely, accurate information sufficient to allow management and the board, each within its scope, to reach informed judgments concerning both the corporation's compliance with law and its business performance.

Obviously the level of detail that is appropriate for such an information system is a question of business judgment. And obviously too, no rationally designed information and reporting system will remove the possibility that the corporation will violate laws or regulations, or that senior officers or directors may nevertheless sometimes be misled or otherwise fail reasonably to detect acts material to the corporation's compliance with the law. But it is important that the board exercise a good faith judgment that the corporation's information and reporting system is in concept and design adequate to assure the board that appropriate information will come to its attention in a timely manner as a matter of ordinary operations, so that it may satisfy its responsibility.

Thus, I am of the view that a director's obligation includes a duty to attempt in good faith to assure that a corporate information and reporting system, which the board concludes is adequate, exists, and that failure to do so under some circumstances may, in theory at least, render a director liable for losses caused by non-compliance with applicable legal standards. . . .

III. ANALYSIS OF THIRD AMENDED COMPLAINT AND SETTLEMENT

A. The Claims

On balance, after reviewing an extensive record in this case, including numerous documents and three depositions, I conclude that this settlement is fair and reasonable. . . .

In order to show that the Caremark directors breached their duty of care by failing adequately to control Caremark's employees, plaintiffs would have to show either (1) that the directors knew or (2) should have known that violations of law were occurring and, in either event, (3) that the directors took no steps in a good faith effort to prevent or remedy that situation, and (4) that such failure proximately resulted in the losses complained of . . . .

1. *Knowing violation of statute:* Concerning the possibility that the Caremark directors knew of violations of law, none of the documents submitted for review, nor any of the deposition transcripts appear to provide evidence of it. Certainly the Board understood that the company had entered into a variety of contracts with physicians, researchers, and health care providers and it was understood that some of these contracts were with persons who had prescribed treatments that Caremark participated in providing. The board was informed that the company's reimbursement for patient care was frequently from government funded sources and that such services were subject to the ARPL. But the Board appears to have been informed by experts that the company's practices while contestable, were lawful. There is no evidence that reliance on such reports was not reasonable. Thus, this case presents no occasion to apply a principle to the effect that knowingly causing the corporation to violate a criminal statute constitutes a breach of a director's fiduciary duty. . . .

2. *Failure to monitor:* Since it does appears that the Board was to some extent unaware of the activities that led to liability, I turn to a consideration of the other potential avenue to director liability that the pleadings take: director inattention or "negligence". Generally where a claim of directorial liability for corporate loss is predicated upon ignorance of liability creating activities within the corporation, as in *Graham* or in this case, in my opinion only a sustained or systematic failure of the board to exercise oversight-such as an utter failure to attempt to assure a reasonable information and reporting system exists-will establish the lack of good faith that is a necessary condition to liability. Such a test of liability-lack of good faith as evidenced by sustained or systematic failure of a director to exercise reasonable oversight-is quite high. But, a demanding test of liability in the oversight context is probably beneficial to corporate shareholders as a class, as it is in the board decision context, since it makes board service by qualified persons more likely, while continuing to act as a stimulus to *good faith performance of duty* by such directors.

Here the record supplies essentially no evidence that the director defendants were guilty of a sustained failure to exercise their oversight function. To the contrary, insofar as I am able to tell on this record, the corporation's information systems appear to have represented a good faith attempt to be informed of relevant facts. If the directors did not know the specifics of the activities that lead to the indictments, they cannot be faulted. . . .

I am today entering an order consistent with the foregoing.

Stone v. Ritter

911 A.2d 362 (Del. Sup. Ct. 2006)

. . . This is an appeal from a final judgment of the Court of Chancery dismissing a derivative complaint against fifteen present and former directors of AmSouth Bancorporation ("AmSouth"), a Delaware corporation. . . .

In this appeal, the plaintiffs acknowledge that the directors neither "knew [n]or should have known that violations of law were occurring," *i.e.,* that there were no "red flags" before the directors. Nevertheless, the plaintiffs argue that the Court of Chancery erred by dismissing the derivative complaint which alleged that "the defendants had utterly failed to implement any sort of statutorily required monitoring, reporting or information controls that would have enabled them to learn of problems requiring their attention." The defendants argue that the plaintiffs' assertions are contradicted by the derivative complaint itself and by the documents incorporated therein by reference.

. . . [W]e hold that *Caremark* articulates the necessary conditions for assessing director oversight liability. . . .

Facts

. . . In 2004, AmSouth and AmSouth Bank paid $40 million in fines and $10 million in civil penalties to resolve government and regulatory investigations pertaining principally to the failure by bank employees to file "Suspicious Activity Reports" ("SARs"), as required by the federal Bank Secrecy Act ("BSA") and various anti-money-laundering ("AML") regulations. . . .

Graham and Caremark

. . . In *Graham* this Court held that "*absent cause for suspicion* there is no duty upon the directors to install and operate a corporate system of espionage to ferret out wrongdoing which they have no reason to suspect exists."

In *Caremark* the Court of Chancery reassessed the applicability of our holding in *Graham* when called upon to approve a settlement of a derivative lawsuit brought against the directors of Caremark International, Inc. The plaintiffs claimed that the Caremark directors should have known that certain officers and employees of Caremark were involved in violations of the federal Anti-Referral Payments Law. That law prohibits health care providers from paying any form of remuneration to induce the referral of Medicare or Medicaid patients. The plaintiffs claimed that the *Caremark* directors breached their fiduciary duty for having "allowed a situation to develop and continue which exposed the corporation to enormous legal liability and that in so doing they violated a duty to be active monitors of corporate performance."

In evaluating whether to approve the proposed settlement agreement in *Caremark* the Court of Chancery narrowly construed our holding in *Graham* "as standing for the proposition that, absent grounds to suspect deception, neither corporate boards nor senior officers can be charged with wrongdoing simply for assuming the integrity of employees and the honesty of their dealings on the company's behalf." . . .

. . . [T]he *Caremark* Court stated, "it is important that the board exercise a good faith judgment that the corporation's information and reporting system is in concept and design adequate to assure the board that appropriate information will come to its attention in a timely manner as a matter of ordinary operations, so that it may satisfy its responsibility." The *Caremark* Court recognized, however, that "the duty to act in good faith to be informed cannot be thought to require directors to possess detailed information about all aspects of the operation of the enterprise." The Court of Chancery then formulated the following standard for assessing the liability of directors where the directors are unaware of employee misconduct that results in the corporation being held liable:

> Generally where a claim of directorial liability for corporate loss is predicated upon ignorance of liability creating activities within the corporation, as in *Graham* or in this case, ... only a sustained or systematic failure of the board to exercise oversight-such as an utter failure to attempt to assure a reasonable information and reporting system exists-will establish the lack of good faith that is a necessary condition to liability.

Caremark Standard Approved

As evidenced by the language quoted above, the *Caremark* standard for so-called "oversight" liability draws heavily upon the concept of director failure to act in good faith. That is consistent with the definition(s) of bad faith recently approved by this Court in its recent *Disney* decision, where we held that a failure to act in good faith requires conduct that is qualitatively different from, and more culpable than, the conduct giving rise to a violation of the fiduciary duty of care (i.e., gross negligence). . . .

We hold that *Caremark* articulates the necessary conditions predicate for director oversight liability: (a) the directors utterly failed to implement any reporting or information system or controls; *or* (b) having implemented such a system or controls, consciously failed to monitor or oversee its operations thus disabling themselves from being informed of risks or problems requiring their attention. In either case, imposition of liability requires a showing that the directors knew that they were not discharging their fiduciary obligations. Where directors fail to act in the face of a known duty to act, thereby demonstrating a conscious disregard for their responsibilities, they breach their duty of loyalty by failing to discharge that fiduciary obligation in good faith. . . .

[In this case, the] findings reflect that the Board received and approved relevant policies and procedures, delegated to certain employees and departments the responsibility for filing the SARs and monitoring compliance, and exercised oversight by relying on periodic reports from them. Although there ultimately may have been failures by employees to report deficiencies to the Board, there is no basis for an oversight claim seeking to hold the directors personally liable for such failures by the employees.

With the benefit of hindsight, the plaintiffs' complaint seeks to equate a bad outcome with bad faith. The lacuna in the plaintiffs' argument is a failure to recognize that the directors' good faith exercise of oversight responsibility may not invariably prevent employees from violating criminal laws, or from causing the corporation to incur significant financial liability, or both, as occurred in *Graham, Caremark* and this very case. In the absence of red flags, good faith in the context of oversight must be measured by the directors' actions "to assure a reasonable information and reporting system exists" and not by second-guessing after the occurrence of employee conduct that results in an unintended adverse outcome. Accordingly, we hold that the Court of Chancery properly applied *Caremark* and dismissed the plaintiffs' derivative complaint for failure to excuse demand by alleging particularized facts that created reason to doubt whether the directors had acted in good faith in exercising their oversight responsibilities.

Conclusion

The judgment of the Court of Chancery is affirmed.

---

(18) FIDUCIARY DUTIES OF CONTROLLING SHAREHOLDERS:

Refer to the following sections in the Text to help you answer the questions below:

Text §§6A-211(a)-(d), 6A-211(f)

Please read the facts of ***Sinclair Oil v. Levien***, below, and answer the following questions:

What fiduciary-duty standard applies to Sinven's decision to issue dividends? Was this a self-dealing transaction? If not, what would a plaintiff have to show to win its case?

Was the decision regarding International a conflicted transaction for the controlling shareholder Sinclair? If so, who would have the burden of proof and what would that party have to prove?

Based on the facts presented in the case, does Sinclair have very strong incentives to divert funds from its subsidiary Sinven to its

other subsidiary, International? (Hint: What percentage of ownership does Sinclair have of each subsidiary?)

Sinclair Oil Corp. v. Levien
280 A.2d 717 (Del. Sup. Ct. 1971)

. . . Sinclair, operating primarily as a holding company, is in the business of exploring for oil and of producing and marketing crude oil and oil products. At all times relevant to this litigation, it owned about 97% Of Sinven's stock. The plaintiff owns about 3000 of 120,000 publicly held shares of Sinven. Sinven, incorporated in 1922, has been engaged in petroleum operations primarily in Venezuela and since 1959 has operated exclusively in Venezuela.

Sinclair nominates all members of Sinven's board of directors. The Chancellor found as a fact that the directors were not independent of Sinclair. Almost without exception, they were officers, directors, or employees of corporations in the Sinclair complex. By reason of Sinclair's domination, it is clear that Sinclair owed Sinven a fiduciary duty. . . . Sinclair concedes this. . . .

. . . [F]rom1960 through 1966, Sinclair caused Sinven to pay out such excessive dividends that the industrial development of Sinven was effectively prevented, and it became in reality a corporation in dissolution.

From 1960 through 1966, Sinven paid out $108,000,000 in dividends ($38,000,000 in excess of Sinven's earnings during the same period). The Chancellor held that Sinclair caused these dividends to be paid during a period when it had a need for large amounts of cash. Although the dividends paid exceeded earnings, the plaintiff concedes that the payments were made in compliance with 8 Del.C. §170, authorizing payment of dividends out of surplus or net profits. However, the plaintiff attacks these dividends on the ground that they resulted from an improper motive-Sinclair's need for cash. . . .

In 1961 Sinclair created Sinclair International Oil Company (hereafter International), a wholly owned subsidiary used for the purpose of coordinating all of Sinclair's foreign operations. All crude purchases by Sinclair were made thereafter through International.

On September 28, 1961, Sinclair caused Sinven to contract with International whereby Sinven agreed to sell all of its crude oil and refined products to International at specified prices. The contract provided for minimum and maximum quantities and prices. The plaintiff contends that Sinclair caused this contract to be breached in two respects. Although the contract called for payment on receipt, International's payments lagged as much as 30 days after receipt. Also, the contract required International to purchase at least a fixed minimum amount of crude and refined products from Sinven. International did not comply with this requirement. [Sinclair did not cause Sinven to enforce the contract with international]. . . .

---

(19) THE CASH-OUT MERGER:

Refer to the following sections in the Text to help you answer the questions below:

Text §§6A-211(c), 6A-211(d)

Please read the facts of ***Weinberger v. UOP***,[5] below, and answer the following question:

> **Imagine a UOP shareholder sues Signal for breaching its fiduciary duty to the minority shareholders of UOP. What is your legal opinion regarding the likelihood of success of the lawsuit? Explain.**

. . . Signal is a . . . company [whose] stock is publicly traded on the New York, Philadelphia and Pacific Stock Exchanges. UOP, formerly known as Universal Oil Products Company, was a . . . company engaged in various lines of business . . .. Its stock was publicly held and listed on the New York Stock Exchange.

[Signal held 50.5% of UOP's outstanding shares.]

Although UOP's board consisted of thirteen directors, Signal nominated and elected only six. Of these, five were either directors or employees of Signal. The sixth, a partner in the banking firm of Lazard Freres & Co., had been one of Signal's representatives in the negotiations and bargaining with UOP concerning the tender offer and purchase price of the UOP shares.

However, the president and chief executive officer of UOP retired during 1975, and Signal caused him to be replaced by James V. Crawford, a long-time employee and senior executive vice president of one of Signal's wholly-owned subsidiaries. Crawford succeeded his predecessor on UOP's board of directors and also was made a director of Signal.

---

[5] 457 A.2d 701 (Del. Sup. Ct. 1983)

. . . The trial court found that at the instigation of certain Signal management personnel, including William W. Walkup, its board chairman, and Forrest N. Shumway, its president, a feasibility study was made concerning the possible acquisition of the balance of UOP's outstanding shares. This study was performed by two Signal officers, Charles S. Arledge, vice president (director of planning), and Andrew J. Chitiea, senior vice president (chief financial officer). Messrs. Walkup, Shumway, Arledge and Chitiea were all directors of UOP in addition to their membership on the Signal board.

Arledge and Chitiea concluded that it would be a good investment for Signal to acquire the remaining 49.5% of UOP shares at any price up to $24 each. Their report was discussed between Walkup and Shumway who, along with Arledge, Chitiea and Brewster L. Arms, internal counsel for Signal, constituted Signal's senior management. In particular, they talked about the proper price to be paid if the acquisition was pursued, purportedly keeping in mind that as UOP's majority shareholder, Signal owed a fiduciary responsibility to both its own stockholders as well as to UOP's minority. It was ultimately agreed that a meeting of Signal's executive committee would be called to propose that Signal acquire the remaining outstanding stock of UOP through a cash-out merger in the range of $20 to $21 per share.

The executive committee meeting was set for February 28, 1978. As a courtesy, UOP's president, Crawford, was invited to attend, although he was not a member of Signal's executive committee. On his arrival, and prior to the meeting, Crawford was asked to meet privately with Walkup and Shumway. He was then told of Signal's plan to acquire full ownership of UOP and was asked for his reaction to the proposed price range of $20 to $21 per share. Crawford said he thought such a price would be "generous", and that it was certainly one which should be submitted to UOP's minority shareholders for their ultimate consideration. He stated, however, that Signal's 100% ownership could cause internal problems at UOP. He believed that employees would have to be given some assurance of their future place in a fully-owned Signal subsidiary. Otherwise, he feared the departure of essential personnel. Also, many of UOP's key employees had stock option incentive programs which would be wiped out by a merger. Crawford therefore urged that some adjustment would have to be made, such as providing a comparable incentive in Signal's shares, if after the merger he was to maintain his quality of personnel and efficiency at UOP.

Thus, Crawford voiced no objection to the $20 to $21 price range, nor did he suggest that Signal should consider paying more than $21 per share for the minority interests. Later, at the executive committee meeting the same factors were discussed, with Crawford repeating the position he earlier took with Walkup and Shumway. Also considered was the 1975 tender offer and the fact that it had been greatly oversubscribed at $21 per share. For many reasons, Signal's management concluded that the acquisition of UOP's minority shares provided the solution to a number of its business problems.

Thus, it was the consensus that a price of $20 to $21 per share would be fair to both Signal and the minority shareholders of UOP. Signal's executive committee authorized its management "to negotiate" with UOP "for a cash acquisition of the minority ownership in UOP, Inc., with the intention of presenting a proposal to [Signal's] board of directors ... on March 6, 1978". Immediately after this February 28, 1978 meeting, Signal issued a press release . . . [which] referred to the fact that the closing price of UOP's common stock on that day was $14.50 per share. . . .

Between Tuesday, February 28, 1978 and Monday, March 6, 1978, a total of four business days, Crawford spoke by telephone with all of UOP's non-Signal, i.e., outside, directors. Also during that period, Crawford retained Lehman Brothers to render a fairness opinion as to the price offered the minority for its stock. He gave two reasons for this choice. First, the time schedule between the announcement and the board meetings was short (by then only three business days) and since Lehman Brothers had been acting as UOP's investment banker for many years, Crawford felt that it would be in the best position to respond on such brief notice. Second, James W. Glanville, a long-time director of UOP and a partner in Lehman Brothers, had acted as a financial advisor to UOP for many years. Crawford believed that Glanville's familiarity with UOP, as a member of its board, would also be of assistance in enabling Lehman Brothers to render a fairness opinion within the existing time constraints.

Crawford telephoned Glanville, who gave his assurance that Lehman Brothers had no conflicts that would prevent it from accepting the task. Glanville's immediate personal reaction was that a price of $20 to $21 would certainly be fair, since it represented almost a 50% premium over UOP's market price. Glanville sought a $250,000 fee for Lehman Brothers' services, but Crawford thought this too much. After further discussions Glanville finally agreed that Lehman Brothers would render its fairness opinion for $150,000.

During this period Crawford also had several telephone contacts with Signal officials. In only one of them, however, was the price of the shares discussed. In a conversation with Walkup, Crawford advised that as a result of his communications with UOP's non-Signal directors, it was his feeling that the price would have to be the top of the proposed range, or $21 per share, if the approval of UOP's outside directors was to be obtained. But again, he did not seek any price higher than $21. . . .

[T]he Lehman Brothers team concluded that "the price of either $20 or $21 would be a fair price for the remaining shares of UOP". They telephoned this impression to Glanville, who was spending the weekend in Vermont.

On Monday morning, March 6, 1978, Glanville and the senior member of the Lehman Brothers team flew to Des Plaines to attend the scheduled UOP directors meeting. Glanville looked over the assembled information during the flight. The two had with them the draft of a "fairness opinion letter" in which the price had been left blank. Either during or immediately prior to the directors' meeting, the two-page "fairness opinion letter" was typed in final form and the price of $21 per share was inserted.

On March 6, 1978, both the Signal and UOP boards were convened to consider the proposed merger. Telephone communications were maintained between the two meetings. Walkup, Signal's board chairman, and also a UOP director, attended UOP's meeting with Crawford in order to present Signal's position and answer any questions that UOP's non-Signal directors might have. Arledge and Chitiea, along with Signal's other designees on UOP's board, participated by conference telephone. All of UOP's outside directors attended the meeting either in person or by conference telephone.

First, Signal's board unanimously adopted a resolution authorizing Signal to propose to UOP a cash merger of $21 per share as outlined in a certain merger agreement and other supporting documents. This proposal required that the merger be approved by a majority of UOP's outstanding minority shares voting at the stockholders meeting at which the merger would be considered, and that the minority shares voting in favor of the merger, when coupled with Signal's 50.5% interest would have to comprise at least two-thirds of all UOP shares. Otherwise the proposed merger would be deemed disapproved.

UOP's board then considered the proposal. Copies of the agreement were delivered to the directors in attendance, and other copies had been forwarded earlier to the directors participating by telephone. They also had before them UOP financial data for 1974-1977, UOP's most recent financial statements, market price information, and budget projections for 1978. In addition they had Lehman Brothers' hurriedly prepared fairness opinion letter finding the price of $21 to be fair. Glanville, the Lehman Brothers partner, and UOP director, commented on the information that had gone into preparation of the letter.

Signal also suggests that the Arledge-Chitiea feasibility study, indicating that a price of up to $24 per share would be a "good investment" for Signal, was discussed at the UOP directors' meeting. The Chancellor made no such finding, and our independent review of the record, detailed *infra,* satisfies us by a preponderance of the evidence that there was no discussion of this document at UOP's board meeting. Furthermore, it is clear beyond peradventure that nothing in that report was ever disclosed to UOP's minority shareholders prior to their approval of the merger.

After consideration of Signal's proposal, Walkup and Crawford left the meeting to permit a free and uninhibited exchange between UOP's non-Signal directors. Upon their return a resolution to accept Signal's offer was then proposed and adopted. While Signal's men on UOP's board participated in various aspects of the meeting, they abstained from voting. However, the minutes show that each of them "if voting would have voted yes".

On March 7, 1978, UOP sent a letter to its shareholders advising them of the action taken by UOP's board with respect to Signal's offer. This document pointed out, among other things, that on February 28, 1978 "both companies had announced negotiations were being conducted".

Despite the swift board action of the two companies, the merger was not submitted to UOP's shareholders until their annual meeting on May 26, 1978. . . .

. . . At the meeting only 56%, or 3,208,652, of the minority shares were voted. Of these, 2,953,812, or 51.9% of the total minority, voted for the merger, and 254,840 voted against it. When Signal's stock was added to the minority shares voting in favor, a total of 76.2% of UOP's outstanding shares approved the merger while only 2.2% opposed it.

By its terms the merger became effective on May 26, 1978, and each share of UOP's stock held by the minority was automatically converted into a right to receive $21 cash. . . .

---

(20) <u>SALE OF CONTROL PREMIA:</u>

Refer to the following sections in the Text to help you answer the questions below:

Text §6A-211(e)

Please read the facts of ***Perlman v. Feldmann***,[6] below, and answer the following questions:

> **Is the controlling shareholder, Feldmann, allowed to sell his shares at a premium over the market price?**
>
> **If you were a judge, what facts below might cause you to answer in the negative?**

. . . This is a derivative action brought by minority stockholders of Newport Steel Corporation to compel accounting for, and restitution of, allegedly illegal

[6] 219 F.2d 173 (1955).

gains which accrued to defendants as a result of the sale in August, 1950, of their controlling interest in the corporation. The principal defendant, C. Russell Feldmann, who represented and acted for the others, members of his family, was at that time not only the dominant stockholder, but also the chairman of the board of directors and the president of the corporation. Newport, an Indiana corporation, operated mills for the production of steel sheets for sale to manufacturers of steel products, first at Newport, Kentucky, and later also at other places in Kentucky and Ohio. The buyers, a syndicate organized as Wilport Company, a Delaware corporation, consisted of end-users of steel who were interested in securing a source of supply in a market becoming ever tighter in the Korean War.

[Wilport paid Feldmann $20 per share for the control block of stock of Newport Steel], although the over-the-counter market price had not exceeded $12 and the book value per share was $17.03. . . .

WORKBOOK

CHAPTER 7

CLOSELY-HELD BUSINESS ENTITIES

CHAPTER 7: EXERCISES:

---

(1) FIDUCIARY DUTIES IN THE CLOSELY-HELD BUSINESS:

Refer to the following sections in the Text to help you answer the questions below:

Text §§7A-200 et seq., 7B-302 et seq., 7C-302

ANSWER THE QUESTIONS THAT FOLLOW THE FACT PATTERN.

Alvin, Bertha, Clyde and Mina are the shareholders of XYZ Inc., a closely-held corporation. The company manufactures and sells widgets.

XYZ is an S-corp. Each shareholder owns roughly 25% of the outstanding shares.

Alvin, Bertha and Clyde sit on the board of directors. They are also the company's executive officers.

Mina is not a director of the company, but she is an employee in charge of shipping.

Over the course of a year:

1) The board decides not to issue any dividends for the fiscal year.

2) The board decides to buy equipment from a company whose only shareholders are Alvin and Bertha.

3) Mina drafts a report detailing suggestions for improving the company's distribution system. Alvin, Bertha and Clyde do not pay attention to her suggestions.

4) The board decides to hold its shareholders meeting in Paris, France. It pays the expenses of the shareholders and their spouses to make the trip.

5) The board never notifies Mina of the annual shareholders meeting.

6) Alvin forms a group of investors to purchase the plot of land next to XYZ's manufacturing plant. XYZ's plant has had insufficient parking for several years and needs to expand its parking lot.

7) The board approves 25% pay raises for the executive officers.

8) Alvin, Bertha and Clyde refuse to elect Mina to the board.

9) The board decides not to insure the manufacturing plant. The plant subsequently burns to the ground and XYZ is left without any manufacturing facilities.

10) The board decides to fire Mina because "she was doing a poor job." Mina was an employee-at-will.

What claims could Mina make against the other shareholders for each of the above items? If you were a law professor, what facts would you add to help or hinder Mina's case?

If Mina wants to compel her fellow shareholders to buy her out at fair market value, what legal claim could she attempt? Explain.

What action could Mina take to force a buyout if this were a partnership, and not a corporation? Could she do the same in an LLC?

---

(2) THE BUY-SELL AGREEMENT 1:

Refer to the following sections in the Text to help you answer the questions below:

Text §7A-300 et seq.

Each of the following provisions comes from a buy-sell agreement (not necessarily the same one).

For each provision, explain briefly:

What issue does the provision address? (i.e., DDD BEER)

What method of purchase/sale does the provision prescribe?

What is the purchase price?

Clause 1:

If during her lifetime, a Stockholder (the "Selling Stockholder") desires to transfer any Stock in the Corporation, she shall give notice to the Corporation and to the other Stockholders (the "Remaining Stockholders"), stating the terms and conditions of the proposed Transfer. Notwithstanding any price terms that may be in the notice, the notice will be deemed to be an offer to sell all of the shares then owned by the Selling Stockholder at a price equal to the Book Value as of the Valuation Date. . . .

If the Corporation declines to purchase all of the shares being offered by the Selling Stockholder, or if the Corporation's option lapses, then the Remaining Stockholders will have the right, exercisable within sixty (60) days after the date of the notice described in Paragraph __, to purchase the shares of Stock being offered by the Selling Stockholder that the Corporation has purchased. . . .

If neither the Corporation nor the Remaining Stockholders timely elect to purchase all of the Stock being offered by the Selling Stockholder, the Selling Stockholder shall be free to transfer all, and not less than all, of such Stock upon the terms and conditions stated in the notice described in Paragraph ___, at any time during the sixty (60) day period after the expiration of the option period described in Paragraph ___. However, if the Selling Stockholder does not sell such Stock, she may not later transfer the Stock without again complying with the provisions of this Article.

Clause 2:

Upon the death of a Stockholder (the "Decedent"), the Decedent's personal representative shall have the right to require the Corporation to purchase, all of the stock owned by the Decedent at a price equal to the Fair Value, upon the terms and conditions provided in Section ___.

Clause 3:

Upon the Termination of Employment of any Stockholder ("the Terminating Stockholder"), the Corporation and/or the Remaining Stockholders shall have the right, exercisable as provided in this Article, to require the Terminating Stockholder to sell all of the Stock owned by the Terminating Stockholder at the date her employment terminated, at a price equal to the Book Value, and upon the terms and conditions described in Section ___. . . .

If the Corporation declines to purchase all of the shares owned by the Terminating Stockholder, or if the Corporation's option lapses, then the Remaining Stockholders will have the right, exercisable within sixty (60) days after the date of the Termination of Employment of the Terminating Stockholder to purchase all of the Stock owned by the Terminating Stockholder at the date her employment terminated that the Corporation has not purchased.

Clause 4:

If at any time a Shareholder proposes to transfer Equity Securities to one or more third parties pursuant to an understanding with such third parties ("Transfer"), then the Shareholder shall give the Company a written notice of the Shareholder's intention to make the Transfer (the "Transfer Notice").

The Shareholder shall include in Transfer Notice (i) a description of the Equity Securities to be transferred ("Offered Shares"), (ii) the identity of the prospective transferee(s) and (iii) the consideration and the material terms and conditions upon which the proposed Transfer is to be made.

The Shareholder shall make a certification in the Transfer Notice that the Shareholder has received an offer from the prospective transferee(s) and in good faith believes a binding agreement for the Transfer is obtainable on the terms set forth in the Transfer Notice. The Transfer Notice shall also include a copy of any written proposal, term sheet or letter of intent or other agreement relating to the proposed Transfer.

The Company will have an option for a period of 30 days from receipt of the Transfer Notice to elect to purchase the Offered Shares at the same price and subject to the same material terms and conditions as described in the Transfer Notice.

Clause 5:

Should a Shareholder (the “Selling Shareholder”) receive a bona fide offer (the “Purchase Offer”) to purchase 50% or more of the Shareholder’s Stock from a third party (the “Offeror”), the Selling Shareholder shall notify the other Shareholders of the terms and provisions of such Purchase Offer.

Each of the other Shareholders has the right to participate in the Selling Shareholder’s sale by selling her pro rata share of its Stock to the Offeror pursuant to the terms of the Purchase Offer.

Clause 6:

If a Stockholder who holds no less than [51]% of the outstanding Common Stock of the Company (the "Selling Stockholder"), receives a bona fide offer from a third party to purchase, in one transaction or a series of related transactions, all of the Company's outstanding Common Stock, the Selling Stockholder shall have the right to require that each other Stockholder participates in such sale in the manner set forth in this Section.

---

(3) THE BUY-SELL AGREEMENT 2:

Refer to the following sections in the Text to help you answer the questions below:

Text §§7C-300 et seq., 7A-303 et seq., 7A-305, 7A-306

Imagine you are drafting the buy-sell provisions of an LLC operating agreement.

Invent a client in your mind and speculate about her particular circumstances, her motivations for investing in the LLC, her long-term or short-term business and financial goals, etc.

Please also consider who her co-investors might be and anything else that will help you imagine how you would draft the buy-sell agreement.

For each of the triggering events listed below:

What purchase price would you choose?

Would you draft a cross purchase, redemption, or hybrid model?

Would you make the purchase and sale mandatory or optional?

How would a purchase under the agreement be funded?

TRIGGERING EVENTS:

Death

Divorce

Disability

Bankruptcy etc.

Employment

Exit

Retirement

---

(4) THE BUY-SELL AGREEMENT 3:

Refer to the following sections in the Text to help you answer the questions below:

Text §§7A-303 et seq., 7C-301

Please refer to the relevant portions of an operating agreement, provided below.

The LLC has five members. How does the operating address each of the following events:

Event 1 – MEMBER A DIES:

> **Member B wants to purchase all of Member A's membership interest. Does she have this right?**

Event 2 – MEMBER C DIES:

> **Neither the corporation nor any of the other members has the funds to purchase the membership interest. What happens?**

Event 3 – MEMBER D RESIGNS FROM HER POSITION WITH THE COMPANY:

> **Member D wants to be bought out. Does she have this right?**

Event 4 – MEMBER E RECEIVES A GREAT CASH OFFER FOR HER MEMBERSHIP INTEREST FROM A THIRD PARTY:

> **May she immediately accept the offer and sell to the third party?**
>
> **If she eventually sells to the third party, after complying with the procedures in the operating agreement, will the third party become a "member?"**
>
> **If the Company and the other members only want to buy a portion of her membership interest, may she sell her entire membership interest to the third party?**

Relevant provisions of the operating agreement begin on the next page.

ARTICLE 5. TRANSFER OF MEMBERSHIP INTERESTS

Section 5.1 Transfers not in Compliance with this Article Void.

Any attempted Transfer of a Membership Interest, or any part thereof, not in compliance with this Article is null and void.

Section 5.2 Right of First Refusal.

5.2(a) Grant of Right of First Refusal. The Company and its Members have a right of first of refusal ("First Refusal Right") in connection with any proposed Transfer of Membership Interest, except for any Transfer described in Section 5.2(g).

5.2(b) Notice of Intended Transfer. In the event a Member desires to accept a bona fide third-party offer for the Transfer of any or all of the Member's Membership Interest (the "Offered Membership Interest"), the Member shall promptly

(i) deliver to the President of the Company and the other Members written notice (the "Transfer Notice") of the terms and conditions of the offer, including the portion of the Member's Membership Interest subject to the offer, the purchase price, the identity of the third-party offeror, and, upon request of the any Member, information verifying the financial ability of the third-party offeror to purchase the Offered Membership Interest, and

(ii) provide satisfactory proof that the Transfer of the Offered Membership Interest to the third-party offeror would not be in contravention of the provisions of this Agreement.

5.2(c) Exercise of Right by the Company. The Company shall, for a period of thirty (30) days following receipt of the Transfer Notice, have the right to purchase all or any portion of the Offered Membership Interest specified in the Transfer Notice for the purchase price in the Transfer Notice (the "Purchase Price"). Such right must be exercised by

(i) delivering written notice to the transferor Member and the other Members prior to the expiration of the 30-day exercise period; and

(ii) consummating the transaction within thirty (30) days after the date of such notice.

5.2(d) Exercise of Right by the Other Members. If the Company does not elect to purchase the entire Offered Membership Interest, then any Member may elect to purchase the portion of the Offered Membership Interest that the Company does not purchase for the Purchase Price during the thirty (30) day period following the decision of the Company not to exercise the Company's First Refusal Right. If more than one Member chooses to exercise such First Refusal Right, such Members will have a right to purchase their Pro Rata Share of the Offered Membership Interest. Such right must be exercised by

(i) delivering written notice to the transferor Member and the Company within thirty (30) days after the expiration of the Company's 30-day exercise period; and

(ii) consummating such transaction within thirty (30) days after the date of such notice.

5.2(e) Payment of Purchase Price. All payments of the Purchase Price shall be made by cash, certified or bank check, wire transfer or such other method as is mutually agreeable to the parties. The Purchase Price for any purchase by one or more Members under this Article 10 shall be paid in three equal installments, the first such installment being due and payable at closing and the second and third such installments being due and payable on the first and second anniversary of the closing, respectively. The balance of the Purchase Price shall be represented by two promissory notes of the purchaser of the Offered Membership Interest, bearing interest from the date of closing at a rate equal to the rate announced from time to time by _____ Bank or its successors, as its prime rate, adjusted on the first day of each calendar quarter after the date of closing and payable on the due date of each such note. Each note must contain a right of prepayment without penalty.

5.2(f) Non-Exercise of Right. In the event the Company and/or the other Members do not purchase all of the Offered Membership Interest, the transferor Member shall have a period of thirty (30) days thereafter in which to Dispose of the Offered Membership Interest to the third-party offeror identified in the Transfer Notice upon terms and conditions specified in the Transfer Notice; provided, however, that any such Transfer must not be effected in contravention of the provisions of this Agreement. In the event the Member does not cause such Transfer of the Offered Membership Interest within the specified thirty (30) day period, the First Refusal Right set forth herein shall continue to be applicable to any subsequent Transfer of the Offered Membership Interest by the Member.

5.2(g) Exception to Right of First Refusal. The First Refusal Right will not apply to a Transfer of any or all of a Member's Membership Interest when the Transfer is to another Member; provided, however, that the transfer is otherwise in accordance with the terms of this Agreement.

The First Refusal Right will not apply to a Transfer of any or all of a Member's Membership Interest when the Transfer is to a spouse or a trust under which a spouse is the sole beneficiary; provided, however, that (i) the transferor Member shall promptly deliver to the President of the Company written notice of the terms and conditions of the Transfer including the portion of the Member's Membership Interest subject to the Transfer and the identity of the transferee Member and (ii) that the transfer is otherwise in accordance with the terms of this Agreement.

Section 5.3 Departure of a Member.

5.3(a) Exercise of Right by the Company. Should any Member cease to be an employee of the Company for any reason, including, but not limited to, death, resignation, illness, discharge or disability, ("Departing Member") for a period of one hundred and ninety (90) days after the date the Member ceases to be so employed, the Company shall have the right to purchase the Departing Member's Membership Interest on the terms and conditions set forth in Sections 5.3(c) and 5.3(d). Such right must be exercised by

(i) delivering written notice to the Departing Member, her guardian or legal representative, or her estate and/or heirs within such 90-day period; and

(ii) consummating such transaction within thirty (30) days after the date of such written notice of exercise.

5.3(b) Exercise of Right by the Remaining Members. If the Company does not elect to purchase the entire Membership Interest of the Departing Member, the remaining Members shall have the right to purchase the portion of such Member's Membership Interest that the Company does not purchase, on the terms and conditions set forth in Sections 5.3(c) and 5.3(d).

Each remaining Member may purchase the percentage of the Departing Member's Membership Interest equal to (x) such remaining Member's percentage Membership Interest divided by (y) the total percentage Membership Interests of all remaining Members who elect to purchase the Departing Member's Membership Interest.

Such right must be exercised by

(i) delivering written notice to the Departing Member, her guardian or legal representative, or her estate and/or heirs, and the Company within fifteen (15) days after the expiration of the Company's 90-day period; and

(ii) consummating such transaction within thirty (30) days after the date of such written notice of exercise.

5.3(c) Non-Exercise of Right. In the event the Company and/or the remaining Members do not purchase the Departing Member's Membership Interest, or do not purchase 100% of the Departing Members Membership Interests, then the Departing Member shall remain a Member, except in the case of the death of the Departing Member, in which case the, the Departing Member's heir(s) becomes an Assignee until such time, if at all, as the Company accepts the heir(s) as a Member.

5.3(d) Purchase Price. The purchase price of the Departing Member's Membership Interest under Section 5.3 will be equal to the fair market value of the Departing Member's Membership Interest in the Company.

Should the parties be unable to mutually agree upon such fair market value within 30 days after the Company and/or the remaining Members have exercised their rights, the purchase price shall be determined by a committee of three independent appraisers, one of whom shall be chosen by the seller, one of whom shall be chosen by the purchaser(s), and the third of whom shall be chosen by the first two appraisers thus chosen.

Each party shall choose such appraiser within ten days after such 30 day period, and in the event either party fails to select an appraiser within such period, such party's right to select an appraiser shall be forfeited and the appraisal shall be conducted solely by the appraiser selected by the other party. Such committee of appraisers shall determine the fair value by computing the average of the three appraisers' individual appraisal amounts.

The purchase price as so determined shall be paid, at the purchaser's option, (i) in cash in one lump sum, (ii) by a promissory note providing for two annual installments (with the first installment not less than 50% of the purchase price) of principal and interest, with interest at the prime rate of ______ Bank or its successors in effect on the date the promissory note is delivered, (iii) by a combination of cash and such a promissory note, or (iv) by any other method of payment mutually agreed upon by the seller and the purchaser. Any promissory note shall contain a right of prepayment without penalty.

---

(5) **THE TRANSFER:**

Refer to the following sections in the Text to help you answer the questions below:

Text §§7A-304, 7C-301, 7B-301, Chapter 5, §5A-208(b)

Mary is a shareholder in a closely-held corporation. Mary and the other shareholders have signed a shareholders agreement that has limitations on their ability to transfer their shares to third parties.

In violation of the shareholders agreement, Mary transfers her shares to Zed, a third party. Zed was unaware that the shares were subject to transfer restrictions. When the other shareholders learned of the transfer to Zed, they formally opposed it by written letter to Mary and the corporate secretary. In the letter, they assert that Zed is not a shareholder.

> **Is Zed a shareholder in the corporation, with all associated economic and control rights that a shareholder has under relevant law, the articles, and the bylaws?**

What steps could the parties have taken to reduce the risk of a transfer of shares in breach of the shareholders agreement?

Would the result be different if the parties were members in an LLC? Partners in a partnership?

---

(6) SQUEEZE HER OUT:

Refer to the following sections in the Text to help you answer the questions below:

Text §7C-200, Chapter 6, §§6C-100, 6B-200 et seq.

ANSWER THE QUESTIONS THAT FOLLOW THE FACT PATTERN.

Alice and Betty are the only two members of Alpha LLC. Each made initial capital contributions of $10,000 to get the business started. The company now has a very profitable and stable business.

Alice feels like she does most of the work for the business and Betty is free-riding on her efforts. Indeed, Alice is right – the business would survive and thrive without Betty, but would come to a grinding halt without Alice. Alice does not get any extra compensation for her efforts. Alice and Betty share equally in the company's profits. Neither receives a salary. Alice has voting control pursuant to the operating agreement.

Nothing in the agreement between Alice and Betty requires Alice to do any work for the company, but Alice knows that if she stopped doing all the work, the company would suffer and the profits would dry up.

Alice comes up with a plan:

Alice plans to cause Alpha LLC to dissolve. The operating agreement gives her enough voting power to approve dissolution, even if Betty opposes.

Alice will form a new LLC, where she is the only member. In the liquidation of the company, Alice will buy the company's assets if necessary. She expects to get a good price because the sum total of the individual assets of the company are not worth as much as the entire business as a going concern.

In fact, she does not actually need to buy the company's assets. She could easily acquire the office equipment and computers from some other source. All she really needs for her new LLC is her own know-how. She suddenly realizes that she is the Alpha's greatest asset.

Once Alpha has dissolved and she has formed her new LLC, she can go into business on her own, doing the same things she was doing for Alpha, but capturing all the benefits of her efforts.

What is your advice to Alice? Explain the risks to her, if any, for her plan.

---

(7) THE CHARGING ORDER:

Refer to the following provisions to answer the questions below:

RULLCA §503

For further help, please refer to the following sections in the Text:

Text §§7C-303, 7B-303

Alice is a member of XYZ LLC. She took out a personal loan from a bank using her car as collateral. After suffering some financial setbacks, she defaulted on the loan, still owing $30,000.

The bank repossessed and foreclosed on Alice's car. The bank was only able to recover $12,000 for the car, leaving a deficit of $18,000.

The bank was able to get a charging order on Alice's LLC membership interest. Soon after the court granted the charging order, the LLC was considering a major capital investment in the expansion of the company's factory. For this type of transaction, the operating agreement required a vote of the members.

Does the bank have a right to vote?

Does Alice have a right to vote?

One year later, the members have decided to cause the LLC to make a distribution to its members. Alice is schedule to receive $25,000.

Who has the right to receive the $25,000 distribution?

---

(8) PROHIBITIONS ON THE TRANSFER OF SHARES:

Refer to the following provisions to answer the questions below:

RMBCA §6.27

Read each of the following restrictions on the transfer of shares that you might in a shareholders agreement. Are they permissible under the RMBCA?

Clause 1:

Each Shareholder understands that her Shares have not been registered under the Securities Act of 1933 ("Act"). Each Shareholder also acknowledges that she has acquired her Shares for investment purposes and not with a view to distribution or resale, and that she may not mortgage, pledge, hypothecate, or otherwise transfer her Shares without an effective registration statement under the Act, or an opinion of counsel for the Corporation that registration is not required under the Act.

Clause 2:

Any attempt by a Shareholder to transfer Shares is void if the transfer would undermine the Corporation's eligibility for tax treatment under Subchapter S of the Internal Revenue Code.

Clause 3:

The Shareholders understand that the Corporation intends to qualify as a Small Disadvantaged Business under the U.S. Small Business Administration's 8(a) Business Development Program. A Shareholder shall not transfer Shares to any person if the transfer might reasonably be expected to adversely affect the Corporation's eligibility for Small Disadvantaged Business status. Any transfer in violation of this provision is void.

---

(9) <u>A DIFFICULT CHOICE:</u>

Refer to the following sections in the Text to help you answer the questions below:

Text §§7C-300, 7A-303(f), 7A-305

Your client is forming an LLC with another party. The other party is represented by her own attorney.

The other party is an established businessperson who has been behind several successful business ventures in the past. She is very wealthy. Based on all the information you have about her, you estimate that she has significant liquid assets and easy access to credit.

Your client is a young professional in the early stages of her career. She has enough liquid assets for this investment, but not much beyond that. She does not have a well-established history of credit. She can make monthly payments on her student loans, her car loans, her credit cards, and her rent, with a moderate amount of disposable income remaining.

The attorney for the other party sends you the first draft of the proposed LLC operating agreement for your review and comment. The draft operating agreement contains the following clause:

> If at any time Member wishes to exercise the buy-sell right of this Section, the Member (the "Offering Member") must deliver to the other Member (the "Responding Member") a written offer ("Offer") with one exclusive cash offer price ("Offer Price").
>
> In the Offer, the Offering Member must make a legally binding offer that gives the Responding Member a choice between (a) selling her entire Membership Interest to the Offering Member for the Offer Price, or (b) purchasing the entire Membership Interest of the Offering Member for the Offer Price.
>
> Within fifteen days (15) days after receiving the Offer, Responding Member must deliver to the Offering Member a written response ("Response") with a legally binding election agreeing to (a) sell her entire Membership Interest to the Offering Member for the Offer Price or (b) purchase the entire Membership Interest of the Offering Member for the Offer Price.
>
> If the Responding Member fails to deliver the Response within fifteen (15) days of receiving the Offer, she is deemed to agree to sell her entire Membership Interest to the Offering Member at the Offer Price.

What is your initial reaction to this clause?

Could you add a provision that might lessen your concern?

---

(10) STALEMATE:

Refer to the following sections in the Text to help you answer the questions below:

Text §7A-400 et seq.

ANSWER THE QUESTIONS THAT FOLLOW THE FACT PATTERN.

Bob and Mary are shareholders in a closely-held corporation. They each hold 50% of the outstanding shares. They each hold one seat on the two-seat board of directors.

The corporation operates a retail clothing store in a local strip mall. The store has several sales clerks and one store manager. The store manager is under contract until the end of the month, which is rapidly approaching. Bob wants to keep the current store manager, even though means giving her a 20% raise. Mary wants to hire a new manager for a lower salary.

Bob and Mary have been arguing about this for three months now. Each has been unable to persuade the other. Their discussions have become increasingly heated, and the relationship between Bob and Mary has suffered because of it.

The store manager is an important position. If Bob and Mary do not re-hire the current manager or hire a new manager, sales will slow to a crawl, the clerks will be without leadership, and the work schedule will become a nightmare. Neither Bob nor Mary is interested in stepping up and doing the job. The sales clerks will be able to fill in here and there, but none of them have the time or experience to do the job properly. Bob and Mary anticipate that profits will drop significantly without a manager, and there may even be moderate losses in the slower months of the year.

Mary comes to you for advice. She is tired of Bob and tired of the business. She is at retirement age and would be happy if she could sell the business. Bob is not interested in buying her out, working with a new investor, or finding a third party to buy the entire business. Mary would just like to exit her investment, get as much cash as possible, and enjoy her retirement. Their shareholder agreement has no relevant provision to address the situation.

Mary wants to know if there is any way to force Bob to sell the business or liquidate its assets. Explain the option she might have and its prospects for success.

Would there have been a good way to structure the corporation or draft a provision in a shareholder's agreement that could have prevented this stalemate? Explain.

---

(11) <u>BUY ME OUT:</u>

Refer to the following sections in the Text to help you answer the questions below:

Text §§7B-302(b), 7B-302(c), 7C-302

What are the results under the relevant default rules for each of the following situations? Please assume the parties' agreements do not have relevant provisions on buy-out or withdrawal-at-will.

Shareholder to the corporation and her fellow shareholders:

"I am tired of this. I withdraw from the corporation. I demand you buy me out at the full market value of my shares."

Partner to the partnership and her fellow partners:

"I am tired of this. I withdraw from the partnership. I demand you buy me out at the full market value of my partnership interest."

[The relevant Partnership Agreement has a 12-year duration, which has not expired.]

Member to the LLC and her fellow members:

"I am tired of this. I withdraw from the LLC. I demand you buy me out at the full market value of my membership interest."

[The relevant Operating Agreement has a 12-year duration, which has not expired.]

WORKBOOK

CHAPTER 8

LITIGATION

CHAPTER 8 – EXERCISES:

---

(1) DIRECT CLAIMS VS. DERIVATIVE CLAIMS:

Refer to the following sections in the Text to help you answer the questions below:

Text §8A-101 et seq.

Are the following shareholder lawsuits direct or derivative?

(1) The articles of incorporation of XYZ Corp. require the corporation to pay Class A shareholders twice the dividend of Class B shareholders. This year, however, XYZ Corp. paid the same amount of dividends to shareholders of both classes. Anna, a Class A shareholder, sues.

(2) Mary is a shareholder of Paper Co. She believes that the management of the Scranton branch is incompetent. She requests access to corporate books and records regarding the performance of the Scranton branch. The corporation refuses. She sues to get access.

(3) Sharon is a shareholder of Goo Enterprises Inc. Several of the corporation's officers have been diverting corporate funds to themselves through huge loans from the corporation at very low interest rates. Sharon sues the board of directors for failing to detect and prevent these loans.

(4) Lenny is a director of XYZ Corp. He is also the sole shareholder of Little Co. XYZ agrees to buy out Little Co. for $5 million. Mary is a shareholder of XYZ and is unhappy with the transaction. She sues Lenny and the other board members of XYZ for breach of fiduciary duties.

(5) Stan is a shareholder of Zed Corp. Stan is unhappy about the direction of the company, so he brings an action for involuntary dissolution.

(6) ABC Corp has been merged into another corporation. Under the law, the shareholders of ABC had a right to vote on the merger, but the board never called a shareholders meeting for approval of the merger. Sally, a shareholder of ABC, sues the directors.

(7) The board of directors of XYZ Corp. entered into a merger transaction with Big Corp. Under the terms of the merger agreement, XYZ Corp. merged into Big Corp. and the shareholders of XYZ were cashed out at $55 per share. After the merger had been completed, Mary, a shareholder of XYZ, was unhappy with the transaction. She sues the board for breach of its fiduciary duty of care.

(8) In a closely-held corporation, the majority shareholder fires the minority shareholder from her position as CFO, increases her own salary, and takes a corporate opportunity.

(9) The board of directors of XYZ Inc. increases the size of the board from 11 to 15 directors. Sally is a shareholder. She challenges the transaction in court, claiming the increase in the size of the board makes it more difficult for a potential acquirer to conduct a successful hostile takeover of the corporation.

---

(2) THE RMBCA APPROACH TO DEMAND:

Refer to the following provisions to answer the questions below:

RMBCA §§7.42, 7.44

For further help, please refer to the following sections in the Text:

Text §§8A-103 et seq., 8A-104 et seq.

Alpha Corp. has nine directors on its board. The board approved the purchase of Blackacre for $30 million from by **BA LLC**.

After the corporation's purchase of Blackacre was consummated, Sharon Shareholder discovered that five of the directors of Alpha Corp. were the sole members of BA LLC at the time of the transaction between the two companies. Each of the five directors owned 20% of BA LLC.

(1) Sharon shareholder brings a derivative lawsuit against the entire board without first making demand on the board of directors.

What is the result under the RMBCA?

(2) Assume that Sharon Shareholder made demand on the board of Alpha Corp. and the board of directors of Alpha Corp. formed a special litigation committee ("SLC") to consider the demand.

The SLC is made up of three directors who were not members of BA LLC. The members of the SLC were appointed by a majority vote of the four directors who were not members of BA LLC.

- The three SLC members have no financial or employment connections with BA LLC or the five directors who own BA LLC.

- The three members of the SLC have been sitting on the Alpha board with the five conflicted directors for 9 years.

- The three members of the SLC voted in favor of the Blackacre transaction and are named as defendants in the derivative lawsuit.

- The three members of the SLC are not independently wealthy. They receive significant fees for serving on the board of Alpha Corp.

- Two of the five conflicted directors serve on the board's nominating committee.

- The three members of the SLC sit on the board of advisors of a local non-profit organization and are very active in the fundraising for the non-profit. The five conflicted members of the board sit on the board of advisors of the same non-profit and are also major donors.

The SLC makes a thorough investigation of the Blackacre transaction and rejects Sharon's demand. Sharon initiates a shareholder derivative lawsuit. The SLC asks the court to dismiss the lawsuit because it is not in the best interests of the corporation.

Should the court dismiss the lawsuit? What is your analysis under the RMBCA?

---

(3) DEMAND IN "DEMAND-EXCUSED" JURISDICTIONS:

Refer to the following sections in the Text to help you answer the questions below:

Text §§8A-103 et seq., 8A-104 et seq.

Alpha Corp. has nine directors on its board. The board approved the purchase of Blackacre for $30 million from **BA LLC**.

After the corporation's purchase of Blackacre was consummated, Sharon Shareholder discovered that five of the directors of Alpha Corp. were the sole members of BA LLC at the time of the transaction between the two companies. Each of the five directors owned 20% of BA LLC.

(1) Sharon shareholder makes demand on the board and the board rejects demand.

What is the result in a demand-excused jurisdiction?

(2) Assume Sharon shareholder brings a derivative action without making demand on the board. The board asks the court to dismiss the lawsuit.

Will a court dismiss the lawsuit (i.e., was demand excused)?

If none of the directors was conflicted in the Blackacre transaction, what other circumstances might result in excusal of demand? Feel free to use your imagination to create new facts.

(3) Assume that board of Alpha Corp. is willing to concede that demand was excused. The board forms a special litigation committee ("SLC") to consider the demand.

The SLC is made up of three directors who were not members of BA LLC.

- The three SLC members have no financial or employment connections with BA LLC or the five directors who own BA LLC.

- The three members of the SLC have been sitting on the Alpha board with the five conflicted directors for 9 years.

- The three members of the SLC voted in favor of the Blackacre transaction and are named as defendants in the derivative lawsuit.

- The three members of the SLC are not independently wealthy. They receive significant fees for serving on the board of Alpha Corp.

- Two of the five conflicted directors serve on the nominating committee.

- The three members of the SLC sit on the board of advisors of a local non-profit organization and are very active in the fundraising for the non-profit. The five conflicted members of the board sit on the board of advisors of the same non-profit and are also major donors.

The SLC makes a thorough investigation of the Blackacre transaction. The SLC asks the court to dismiss Sharon's derivative lawsuit because it is not in the best interests of the corporation.

Should the court dismiss the lawsuit?

---

(4) THE INDEPENDENCE OF THE SLC:

Refer to the following sections in the Text to help you answer the questions below:

Text §§8A-104 et seq.

Read the documents below and answer the following questions:

What steps does the board take to create an SLC?

How does the board attempt to make the SLC independent?

Excerpts from bylaws of Goo Corp.

"**Article 2 - The Board of Directors**

"**Section 1- Board Size:** The number of directors constituting the board shall be seven (7) . . .

"**Section 4. Board Committees.** The board of directors may create committees composed of one or more directors. Each committee will have the powers granted to it by the board of directors to the extent permitted by the relevant law. A majority of the members of any committee of the Board of Directors will constitute a quorum for all committee action. Committees may include a special litigation committee, consisting of one or more independent directors, to determine whether any rights and remedies the corporation might have should be pursued. Each such committee, with the exception of the special litigation committee, shall be subject to the direction and control of the board of directors."

Goo Corp.
Minutes of the Board of Directors Meeting of December 3, 2015

The board of directors of Goo Corp. (the "Company") held a meeting on December 3, 2015 at 3:00 p.m. The following directors were in attendance and constituted a quorum of the board:

Penelope Piscine
Barry Bovine
Lois Lupine
Ellen Equine
Oliver Ovine
Mary Murine
Veronica Vulpine

The meeting was called to order and it was moved, seconded, and carried that Lois Lupine act as chair of the meeting and Barry Bovine act as secretary.

The following resolutions were adopted by the Company's board of directors:

WHEREAS, a shareholder derivative action has been filed against this corporation and each of the corporation's current directors alleging breach of fiduciary duties in connection with the corporation's acquisition of certain assets of Alpha Inc., which was consummated on October 1, 2015 (the "Claims");

WHEREAS, the board of directors believes it is proper and in the best interests of the corporation to (1) establish a Special Litigation Committee of directors who do not have an individual interest in the outcome of the litigation of the Claims, and (2) delegate to such committee the duty to investigate and evaluate the Claims and to determine whether pursuing any of the Claims is in the best interests of the corporation and its shareholders;

NOW, THEREFORE, the board adopts the following resolutions:

RESOLVED, the board establishes a Special Litigation Committee pursuant to the corporation's bylaws.

The board authorizes the Special Litigation Committee to exercise all corporate authority to determine what action, if any, the corporation should take in response to the Claims and any similar lawsuits that have been or may be filed.

The Special Litigation Committee is authorized to select, retain, direct, and discharge independent legal counsel and such other advisors as the committee deems appropriate to assist the committee in investigating and evaluating the legal and factual bases for the allegations in the Claims and cause the corporation to pay the fees and expenses of such advisors.

The Special Litigation Committee is authorized to take such actions and to execute and deliver instruments that it determines to be necessary or appropriate to perform its functions.

The determinations of the Special Litigation Committee shall be final and binding on the corporation and will not be subject to review by the board of directors.

The corporation shall provide reasonable compensation to the members of the Special Litigation Committee for their service on the committee and reimburse them for expenses they incur in their capacity as members of the Special Litigation Committee.

The corporation shall indemnify each member of the Special Litigation committee to the fullest extent allowable under law and the corporation's articles and bylaws against all expenses, liabilities, and losses incurred by the member in connection with her service on the committee.

RESOLVED, the board increases the size of the board by two (2) directors by amending Article 2, Section 1 of the Company's bylaws to read as follows:

> "The number of directors constituting the board shall be nine (9)."

RESOLVED, the board appoints the following persons to the board of directors to fill the two (2) vacancies created by the increase in the size of the board and to serve until their successors are qualified and elected at the next annual meeting of shareholders:

Lisa Lapine
Carl Caprine

RESOLVED, the board appoints the following directors to the Special Litigation Committee; These directors have no individual stake in the outcome of the Claims as they were not named as defendants to the Claims and were not members of the board of directors or officers of the corporation at the time of the transaction that is the basis for the Claims:

Lisa Lapine
Carl Caprine

These resolutions are effectively immediately.

(5) LITIGATION EXPENSES FOR SHAREHOLDER LAWSUITS:

Refer to the following sections in the Text to help you answer the questions below:

Text §§8A-105, 8A-102

You represent an institutional investor. Your client has significant shareholdings in numerous public corporations. One of these public corporations has just amended its bylaws to include the following provision:

> To the fullest extent permitted by law, in the event that (i) any current or prior stockholder or anyone on their behalf ("Claiming Party") initiates or asserts any claim or counterclaim ("Claim") or joins, offers substantial assistance to, or has a direct financial interest in any Claim against the Corporation and/or any Director, Officer, Employee or Affiliate, and (ii) the Claiming Party (or the third party that received substantial assistance from the Claiming Party or in whose Claim the Claiming Party had a direct financial interest) does not obtain a judgment on the merits that substantially achieves, in substance and amount, the full remedy sought, then each Claiming Party shall be obligated jointly and severally to reimburse the Corporation and any such Director, Officer, Employee or Affiliate, the greatest amount permitted by law of all fees, costs and expenses of every kind and description (including but not limited to, all reasonable attorney's fees and other litigation expenses) (collectively, "Litigation Costs") that the parties may incur in connection with such Claim.

Your client asks you to explain the provision.

What is the purpose of the provision?

Is it good for shareholders?

(6) INDEMNIFICATION AND ADVANCEMENT OF EXPENSES:

Refer to the following provisions to answer the questions below:

RMBCA §§8.50 – 8.56

For further help, please refer to the following sections in the Text:

Text §8A-200 et seq.

Jane A is a director of ABC Co.

1) The shareholders bring a suit against Jane for self-dealing.

    If **Jane loses** the lawsuit, would the corporation be permitted (or required) to indemnify Jane for her legal expenses or her liability?

    If **Jane wins** the lawsuit because the statute of limitations has run, would the corporation be permitted (or required) to indemnify Jane for her legal expenses?

    If **Jane settles** the lawsuit for $500, would the corporation be permitted (or required) to indemnify Jane for her legal expenses or her settlement?

    If **the corporation settles** the lawsuit for $50,000 on Jane's behalf, with Jane paying nothing, would the corporation be permitted (or required) to indemnify Jane for her legal expenses or her settlement?

2) A former employee of the corporation is threatening to sue Jane (and the entire board) for discrimination.

    If the **employee never sues**, but Jane had consulted an expensive lawyer, would the corporation be permitted (or required) to indemnify Jane for her legal expenses?

    If the employee sues Jane and **Jane loses**, would the corporation be permitted (or required) to indemnify Jane for her legal expenses or her liability?

    If the employee eventually sues Jane and **Jane wins**, would the corporation be permitted (or required) to indemnify Jane for her legal expenses?

If **Jane settles** the lawsuit for $10,000, would the corporation be permitted (or required) to indemnify Jane for her legal expenses or her settlement?

3) The state attorney general indicts Jane for attempting to bribe a government official in connection with the corporation's bid to procure a government contract.

If **Jane is acquitted**, would the corporation be permitted (or required) to indemnify Jane for her legal expenses?

If **Jane is convicted** and must pay a fine, would the corporation be permitted (or required) to indemnify Jane for her legal expenses and the fine?

If **Jane pleads guilty or no contest** and must pay a fine, would the corporation be permitted (or required) to indemnify Jane for her legal expenses and the fine?

Who should make the necessary determinations required by the law in the above situations?

May ABC Co. advance her legal expenses in the above situations?

---

(7) INDEMNIFICATION AGREEMENT:

Refer to the following provisions to answer the questions below:

RMBCA §§8.50 – 8.56

For further help, please refer to the following sections in the Text:

Text §8A-201(c)

You represent a client who has been nominated for election to the board of directors of XYZ Corp. She has provided you with XYZ Corp.'s standard indemnification agreement for its directors and officers.

Please review the agreement for your client and note where it provides greater protection than the default provisions of the RMBCA.

Could the agreement allow the corporation to indemnify an officer or director who . . .

acted in bad faith?

did not act in a manner she reasonably believed to be in the best interests of the corporation?

had reasonable cause to believe her conduct was unlawful?

INDEMNIFICATION AGREEMENT

This indemnification agreement ("**Agreement**") is made as of ________, 20___, by and between XYZ Corp. ("**Company**") and ____________________ ("**Indemnitee**").

I. DEFINITIONS:

"**Change in Control**" means the occurrence after the date of this Agreement of any of the following events:

(i) any Person is or becomes the beneficial owner, directly or indirectly, of securities of the Company representing more than fifty percent (50%) of the Company's then outstanding common stock;

(ii) the consummation of a reorganization, merger or consolidation, unless immediately following such reorganization, merger or consolidation, all of the beneficial owners of the common stock of the Company immediately prior to such transaction beneficially own, directly or indirectly, more than 50% of the combined voting power of the outstanding Voting Securities of the entity resulting from such transaction;

(iii) during any period of two consecutive years, not including any period prior to the execution of this Agreement, individuals who at the beginning of such period constituted the Board (including for this purpose any new directors whose election by the Board or nomination for election by the Company's shareholders was approved by a vote of at least two-thirds (2/3) of the directors then still in office who either were directors at the beginning of the period or whose election or nomination for election was previously so approved) cease for any reason to constitute at least a majority of the Board; or

(iv) the shareholders of the Company approve a plan of complete liquidation or dissolution of the Company or an agreement for the sale or disposition by the Company of all or substantially all of the Company's assets.

"**Event**" means any event or occurrence, whether occurring on or after the date of this Agreement, related to the fact that Indemnitee is or was a director, officer, employee or agent of the Company or any subsidiary of the Company, or is or was serving at the request of the Company as a director, officer, employee, member, manager, trustee or agent of any other corporation, limited liability company, partnership, joint venture, trust or other entity or enterprise or by reason of an action or inaction by Indemnitee in any such capacity (whether or not serving in such capacity at the time any Loss is incurred for which indemnification can be provided under this Agreement).

"**Proceeding**" means any threatened, pending or completed action, suit, proceeding or alternative dispute resolution mechanism, by reason of or arising in part out of an Event, whether civil, criminal, administrative, arbitrative, investigative or other, and whether made pursuant to federal, state or other law; or any inquiry, hearing or investigation that the Indemnitee determines might lead to the institution of any such action, suit, proceeding or alternative dispute resolution mechanism.

"**Expenses**" means any and all expenses, including attorneys' and experts' fees, court costs, transcript costs, travel expenses, duplicating, printing and binding costs, telephone charges, and all other costs and expenses actually and reasonably paid or incurred in connection with investigating, defending, being a witness in or participating in (including on appeal), or preparing to defend, be a witness or participate in, any Proceeding. Expenses also include any of the forgoing expenses incurred in connection with any appeal resulting from any Proceeding, including the principal, premium, security for, and other costs relating to any costs bond, supersedes bond, or other appeal bond or its equivalent. Expenses also include any interest, assessment or other charges imposed thereon and costs incurred in preparing statements in support of payment requests hereunder. Expenses, however, do not include amounts paid in settlement by Indemnitee or the amount of judgments or fines against Indemnitee.

"**Losses**" means any and all damages, losses, liabilities, judgments, fines, penalties (whether civil, criminal or other), amounts paid or payable in settlement, including any interest, and assessments,

II. INDEMNIFICATION.

(A) Third party claims: The Company shall indemnify Indemnitee, to the fullest extent permitted under applicable law, against any and all Expenses and Losses if Indemnitee becomes a party to, or is threatened to be made a party to, any Proceeding, other than a Proceeding by or in the right of the Company, if the Indemnitee acted in good faith and in a manner she reasonably believed to be in or not opposed to the best interests of the Company and, in the case of a criminal Proceeding, had no reasonable cause to believe her conduct was unlawful.

The Company's obligation to indemnify Indemnitee for any settlement in connection with a Proceeding under this subsection is conditioned on approval of the settlement by the Company in advance. The Company shall not unreasonably withhold its approval.

(B) Claims by or in the right of the Company: The Company shall indemnify Indemnitee, to the fullest extent permitted under applicable law, against any and all Expenses if Indemnitee becomes a party to, or is threatened to be made a party to, any Proceeding by or in the right of the Company to procure a judgment in the Company's favor, if the Indemnitee acted in good faith and in a manner she reasonably believed to be in or not opposed to the best interests of the Company, *provided, however* that the Company has no obligation to indemnify Indemnitee and is not permitted to indemnify Indemnitee where Indemnitee has been finally adjudicated to be liable to the Company by court order or judgment, unless a court of competent jurisdiction otherwise determines that Indemnitee is entitled to indemnification.

(C) Successful on the Merits: The Company shall indemnify Indemnitee, to the fullest extent permitted under applicable law, against any and all Expenses to the extent that Indemnitee is successful on the merits or otherwise in defense of any Proceeding.

For the purposes of this Agreement, an indemnitee is considered "successful on the merits or otherwise" in any Proceeding that is disposed of on the merits or otherwise (including a disposition without prejudice) only when the Indemnitee did not enter a plea of guilty and there was no final adjudication that the Indemnitee:

1. Was liable to the Company;
2. Failed to act in good faith and in a manner she reasonably believed to be in or not opposed to the best interests of the Company; or
3. Had reasonable cause to believe her conduct was unlawful with respect to any criminal Proceeding.

(D) Participant in a Proceeding: The Company shall indemnify Indemnitee, to the fullest extent permitted under applicable law, against any and all Expenses if the Indemnitee is a witness or otherwise asked to participate in any Proceeding where Indemnitee is not a party.

III. ADVANCEMENT OF EXPENSES.

(A) The Company shall advance Expenses to Indemnitee within thirty (30) days after receiving a written request from Indemnitee, whether prior to or after final disposition of any Proceeding. Indemnitee's right to such advancement is not subject to satisfaction of any standard of conduct.

(B) As a condition to receiving any advancement, Indemnitee must provide documentation of the Proceeding before the Company is obligated to advance Expenses.

(C) Indemnitee agrees to repay any amounts the Company has advanced under this Agreement or pursuant to applicable law only to the extent that it is ultimately determined, following the final disposition of such Proceeding, that Indemnitee is not entitled to indemnification under this Agreement or applicable law. Other than the execution and delivery of this Agreement, no other form of undertaking, security, or collateral, will be required from Indemnitee to qualify for advances under this Agreement or applicable law.

IV. INDEMNIFICATION FOR EXPENSES IN ENFORCING RIGHTS.

To the fullest extent allowable under applicable law, the Company shall indemnify against, and if requested by Indemnitee, shall advance to Indemnitee subject to Section III, any Expenses in connection with any Proceeding by Indemnitee to enforce Indemnitee's rights under this Agreement.

Indemnitee shall reimburse the Company for Expenses in connection with any Proceeding threatened or brought by Indemnitee to enforce Indemnitee's rights under this Agreement if a final judicial determination is made that the Indemnitee's claim was frivolous or not made in good faith.

V. DETERMINATION OF RIGHT TO INDEMNIFICATION.

(A) To the extent that any applicable standard of conduct under this Agreement or applicable law is a condition to the Company's indemnification obligations or a condition to Indemnitee's obligations to repay advances, the determination of whether Indemnitee has satisfied the standard of conduct will be made by the Company's board of directors, a committee of the board of directors, or by independent counsel, *provided, however* that if a Change in Control has occurred, Indemnitee will have the right to demand that independent counsel make the determination in a written opinion addressed to the board of directors, with a copy delivered to Indemnitee.

(B) In making any determination of the standard of conduct, the person(s) making such determination shall presume that Indemnitee has satisfied the applicable standard of conduct and is entitled to indemnification. The Company shall have the burden of proof to overcome that presumption. The termination of any Proceeding by judgment, order, settlement, conviction, or upon a plea of *nolo contendere* or its equivalent, will not, of itself, create a presumption that Indemnitee did not act in good faith and in a manner which she reasonably believed to be in or not opposed to the best interests of the Company, or in the case of a criminal Proceeding, that she had reasonable cause to believe her conduct was unlawful.

(C) Without limiting the broad presumptions in Section V.B, Indemnitee is deemed to have acted in good faith and in a manner she reasonably believed to be in or not opposed to the best interests of the Company if Indemnitee's actions or omissions are in good faith reliance on the records of the Company, or on information, opinions, reports or statements furnished to Indemnitee by the officers or employees of the Company or any of its subsidiaries in the course of their duties, or by committees of the board or by any other person (including legal counsel, accountants and financial advisors) as to matters Indemnitee reasonably believed were within such person's professional or expert competence.

(8) D&O INSURANCE POLICY:

Refer to the following sections in the Text to help you answer the questions below:

Text §8-201(d)

Also refer to the following provisions:

RMBCA §§8.50 – 8.56

The Company has a D&O insurance policy. The relevant provisions are provided below.

You are the legal counsel for one of the directors. Does this policy provide her with the coverage she wants? Explain using specific examples of potential claims.

Does it provide her any protection beyond the default indemnification provisions of the RMBCA?

You are the legal counsel for the Company. Does this provide it with the coverage it wants? Explain using specific examples of potential claims.

. . .

ARTICLE I. AGREEMENT TO INSURE

The Insurer shall pay on behalf of an Insured Person all Loss from Claims against the Insured Person for Wrongful Acts first made during the Policy Period, excluding any Loss the Company actually pays to or on behalf of the Insured Person as indemnification.

The Insurer shall pay on behalf of the Company all Loss from Claims against the Insured Person for Wrongful Acts first made during the Policy Period that the Company pays to or on behalf of the Insured Person as indemnification, but only to the extent the Company is required or permitted by law, to the fullest extent possible, to indemnify the Insured Person.

ARTICLE II. DEFINITIONS

. . .

"Claim" means any civil, criminal, governmental, regulatory, administrative, or arbitration proceeding made against any Insured Person, seeking monetary or non-monetary relief and commenced by the service of a complaint or similar pleading, the return of an indictment, or the receipt or the filing of a notice of charges or similar document, including any proceeding initiated against any Insured Person before the Equal Employment Opportunity Commission, or any similar governmental body, or other written demand for monetary or non-monetary relief made against any Insured Person.

. . .

"Insured Person" means the directors and officers of the Company, past present or future.

. . .

"Loss" means compensatory damages, punitive or exemplary damages, the multiple portion of any multiplied damage award, judgments, settlements, and costs of defense, provided, however, Loss shall not include criminal or civil fines or penalties, taxes, or any matter which may be deemed uninsurable under the law pursuant to which this Policy is construed.

. . .

"Wrongful Act" means (a) any actual or alleged act, omission, error, misstatement, misleading statement, neglect, or breach of duty by any Insured Person in their capacity as such with the Company; or (b) any matter claimed against any Insured Person solely by reason of their capacity with the Company.

. . .

ARTICLE III. EXCLUSIONS

A. The Insurer will not pay Loss for Claims made against an Insured Person alleging, arising out of, based upon, or attributable to the following conduct:

1. an Insured Person gaining any profit, advantage or remuneration to which they were not legally entitled; or

2. fraudulent or criminal acts of an Insured Person,

provided, however, this exclusion shall only apply when it is finally adjudicated that such conduct occurred.

B. Any Claim made against an Insured Person for a Wrongful Act in connection with any pension or welfare plan of the Company, including, without limitation, any Claim against an Insured Person for a violation of the duties, obligations and responsibilities under the Employee Retirement Income Security Act of 1974 and its relevant rules, regulations, and amendments;

C. Any Claim made against an Insured Person for actual or alleged bodily injury, sickness, disease, or death of any person; damage to or destruction of any tangible property, including the loss of use; or mental anguish, emotional distress, invasion of privacy, wrongful entry, eviction, false arrest, false imprisonment, malicious prosecution, libel or slander.

D. Any Claim made against any Insured Person that is brought by or on behalf of the Company or by any Insured Person, provided however, this exclusion shall not apply to:

1. Any Claim brought by a security holder or member of the Company, whether directly or derivatively, and such security holder's or member's Claim is instigated and continued totally independent of, and totally without solicitation of, or assistance of, or active participation of, or intervention of, the Company or any Insured Person;

2. Any Claim brought by an Insured Person in the form of a cross-claim or third-party claim for contribution or indemnity which is part of and results directly from a Claim that is covered by this Policy;

3. Any Claim brought against an Insured Person engaging in protected activity specified in any "whistleblower" protection under any state, local or foreign securities laws; or

4. Any Claim for the actual or alleged wrongful termination of an Insured Person.

E. Any Claim made against any Insured Person alleging, arising out of, based upon, or attributable to, directly or indirectly resulting from, or in consequence of, or in any way involving, Pollution including but not limited to any Claim for financial loss to the Company, its security holders or its creditors.

---

(9) <u>DEMAND FUTILITY:</u>

Refer to the following sections in the Text to help you answer the questions below:

Text §§8A-103(a), 8A-103(b), 8A-103(c), Chapter 6, 6A-205(e)

Read the ***Citigroup*** case below and answer these questions:

Generally, what standard do Delaware courts apply to determine demand futility?

What standard does the court apply to determine futility in a derivative lawsuit that alleges a failure of the board to fulfill its duty to monitor?

Why did the plaintiff's pleadings for the duty to monitor claim fail?

Why did the plaintiff's pleadings for the waste claim succeed?

In re Citigroup Inc. Shareholder Derivative Litigation

964 A.2d 106 (Del. Ch. 2009)

CHANDLER, Chancellor.

This is a shareholder derivative action brought on behalf of Citigroup Inc. ("Citigroup" or the "Company"), seeking to recover for the Company its losses arising from exposure to the subprime lending market. Plaintiffs, shareholders of Citigroup, brought this action against current and former directors and officers of Citigroup, alleging, in essence, that the defendants breached their fiduciary duties by failing to properly monitor and manage the risks the Company faced from problems in the subprime lending market and for failing to properly disclose Citigroup's exposure to subprime assets. Plaintiffs allege that there were extensive "red flags" that should have given defendants notice of the problems that were brewing in the real estate and credit markets and that defendants ignored these warnings in the pursuit of short term profits and at the expense of the Company's long term viability.

Plaintiffs further allege that certain defendants are liable to the Company for corporate waste for . . . approving a multi-million dollar payment and benefit package for defendant Charles Prince, whom plaintiffs describe as largely responsible for Citigroup's problems, upon his retirement as Citigroup's CEO in November 2007. . . .

I. BACKGROUND

A. The Parties

Citigroup is a global financial services company whose businesses provide a broad range of financial services to consumers and businesses. Citigroup was incorporated in Delaware in 1988 and maintains its principal executive offices in New York, New York.

Defendants in this action are current and former directors and officers of Citigroup. The complaint names thirteen members of the Citigroup board of directors on November 9, 2007, when the first of plaintiffs' now-consolidated derivative actions was filed. Plaintiffs allege that a majority of the director defendants were members of the Audit and Risk Management Committee ("ARM Committee") in 2007 and were considered audit committee financial experts as defined by the Securities and Exchange Commission.

Plaintiffs . . . are all owners of shares of Citigroup stock.

B. Citigroup's Exposure to the Subprime Crisis

Plaintiffs allege that since as early as 2006, defendants have caused and allowed Citigroup to engage in subprime lending that ultimately left the Company exposed to massive losses by late 2007. Beginning in late 2005, house prices, which many believe were artificially inflated by speculation and easily available credit, began to plateau, and then deflate. Adjustable rate mortgages issued earlier in the decade began to reset, leaving many homeowners with significantly increased monthly payments. Defaults and foreclosures increased, and assets backed by income from residential mortgages began to decrease in value. By February 2007, subprime mortgage lenders began filing for bankruptcy and subprime mortgages packaged into securities began experiencing increasing levels of delinquency. In mid-2007, rating agencies downgraded bonds backed by subprime mortgages.

Much of Citigroup's exposure to the subprime lending market arose from its involvement with collateralized debt obligations ("CDOs") – repackaged pools of lower rated securities that Citigroup created by acquiring asset-backed securities, including residential mortgage backed securities ("RMBSs"), and then selling rights to the cash flows from the securities in classes, or tranches, with different levels of risk and return. Included with at least some of the CDOs created by Citigroup was a "liquidity put"-an option that allowed the purchasers of the CDOs to sell them back to Citigroup at original value. . . .

By late 2007, it was apparent that Citigroup faced significant losses on its subprime-related assets. . . .

C. Plaintiffs' Claims

Plaintiffs allege that defendants are liable to the Company for breach of fiduciary duty for (1) failing to adequately oversee and manage Citigroup's exposure to the problems in the subprime mortgage market, even in the face of alleged "red flags" . . .. As will be more fully explained below, the "red flags" alleged in the eighty-six page Complaint are generally statements from public documents that reflect worsening conditions in the financial markets, including the subprime and credit markets, and the effects those worsening conditions had on market participants, including Citigroup's peers. . . .

Plaintiffs also allege that the director defendants and certain other defendants are liable to the Company for waste for: . . . approving a multi-million dollar payment and benefit package for defendant Prince upon his retirement as Citigroup's CEO in November 2007. . . .

III. THE MOTION TO DISMISS UNDER [DELAWARE] RULE 23.1 [REGARDING DERIVATIVE SHAREHOLDER LAWSUITS]

A. The Legal Standard for Demand Excused

The decision whether to initiate or pursue a lawsuit on behalf of the corporation is generally within the power and responsibility of the board of directors. This follows from the "cardinal precept of the General Corporation Law of the State of Delaware . . . that directors, rather than shareholders, manage the business and affairs of the corporation." Accordingly, in order to cause the corporation to pursue litigation, a shareholder must either (1) make a pre-suit demand by presenting the allegations to the corporation's directors, requesting that they bring suit, and showing that they wrongfully refused to do so, or (2) plead facts showing that demand upon the board would have been futile. Where, as here, a plaintiff does not make a pre-suit demand on the board of directors, the complaint must plead with particularity facts showing that a demand on the board would have been futile. The purpose of the demand requirement is not to insulate defendants from liability; rather, the demand requirement and the strict requirements of factual particularity . . . "exist[ ] to preserve the primacy of board decisionmaking regarding legal claims belonging to the corporation."

Under the familiar *Aronson* test, to show demand futility, plaintiffs must provide particularized factual allegations that raise a reasonable doubt that "(1) the directors are disinterested and independent [or] (2) the challenged transaction was otherwise the product of a valid exercise of business judgment." Where, however, plaintiffs complain of board inaction and do not challenge a specific decision of the board, there is no "challenged transaction," and the ordinary *Aronson* analysis does not apply. Instead, to show demand futility where the subject of the derivative suit is not a business decision of the board, a plaintiff must allege particularized facts that "create a reasonable doubt that, as of the time the complaint is filed, the board of directors could have properly exercised its independent and disinterested business judgment in responding to a demand."

In evaluating whether demand is excused, . . . the pleadings must comply with "stringent requirements of factual particularity" and set forth "particularized factual statements that are essential to the claim." "A prolix complaint larded with conclusory language ... does not comply with these fundamental pleading mandates."

Plaintiffs have not alleged that a majority of the board was not independent for purposes of evaluating demand. Rather, as to the claims for waste asserted in Count III, plaintiffs allege that the approval of certain transactions did not constitute a valid exercise of business judgment under the second prong of the *Aronson* test. Plaintiffs allege that demand is futile as to Counts I, II, and IV because the director defendants are not able to exercise disinterested business judgment in responding to a demand because their failure of oversight subjects them to a substantial likelihood of personal liability. According to plaintiffs, the director defendants face a substantial threat of personal liability because their conscious disregard of their duties and lack of proper supervision and oversight caused the Company to be overexposed to risk in the subprime mortgage market.

Demand is not excused solely because the directors would be deciding to sue themselves. Rather, demand will be excused based on a possibility of personal director liability only in the rare case when a plaintiff is able to show director conduct that is "so egregious on its face that board approval cannot meet the test of business judgment, and a substantial likelihood of director liability therefore exists."

B. Demand Futility Regarding Plaintiffs' Fiduciary Duty Claims

Plaintiffs' argument is based on a theory of director liability famously articulated by former-Chancellor Allen in *In re Caremark*. Before *Caremark*, in *Graham* . . ., the Delaware Supreme Court, in response to a theory that the Allis-Chalmers directors were liable because they should have known about employee violations of federal anti-trust laws, held that "absent cause for suspicion there is no duty upon the directors to install and operate a corporate system of espionage to ferret out wrongdoing which they have no reason to suspect exists." . . .

With regard to director liability standards, the Court distinguished between (1) "*a board decision* that results in a loss because that decision was ill advised or 'negligent' " and (2) "an *unconsidered failure of the board to act* in circumstances in which due attention would, arguably, have prevented the loss." In the former class of cases, director action is analyzed under the business judgment rule, which prevents judicial second guessing of the decision if the directors employed a rational process and considered all material information reasonably available-a standard measured by concepts of gross negligence. . . .

In the latter class of cases, where directors are alleged to be liable for a failure to monitor liability creating activities, the *Caremark* Court, in a reassessment of the holding in *Graham*, stated that while directors could be liable for a failure to monitor, "only a sustained or systematic failure of the board to exercise oversight-such as an utter failure to attempt to assure a reasonable information and reporting system exists-will establish the lack of good faith that is a necessary condition to liability."

In *Stone v. Ritter*, the Delaware Supreme Court approved the *Caremark* standard for director oversight liability and made clear that liability was based on the concept of good faith, which the *Stone* Court held was embedded in the fiduciary duty of loyalty and did not constitute a freestanding fiduciary duty that could independently give rise to liability. . . .

Thus, to establish oversight liability a plaintiff must show that the directors *knew* they were not discharging their fiduciary obligations or that the directors demonstrated a *conscious* disregard for their responsibilities such as by failing to act in the face of a known duty to act. The test is rooted in concepts of bad faith; indeed, a showing of bad faith is a *necessary condition* to director oversight liability.

1. *Plaintiffs' Caremark Allegations*

Plaintiffs' theory of how the director defendants will face personal liability is a bit of a twist on the traditional *Caremark* claim. In a typical *Caremark* case, plaintiffs argue that the defendants are liable for damages that arise from a failure to properly monitor or oversee employee misconduct or violations of law. For example, in *Caremark* the board allegedly failed to monitor employee actions in violation of the federal Anti-Referral Payments Law; in *Stone*, the directors were charged with a failure of oversight that resulted in liability for the company because of employee violations of the federal Bank Secrecy Act.

In contrast, plaintiffs' . . claims [in the case before the court now] are based on defendants' alleged failure to properly monitor Citigroup's *business risk*, specifically its exposure to the subprime mortgage market. In their answering brief, plaintiffs allege that the director defendants are personally liable under *Caremark* for failing to "make a good faith attempt to follow the procedures put in place or fail[ing] to assure that adequate and proper corporate information and reporting systems existed that would enable them to be fully informed regarding Citigroup's risk to the subprime mortgage market." Plaintiffs point to so-called "red flags" that should have put defendants on notice of the problems in the subprime mortgage market and further allege that the board should have been especially conscious of these red flags because a majority of the directors (1) served on the Citigroup board during its previous Enron related conduct and (2) were members of the ARM Committee and considered financial experts.

Although these claims are framed by plaintiffs as *Caremark* claims, plaintiffs' theory essentially amounts to a claim that the director defendants should be personally liable to the Company because they failed to fully recognize the risk posed by subprime securities. When one looks past the lofty allegations of duties of oversight and red flags used to dress up these claims, what is left appears to be plaintiff shareholders attempting to hold the director defendants personally liable for making (or allowing to be made) business decisions that, in hindsight, turned out poorly for the Company. Delaware Courts have faced these types of claims many times and have developed doctrines to deal with them-the fiduciary duty of care and the business judgment rule. These doctrines properly focus on the decision-making process rather than on a substantive evaluation of the merits of the decision. This follows from the inadequacy of the Court, due in part to a concept known as hindsight bias, to properly evaluate whether corporate decision-makers made a "right" or "wrong" decision.

The business judgment rule "is a presumption that in making a business decision the directors of a corporation acted on an informed basis, in good faith and in the honest belief that the action taken was in the best interests of the company." . . . Thus, absent an allegation of interestedness or disloyalty to the corporation, the business judgment rule prevents a judge or jury from second guessing director decisions if they were the product of a rational process and the directors availed themselves of all material and reasonably available information. The standard of director liability under the business judgment rule "is predicated upon concepts of gross negligence."

Additionally, Citigroup has adopted a provision in its certificate of incorporation pursuant to [Delaware law] that exculpates directors from personal liability for violations of fiduciary duty, except for, among other things, breaches of the duty of loyalty or actions or omissions not in good faith or that involve intentional misconduct or a knowing violation of law. . . Here, plaintiffs have not alleged that the directors were interested in the transaction and instead root their theory of director personal liability in bad faith.

The Delaware Supreme Court has stated that bad faith conduct may be found where a director "intentionally acts with a purpose other than that of advancing the best interests of the corporation, ... acts with the intent to violate applicable positive law, or ... intentionally fails to act in the face of a known duty to act, demonstrating a conscious disregard for his duties." More recently, the Delaware Supreme Court held that when a plaintiff seeks to show that demand is excused because directors face a substantial likelihood of liability where "directors are exculpated from liability except for claims based on 'fraudulent,' 'illegal' or 'bad faith' conduct, a plaintiff must also plead particularized facts that demonstrate that the directors acted with scienter, *i.e.*, that they had 'actual or constructive knowledge' that their conduct was legally improper." A plaintiff can thus plead bad faith by alleging with particularity that a director *knowingly* violated a fiduciary duty or failed to act in violation of a *known* duty to act, demonstrating a *conscious* disregard for her duties.

Turning now specifically to plaintiffs' *Caremark* claims, one can see a similarity between the standard for assessing oversight liability and the standard for assessing a disinterested director's decision under the duty of care when the company has adopted an exculpatory provision pursuant to [Delaware law]. In either case, a plaintiff can show that the director defendants will be liable if their acts or omissions constitute bad faith. A plaintiff can show bad faith conduct by, for example, properly alleging particularized facts that show that a director *consciously* disregarded an obligation to be reasonably informed about the business and its risks or *consciously* disregarded the duty to monitor and oversee the business.

The Delaware Supreme Court made clear in *Stone* that directors of Delaware corporations have certain responsibilities to implement and monitor a system of oversight; however, this obligation does not eviscerate the core protections of the business judgment rule-protections designed to allow corporate managers and directors to pursue risky transactions without the specter of being held personally liable if those decisions turn out poorly. Accordingly, the burden required for a plaintiff to rebut the presumption of the business judgment rule by showing gross negligence is a difficult one, and the burden to show bad faith is even higher. Additionally, as former-Chancellor Allen noted in *Caremark*, director liability based on the duty of oversight "is possibly the most difficult theory in corporation law upon which a plaintiff might hope to win a judgment." The presumption of the business judgment rule, the protection of an exculpatory §102(b)(7) provision, and the difficulty of proving a *Caremark* claim together function to place an extremely high burden on a plaintiff to state a claim for personal director liability for a failure to see the extent of a company's business risk.

To the extent the Court allows shareholder plaintiffs to succeed on a theory that a director is liable for a failure to monitor business risk, the Court risks undermining the well settled policy of Delaware law by inviting Courts to perform a hindsight evaluation of the reasonableness or prudence of directors' business decisions. Risk has been defined as the chance that a return on an investment will be different that expected. The essence of the business judgment of managers and directors is deciding how the company will evaluate the trade-off between risk and return. Businesses-and particularly financial institutions-make returns by taking on risk; a company or investor that is willing to take on more risk can earn a higher return. Thus, in almost any business transaction, the parties go into the deal with the knowledge that, even if they have evaluated the situation correctly, the return could be different than they expected.

It is almost impossible for a court, in hindsight, to determine whether the directors of a company properly evaluated risk and thus made the "right" business decision. . . . It is also possible that the decision-maker improperly evaluated the risk posed by an investment and that the company suffered large losses as a result.

Business decision-makers must operate in the real world, with imperfect information, limited resources, and an uncertain future. To impose liability on directors for making a "wrong" business decision would cripple their ability to earn returns for investors by taking business risks. Indeed, this kind of judicial second guessing is what the business judgment rule was designed to prevent, and even if a complaint is framed under a *Caremark* theory, this Court will not abandon such bedrock principles of Delaware fiduciary duty law. With these considerations and the difficult standard required to show director oversight liability in mind, I turn to an evaluation of the allegations in the Complaint.

a. The Complaint Does Not Properly Allege Demand Futility for Plaintiffs' Fiduciary Duty Claims

In this case, plaintiffs allege that the defendants are liable for failing to properly monitor the risk that Citigroup faced from subprime securities. While it may be possible for a plaintiff to meet the burden under some set of facts, plaintiffs in this case have failed to state a *Caremark* claim sufficient to excuse demand based on a theory that the directors did not fulfill their oversight obligations by failing to monitor the business risk of the company.

The allegations in the Complaint amount essentially to a claim that Citigroup suffered large losses and that there were certain warning signs that could or should have put defendants on notice of the business risks related to Citigroup's investments in subprime assets. Plaintiffs then conclude that because defendants failed to prevent the Company's losses associated with certain business risks, they must have consciously ignored these warning signs or knowingly failed to monitor the Company's risk in accordance with their fiduciary duties. Such conclusory allegations, however, are not sufficient to state a claim for failure of oversight that would give rise to a substantial likelihood of personal liability, which would require particularized factual allegations demonstrating bad faith by the director defendants.

Plaintiffs do not contest that Citigroup had procedures and controls in place that were designed to monitor risk. . . .

Plaintiffs nevertheless argue that the director defendants breached their duty of oversight either because the oversight mechanisms were not adequate or because the director defendants did not make a good faith effort to comply with the established oversight procedures. To support this claim, the Complaint alleges numerous facts that plaintiffs argue should have put the director defendants on notice of the impending problems in the subprime mortgage market and Citigroup's exposure thereto. Plaintiffs summarized some of these "red flags" in their answering brief as follows:

- the steady decline of the housing market and the impact the collapsing bubble would have on mortgages and subprime backed securities since as early as 2005;
- December 2005 guidance from the FASB staff-"The FASB staff is aware of loan products whose contractual features may increase the exposure of the originator, holder, investor, guarantor, or servicer to risk of nonpayment or realization.";
- the drastic rise in foreclosure rates starting in 2006;
- several large subprime lenders reporting substantial losses and filing for bankruptcy starting in 2006;

- billions of dollars in losses reported by Citigroup's peers, such as Bear Stearns and Merrill Lynch.

Plaintiffs argue that demand is excused because a majority of the director defendants face a substantial likelihood of personal liability because they were charged with management of Citigroup's risk as members of the ARM Committee and as audit committee financial experts and failed to properly oversee and monitor such risk. As explained above, however, to establish director oversight liability plaintiffs would ultimately have to prove bad faith conduct by the director defendants. Plaintiffs fail to plead any particularized factual allegations that raise a reasonable doubt that the director defendants acted in good faith.

The warning signs alleged by plaintiffs are not evidence that the directors consciously disregarded their duties or otherwise acted in bad faith; at most they evidence that the directors made bad business decisions. The "red flags" in the Complaint amount to little more than portions of public documents that reflected the worsening conditions in the subprime mortgage market and in the economy generally. Plaintiffs fail to plead "particularized facts suggesting that the Board was presented with 'red flags' alerting it to potential misconduct" at the Company. That the director defendants knew of signs of a deterioration in the subprime mortgage market, or even signs suggesting that conditions could decline further, is not sufficient to show that the directors were or should have been aware of any wrongdoing at the Company or were consciously disregarding a duty somehow to prevent Citigroup from suffering losses. Nothing about plaintiffs' "red flags" supports plaintiffs' conclusory allegation that "defendants have not made a good faith attempt to assure that adequate and proper corporate information and reporting systems existed that would enable them to be fully informed regarding Citigroup's risk to the subprime mortgage market." Indeed, plaintiffs' allegations do not even specify how the board's oversight mechanisms were inadequate or how the director defendants knew of these inadequacies and consciously ignored them. Rather, plaintiffs seem to hope the Court will accept the conclusion that since the Company suffered large losses, and since a properly functioning risk management system would have avoided such losses, the directors must have breached their fiduciary duties in allowing such losses. . . .

The Complaint and plaintiffs' answering brief repeatedly make the conclusory allegation that the defendants have breached their duty of oversight, but nowhere do plaintiffs adequately explain what the director defendants actually did or failed to do that would constitute such a violation. Even while admitting that Citigroup had a risk monitoring system in place, plaintiffs seem to conclude that, because the director defendants (and the ARM Committee members in particular) were charged with monitoring Citigroup's risk, then they must be found liable because Citigroup experienced losses as a result of exposure to the subprime mortgage market. The only factual support plaintiffs provide for this conclusion are "red flags" that actually amount to nothing more than signs of continuing deterioration in the subprime mortgage market. These types of conclusory allegations are exactly the kinds of allegations that do not state a claim for relief under *Caremark*.

To recognize such claims under a theory of director oversight liability would undermine the long established protections of the business judgment rule. . . . What plaintiffs are asking the Court to conclude from the presence of these "red flags" is that the directors failed to see the extent of Citigroup's business risk and therefore made a "wrong" business decision by allowing Citigroup to be exposed to the subprime mortgage market.

This Court's recent decision in *American International Group, Inc. Consolidated Derivative Litigation [("AIG")]* demonstrates the stark contrast between the allegations here and allegations that are sufficient to survive a motion to dismiss. In *AIG* the Court faced a motion to dismiss a complaint that included "well-pled allegations of pervasive, diverse, and substantial financial fraud involving managers at the highest levels of AIG." . . . [T]he Court held that the factual allegations in the complaint were sufficient to support an inference that AIG executives running those divisions knew of and approved much of the wrongdoing. The Court reasoned that huge fraudulent schemes were unlikely to be perpetrated without the knowledge of the executive in charge of that division of the company. Unlike the allegations in this case, the defendants in *AIG* allegedly failed to exercise reasonable oversight over pervasive *fraudulent* and *criminal* conduct. Indeed, the Court in *AIG* even stated that the complaint there supported the assertion that top AIG officials were leading a "criminal organization" and that "[t]he diversity, pervasiveness, and materiality of the alleged financial wrongdoing at AIG is extraordinary."

Contrast the *AIG* claims with the claims in this case. Here, plaintiffs argue that the Complaint supports the reasonable conclusion that the director defendants acted in bad faith by failing to see the warning signs of a deterioration in the subprime mortgage market and failing to cause Citigroup to change its investment policy to limit its exposure to the subprime market. Director oversight duties are designed to ensure reasonable reporting and information systems exist that would allow directors to know about and prevent wrongdoing that could cause losses for the Company. There are significant differences between failing to oversee employee fraudulent or criminal conduct and failing to recognize the extent of a Company's business risk. Directors should, indeed must under Delaware law, ensure that reasonable information and reporting systems exist that would put them on notice of fraudulent or criminal conduct within the company. Such oversight programs allow directors to intervene and prevent frauds or other wrongdoing that could expose the company to risk of loss as a result of such conduct. While it may be tempting to say that directors have the same duties to monitor and oversee business risk, imposing *Caremark*-type duties on directors to monitor business risk is fundamentally different. Citigroup was in the business of taking on and managing investment and other business risks. To impose oversight liability on directors for failure to monitor "excessive" risk would involve courts in conducting hindsight evaluations of decisions at the heart of the business judgment of directors. Oversight duties under Delaware law are not designed to subject directors, even expert directors, to *personal liability* for failure to predict the future and to properly evaluate business risk.

Instead of alleging facts that could demonstrate bad faith on the part of the directors, by presenting the Court with the so called "red flags," plaintiffs are inviting the Court to engage in the exact kind of judicial second guessing that is proscribed by the business judgment rule. In any business decision that turns out poorly there will likely be signs that one could point to and argue are evidence that the decision was wrong. Indeed, it is tempting in a case with such staggering losses for one to think that they could have made the "right" decision if they had been in the directors' position. This temptation, however, is one of the reasons for the presumption against an objective review of business decisions by judges, a presumption that is no less applicable when the losses to the Company are large. . . .

C. Demand Futility Allegations Regarding Plaintiffs' Waste Claims

Count III of the Complaint alleges that certain of the defendants are liable for waste for . . . approving the Letter Agreement dated November 4, 2007 between Citigroup and defendant Prince. . . .

Demand futility is analyzed under *Aronson* when plaintiffs have challenged board action or approval of a transaction. With regard to the claims based on the approval of the Letter Agreement . . . , plaintiffs do not argue that a majority of the director defendants were not disinterested and independent. Rather, plaintiffs argue that demand is excused under the second prong of the *Aronson* analysis, which requires that the plaintiffs plead particularized factual allegations that raise a reasonable doubt as to whether "the challenged transaction was otherwise the product of a valid exercise of business judgment."

Delaware law provides stringent requirements for a plaintiff to state a claim for corporate waste, and to excuse demand on grounds of waste the Complaint must allege particularized facts that lead to a reasonable inference that the director defendants authorized "an exchange that is so one sided that no business person of ordinary, sound judgment could conclude that the corporation has received adequate consideration." The test to show corporate waste is difficult for any plaintiff to meet; indeed, "[t]o prevail on a waste claim ... the plaintiff must overcome the general presumption of good faith by showing that the board's decision was so egregious or irrational that it could not have been based on a valid assessment of the corporation's best interests." . . .

2. *Approval of the Letter Agreement*

Plaintiffs allege that the board's approval of the November 4, 2007 letter agreement constituted corporate waste. Because approval of the letter was board action, demand is evaluated under the *Aronson* standard. Plaintiffs claim that demand is excused under the second prong of *Aronson* because the particularized factual allegations in the Complaint raise a reasonable doubt as to whether the approval was "the product of a valid exercise of business judgment."

The directors of a Delaware corporation have the authority and broad discretion to make executive compensation decisions. The standard under which the Court evaluates a waste claim is whether there was "an exchange of corporate assets for consideration so disproportionately small as to lie beyond the range at which any reasonable person might be willing to trade." It is also well settled in our law, however, that the discretion of directors in setting executive compensation is not unlimited. Indeed, the Delaware Supreme Court was clear when it stated that "there is an outer limit" to the board's discretion to set executive compensation, "at which point a decision of the directors on executive compensation is so disproportionately large as to be unconscionable and constitute waste."

According to plaintiffs' allegations, the November 4, 2007 letter agreement provides that Prince will receive $68 million upon his departure from Citigroup, including bonus, salary, and accumulated stockholdings. Additionally, the letter agreement provides that Prince will receive from Citigroup an office, an administrative assistant, and a car and driver for the lesser of five years or until he commences full time employment with another employer. Plaintiffs allege that this compensation package constituted waste and met the "so one sided" standard because, in part, the Company paid the multi-million dollar compensation package to a departing CEO whose failures as CEO were allegedly responsible, in part, for billions of dollars of losses at Citigroup. In exchange for the multi-million dollar benefits and perquisites package provided for in the letter agreement, the letter agreement contemplated that Prince would sign a non-compete agreement, a non-disparagement agreement, a non-solicitation agreement, and a release of claims against the Company. Even considering the text of the letter agreement, I am left with very little information regarding (1) how much additional compensation Prince actually received as a result of the letter agreement and (2) the real value, if any, of the various promises given by Prince. Without more information and taking. . . plaintiffs' well pleaded allegations as true, there is a reasonable doubt as to whether the letter agreement meets the admittedly stringent "so one sided" standard or whether the letter agreement awarded compensation that is beyond the "outer limit" described by the Delaware Supreme Court. Accordingly, the Complaint has adequately alleged, . . . that demand is excused with regard to the waste claim based on the board's approval of Prince's compensation under the letter agreement. . . .

IV. CONCLUSION

Citigroup has suffered staggering losses, in part, as a result of the recent problems in the United States economy, particularly those in the subprime mortgage market. It is understandable that investors, and others, want to find someone to hold responsible for these losses, and it is often difficult to distinguish between a desire to blame *someone* and a desire to force those responsible to account for their wrongdoing. Our law, fortunately, provides guidance for precisely these situations in the form of doctrines governing the duties owed by officers and directors of Delaware corporations. This law has been refined over hundreds of years, which no doubt included many crises, and we must not let our desire to blame someone for our losses make us lose sight of the purpose of our law. Ultimately, the discretion granted directors and managers allows them to maximize shareholder value in the long term by taking risks without the debilitating fear that they will be held personally liable if the company experiences losses. This doctrine also means, however, that when the company suffers losses, shareholders may not be able to hold the directors personally liable.

For the foregoing reasons, the motion to dismiss or stay in favor of the New York Action is denied. Defendants' motion to dismiss is denied as to the claim in Count III of the Complaint for waste for approval of the November 4, 2007 Prince letter agreement. All other claims in the complaint are dismissed for failure to adequately plead demand futility. . .. . . .

---

(10) THE INDEPENDENCE OF THE SLC REDUX:

Refer to the following sections in the Text to help you answer the questions below:

Text §8A-104 et seq.

Read the following case and answer these questions.

Assuming the entire board was disabled, how was the SLC established? The facts are not clear, so do your best to imagine how it happened.

What is the court's level of deference to the SLC decision?

Why did the court find the members of the SLC were not independent? Were they dominated or controlled by the defendant-directors?

What would have happened if the board had not set up an SLC, but had simply argued that demand was not futile? You may need to speculate on some of the facts to answer.

IN RE ORACLE CORP. DERIVATIVE LITIGATION

824 A.2d 917 (Del. Ch. 2003)

STRINE Vice Chancellor.

In this opinion, I address the motion of the special litigation committee ("SLC") of Oracle Corporation to terminate this action, "the Delaware Derivative Action," and other such actions pending in the name of Oracle against certain Oracle directors and officers. These actions allege that these Oracle directors engaged in insider trading while in possession of material, non-public information showing that Oracle would not meet the earnings guidance it gave to the market for the third quarter of Oracle's fiscal year 2001. The SLC bears the burden of persuasion on this motion and must convince me that there is no material issue of fact calling into doubt its independence. This requirement is set forth in *Zapata Corp. v. Maldonado* and its progeny.

The question of independence "turns on whether a director is, *for any substantial reason,* incapable of making a decision with only the best interests of the corporation in mind." That is, the independence test ultimately "focus[es] on impartiality and objectivity." In this case, the SLC has failed to demonstrate that no material factual question exists regarding its independence. . . .

I. *Factual Background*

A. *Summary of the Plaintiffs' Allegations*

The Delaware Derivative Complaint centers on alleged insider trading by four members of Oracle's board of directors – Lawrence Ellison, Jeffrey Henley, Donald Lucas, and Michael Boskin (collectively, the "Trading Defendants"). Each of the Trading Defendants had a very different role at Oracle.

Ellison is Oracle's Chairman, Chief Executive Officer, and its largest stockholder, owning nearly twenty-five percent of Oracle's voting shares. . . .

Henley is Oracle's Chief Financial Officer, Executive Vice President, and a director of the corporation. . . .

Lucas is a director who chairs Oracle's Executive Committee and its Finance and Audit Committee. . . .

Boskin is a director, Chairman of the Compensation Committee, and a member of the Finance and Audit Committee. . . .

According to the plaintiffs, each of these Trading Defendants possessed material, non-public information demonstrating that Oracle would fail to meet the earnings and revenue guidance it had provided to the market in December 2000. . . .

. . . [T]he plaintiffs contend more generally that the Trading Defendants received material, non-public information that the sales growth for Oracle's other products was slowing in a significant way, which made the attainment of the earnings and revenue guidance extremely difficult. This information grew in depth as the quarter proceeded, as various sources of information that Oracle's top managers relied upon allegedly began to signal weakness in the company's revenues. These signals supposedly included a slowdown in the “pipeline” of large deals that Oracle hoped to close during the quarter and weak revenue growth in the first month of the quarter.

During the time when these disturbing signals were allegedly being sent, the Trading Defendants [traded in Oracle stock]. . . .

B. *The Plaintiffs' Claims in the Delaware Derivative Action*

The plaintiffs make two central claims in their amended complaint in the Delaware Derivative Action. First, the plaintiffs allege that the Trading Defendants breached their duty of loyalty by misappropriating inside information and using it as the basis for trading decisions. This claim rests its legal basis on the venerable case of *Brophy v. Cities Service Co.* Its factual foundation is that the Trading Defendants were aware (or at least possessed information that should have made them aware) that the company would miss its December guidance by a wide margin and used that information to their advantage in selling at artificially inflated prices.

Second, as to the other defendants-who are the members of the Oracle board who did not trade-the plaintiffs allege a *Caremark* violation, in the sense that the board's indifference to the deviation between the company's December guidance and reality was so extreme as to constitute subjective bad faith. . . .

D. *The Formation of the Special Litigation Committee*

On February 1, 2002, Oracle formed the SLC in order to investigate the Delaware Derivative Action and to determine whether Oracle should press the claims raised by the plaintiffs, settle the case, or terminate it. Soon after its formation, the SLC's charge was broadened to give it the same mandate as to all the pending derivative actions, wherever they were filed.

The SLC was granted full authority to decide these matters without the need for approval by the other members of the Oracle board.

E. *The Members of the Special Litigation Committee*

Two Oracle board members were named to the SLC. Both of them joined the Oracle board on October 15, 2001, more than a half a year after Oracle's 3Q FY 2001 closed. The SLC members also share something else: both are tenured professors at Stanford University.

Professor Hector Garcia-Molina is Chairman of the Computer Science Department at Stanford and holds the Leonard Bosack and Sandra Lerner Professorship in the Computer Science and Electrical Engineering Departments at Stanford. . . .

The other SLC member, Professor Joseph Grundfest, is the W.A. Franke Professor of Law and Business at Stanford University. . . . Like Garcia-Molina, Grundfest's appointment at Stanford was a homecoming, because he obtained his law degree and performed significant post-graduate work in economics at Stanford. . . .

For their services, the SLC members were paid $250 an hour, a rate below that which they could command for other activities, such as consulting or expert witness testimony. Nonetheless, during the course of their work, the SLC members became concerned that (arguably scandal-driven) developments in the evolving area of corporate governance as well as the decision in *Telxon v. Meyerson,* might render the amount of their compensation so high as to be an argument against their independence. Therefore, Garcia-Molina and Grundfest agreed to give up any SLC-related compensation if their compensation was deemed by this court to impair their impartiality.

F. *The SLC Members Are Recruited to the Board*

The SLC members were recruited to the board primarily by defendant Lucas, with help from defendant Boskin. The wooing of them began in the summer of 2001. Before deciding to join the Oracle board, Grundfest, in particular, did a good deal of due diligence. . . .

G. *The SLC's Advisors*

The most important advisors retained by the SLC were its counsel from Simpson Thacher & Bartlett LLP. Simpson Thacher had not performed material amounts of legal work for Oracle or any of the individual defendants before its engagement, and the plaintiffs have not challenged its independence.

National Economic Research Advisors ("NERA") was retained by the SLC to perform some analytical work. The plaintiffs have not challenged NERA's independence.

H. *The SLC's Investigation and Report*

The SLC's investigation was, by any objective measure, extensive. . . .

During the course of the investigation, the SLC met with its counsel thirty-five times for a total of eighty hours. In addition to that, the SLC members, particularly Professor Grundfest, devoted many more hours to the investigation.

In the end, the SLC produced an extremely lengthy Report totaling 1,110 pages (excluding appendices and exhibits) that concluded that Oracle should not pursue the plaintiffs' claims against the Trading Defendants or any of the other Oracle directors serving during the 3Q FY 2001. . . .

For [reasons set out in the Report], the SLC concluded that the plaintiffs' allegations that the Trading Defendants had breached their fiduciary duty of loyalty by using inside information about Oracle to reap illicit trading gains were without merit. The SLC also determined that, consistent with this determination, there was no reason to sue the other members of the Oracle board who were in office as of 3Q FY 2001. Therefore, the SLC determined to seek dismissal of the Delaware Derivative Action and the other derivative actions.

II. *The SLC Moves to Terminate*

Consistent with its Report, the SLC moved to terminate this litigation. The plaintiffs were granted discovery focusing on three primary topics: the independence of the SLC, the good faith of its investigative efforts, and the reasonableness of the bases for its conclusion that the lawsuit should be terminated. Additionally, the plaintiffs received a large volume of documents comprising the materials that the SLC relied upon in preparing its Report.

III. *The Applicable Procedural Standard*

In order to prevail on its motion to terminate the Delaware Derivative Action, the SLC must persuade me that: (1) its members were independent; (2) that they acted in good faith; and (3) that they had reasonable bases for their recommendations. If the SLC meets that burden, I am free to grant its motion or may, in my discretion, undertake my own examination of whether Oracle should terminate and permit the suit to proceed if I, in my oxymoronic judicial "business judgment," conclude that procession is in the best interests of the company. This two-step analysis comes, of course, from *Zapata.*

. . . [T]he Oracle SLC here "should be prepared to meet the normal burden under Rule 56 that there is no genuine issue as to any material fact and that [it] is entitled to dismiss as a matter of law." . . .

As I understand it, this standard requires me to determine whether, on the basis of the undisputed factual record, I am convinced that the SLC was independent, acted in good faith, and had a reasonable basis for its recommendation. If there is a material factual question about these issues causing doubt about any of these grounds, I read *Zapata* and its progeny as requiring a denial of the SLC's motion to terminate.

In this case, the plaintiffs principally challenge the SLC's independence and the reasonableness of its recommendation. For reasons I next explain, I need examine only the more difficult question, which relates to the SLC's independence.

IV. *Is the SLC Independent?*

A. *The Facts Disclosed in the Report*

. . . Noticeably absent from the SLC Report was any disclosure of several significant ties between Oracle or the Trading Defendants and Stanford University, the university that employs both members of the SLC. In the Report, it was only disclosed that:

- defendant Boskin was a Stanford professor;
- the SLC members were aware that Lucas [, one of the defendants] had made certain donations to Stanford; and
- among the contributions was a donation of $50,000 worth of stock that Lucas donated to Stanford Law School after Grundfest delivered a speech to a venture capital fund meeting in response to Lucas's request. It happens that Lucas's son is a partner in the fund and that approximately half the donation was allocated for use by Grundfest in his personal research.

B. *The "Stanford" Facts that Emerged During Discovery*

In view of the modesty of these disclosed ties, it was with some shock that a series of other ties among Stanford, Oracle, and the Trading Defendants emerged during discovery. Although the plaintiffs have embellished these ties considerably beyond what is reasonable, the plain facts are a striking departure from the picture presented in the Report.

Before discussing these facts, I begin with certain features of the record-as I read it-that are favorable to the SLC. Initially, I am satisfied that neither of the SLC members is compromised by a fear that support for the procession of this suit would endanger his ability to make a nice living. Both of the SLC members are distinguished in their fields and highly respected. Both have tenure, which could not have been stripped from them for making a determination that this lawsuit should proceed.

Nor have the plaintiffs developed evidence that either Grundfest or Garcia-

Molina have fundraising responsibilities at Stanford. . . .

[O]ne must acknowledge that the question is whether the ties I am about to identify would be of a material concern to two distinguished, tenured faculty members whose current jobs would not be threatened by whatever good faith decision they made as SLC members.

With this question in mind, I begin to discuss the specific ties that allegedly compromise the SLC's independence, beginning with those involving Professor Boskin.

1. *Boskin*

Defendant Michael J. Boskin is the T.M. Friedman Professor of Economics at Stanford University. . . .

During the 1970s, Boskin taught Grundfest when Grundfest was a Ph.D. candidate. Although Boskin was not Grundfest's advisor and although they do not socialize, the two have remained in contact over the years, speaking occasionally about matters of public policy.

Furthermore, both Boskin and Grundfest are senior fellows and steering committee members at the Stanford Institute for Economic Policy Research, which was previously defined as "SIEPR." According to the SLC, the title of senior fellow is largely an honorary one. According to SIEPR's own web site, however, "[s]enior fellows actively participate in SIEPR research and participate in its governance." . . .

2. *Lucas*

As noted in the SLC Report, the SLC members admitted knowing that Lucas was a contributor to Stanford. They also acknowledged that he had donated $50,000 to Stanford Law School in appreciation for Grundfest having given a speech at his request. About half of the proceeds were allocated for use by Grundfest in his research.

But Lucas's ties with Stanford are far, far richer than the SLC Report lets on. To begin, Lucas is a Stanford alumnus, having obtained both his undergraduate and graduate degrees there. By any measure, he has been a very loyal alumnus.

In showing that this is so, I start with a matter of some jousting between the SLC and the plaintiffs. Lucas's brother, Richard, died of cancer and by way of his will established a foundation. Lucas became Chairman of the Foundation and serves as a director along with his son, a couple of other family members, and some non-family members. A principal object of the Foundation's beneficence has been Stanford. The Richard M. Lucas Foundation has given $11.7 million to Stanford since its 1981 founding. Among its notable contributions, the Foundation funded the establishment of the Richard M. Lucas Center for Magnetic Resonance Spectroscopy and Imaging at Stanford's Medical School. Donald Lucas was a founding member and lead director of the Center.

The SLC Report did not mention the Richard M. Lucas Foundation or its grants to Stanford. In its briefs on this motion, the SLC has pointed out that Donald Lucas is one of nine directors at the Foundation and does not serve on its Grant Review Committee. Nonetheless, the SLC does not deny that Lucas is Chairman of the board of the Foundation and that the board approves all grants.

Lucas's connections with Stanford as a contributor go beyond the Foundation, however. From his own personal funds, Lucas has contributed $4.1 million to Stanford, a substantial percentage of which has been donated within the last half-decade. Notably, Lucas has, among other things, donated $424,000 to SIEPR and approximately $149,000 to Stanford Law School. Indeed, Lucas is not only a major contributor to SIEPR, he is the Chair of its Advisory Board. At SIEPR's facility at Stanford, the conference center is named the Donald L. Lucas Conference Center.

From these undisputed facts, it is inarguable that Lucas is a very important alumnus of Stanford and a generous contributor to not one, but two, parts of Stanford important to Grundfest: the Law School and SIEPR.

With these facts in mind, it remains to enrich the factual stew further, by considering defendant Ellison's ties to Stanford.

3. *Ellison*

There can be little doubt that Ellison is a major figure in the community in which Stanford is located. The so-called Silicon Valley has generated many success stories, among the greatest of which is that of Oracle and its leader, Ellison. One of the wealthiest men in America, Ellison is a major figure in the nation's increasingly important information technology industry. Given his wealth, Ellison is also in a position to make-and, in fact, he has made-major charitable contributions.

Some of the largest of these contributions have been made through the Ellison Medical Foundation, which makes grants to universities and laboratories to support biomedical research relating to aging and infectious diseases. Ellison is the sole director of the Foundation. Although he does not serve on the Foundation's Scientific Advisory Board that sifts through grant applications, he has reserved the right-as the Foundation's sole director-to veto any grants, a power he has not yet used but which he felt it important to retain. The Scientific Advisory Board is comprised of distinguished physicians and scientists from many institutions, but not including Stanford.

Although it is not represented on the Scientific Advisory Board, Stanford has nonetheless been the beneficiary of grants from the Ellison Medical Foundation-to the tune of nearly $10 million in paid or pledged funds. Although the Executive Director of the Foundation asserts by way of an affidavit that the grants are awarded to specific researchers and may be taken to another institution if the researcher leaves, the grants are conveyed under contracts between the Foundation and Stanford itself and purport by their terms to give Stanford the right (subject to Foundation approval) to select a substitute principal investigator if the original one becomes unavailable.

During the time Ellison has been CEO of Oracle, the company itself has also made over $300,000 in donations to Stanford. Not only that, when Oracle established a generously endowed educational foundation-the Oracle Help Us Help Foundation-to help further the deployment of educational technology in schools serving disadvantaged populations, it named Stanford as the "appointing authority," which gave Stanford the right to name four of the Foundation's seven directors. Stanford's acceptance reflects the obvious synergistic benefits that might flow to, for example, its School of Education from the University's involvement in such a foundation, as well as the possibility that its help with the Foundation might redound to the University's benefit when it came time for Oracle to consider making further donations to institutions of higher learning.

Taken together, these facts suggest that Ellison (when considered as an individual and as the key executive and major stockholder of Oracle) had, at the very least, been involved in several endeavors of value to Stanford.

Beginning in the year 2000 and continuing well into 2001-the same year that Ellison made the trades the plaintiffs contend were suspicious and the same year the SLC members were asked to join the Oracle board-Ellison and Stanford discussed a much more lucrative donation. The idea Stanford proposed for discussion was the creation of an Ellison Scholars Program modeled on the Rhodes Scholarship at Oxford. The proposed budget for Stanford's answer to Oxford: $170 million. The Ellison Scholars were to be drawn from around the world and were to come to Stanford to take a two-year interdisciplinary graduate program in economics, political science, and computer technology. During the summer between the two academic years, participants would work in internships at, among other companies, Oracle. . . .

In order to buttress the argument that Stanford did not feel beholden to him, Ellison shared with the court the (otherwise private) fact that one of his children had applied to Stanford in October 2000 and was not admitted. If Stanford felt comfortable rejecting Ellison's child, the SLC contends, why should the SLC members hesitate before recommending that Oracle press insider trading-based fiduciary duty claims against Ellison?

But the fact remains that Ellison was still talking very publicly and seriously about the possibility of endowing a graduate interdisciplinary studies program at Stanford during the summer *after* his child was rejected from Stanford's undergraduate program. . . .

C. *The SLC's Argument*

[T]he SLC argues that university professors simply are not inhibited types, unwilling to make tough decisions even as to fellow professors and large contributors. What is tenure about if not to provide professors with intellectual freedom, even in non-traditional roles such as special litigation committee members? No less ardently-but with no record evidence that reliably supports its ultimate point-the SLC contends that Garcia-Molina and Grundfest are extremely distinguished in their fields and were not, in fact, influenced by the facts identified heretofore. Indeed, the SLC argues, how could they have been influenced by many of these facts when they did not learn them until the post-Report discovery process? If it boils down to the simple fact that both share with Boskin the status of a Stanford professor, how material can this be when there are 1,700 others who also occupy the same position? . . .

E. *The Court's Analysis of the SLC's Independence*

Having framed the competing views of the parties, it is now time to decide.

I begin with an important reminder: the SLC bears the burden of proving its independence. It must convince me.

But of what? According to the SLC, its members are independent unless they are essentially subservient to the Trading Defendants – *i.e.,* they are under the "domination and control" of the interested parties. If the SLC is correct and this is the central inquiry in the independence determination, they would win. Nothing in the record suggests to me that either Garcia-Molina or Grundfest are dominated and controlled by any of the Trading Defendants, by Oracle, or even by Stanford.

But, in my view, an emphasis on "domination and control" would serve only to fetishize much-parroted language, at the cost of denuding the independence inquiry of its intellectual integrity. Take an easy example. Imagine if two brothers were on a corporate board, each successful in different businesses and not dependent in any way on the other's beneficence in order to be wealthy. The brothers are brothers, they stay in touch and consider each other family, but each is opinionated and strong-willed. A derivative action is filed targeting a transaction involving one of the brothers. The other brother is put on a special litigation committee to investigate the case. If the test is domination and control, then one brother could investigate the other. Does any sensible person think that is our law? I do not think it is.

And it should not be our law. Delaware law should not be based on a reductionist view of human nature that simplifies human motivations on the lines of the least sophisticated notions of the law and economics movement. *Homo sapiens* is not merely *homo economicus.* We may be thankful that an array of other motivations exist that influence human behavior; not all are any better than greed or avarice, think of envy, to name just one. But also think of motives like love, friendship, and collegiality, think of those among us who direct their behavior as best they can on a guiding creed or set of moral values.

Nor should our law ignore the social nature of humans. To be direct, corporate directors are generally the sort of people deeply enmeshed in social institutions. Such institutions have norms, expectations that, explicitly and implicitly, influence and channel the behavior of those who participate in their operation. Some things are "just not done," or only at a cost, which might not be so severe as a loss of position, but may involve a loss of standing in the institution. In being appropriately sensitive to this factor, our law also cannot assume-absent some proof of the point-that corporate directors are, as a general matter, persons of unusual social bravery, who operate heedless to the inhibitions that social norms generate for ordinary folk.

For all these reasons, this court has previously held that the Delaware Supreme Court's teachings on independence can be summarized thusly:

> At bottom, the question of independence turns on whether a director is, *for any substantial reason,* incapable of making a decision with only the best interests of the corporation in mind. That is, the Supreme Court cases ultimately focus on impartiality and objectivity. . . .

Without backtracking from these general propositions, it would be less than candid if I did not admit that Delaware courts have applied these general standards in a manner that has been less than wholly consistent. Different decisions take a different view about the bias-producing potential of family relationships, not all of which can be explained by mere degrees of consanguinity. Likewise, there is admittedly case law that gives little weight to ties of friendship in the independence inquiry. In this opinion, I will not venture to do what I believe to be impossible: attempt to rationalize all these cases in their specifics. Rather, I undertake what I understand to be my duty and what is possible: the application of the independence inquiry that our Supreme Court has articulated in a manner that is faithful to its essential spirit.

1. *The Contextual Nature of the Independence Inquiry Under Delaware Law*

. . . Special litigation committees are permitted as a last chance for a corporation to control a derivative claim in circumstances when a majority of its directors cannot impartially consider a demand. By vesting the power of the board to determine what to do with the suit in a committee of independent directors, a corporation may retain control over whether the suit will proceed, so long as the committee meets the standard set forth in *Zapata.*

In evaluating the independence of a special litigation committee, this court must take into account the extraordinary importance and difficulty of such a committee's responsibility. . . .

The difficulty of making this decision is compounded in the special litigation committee context because the weight of making the moral judgment necessarily falls on less than the full board. A small number of directors feels the moral gravity-and social pressures-of this duty alone.

For all these reasons, the independence inquiry is critically important if the special litigation committee process is to retain its integrity, a quality that is, in turn, essential to the utility of that process. . . .

Therefore, I necessarily measure the SLC's independence contextually, and my ruling confronts the SLC's ability to decide impartially whether the Trading Defendants should be pursued for insider trading.

This contextual approach is a strength of our law, as even the best minds have yet to devise across-the-board definitions that capture all the circumstances in which the independence of directors might reasonably be questioned. By taking into account all circumstances, the Delaware approach undoubtedly results in some level of indeterminacy, but with the compensating benefit that independence determinations are tailored to the precise situation at issue. . .

Likewise, Delaware law requires courts to consider the independence of directors based on the facts known to the court about them specifically, the so-called "subjective 'actual person' standard." That said, it is inescapable that a court must often apply to the known facts about a specific director a consideration of how a reasonable person similarly situated to that director would behave, given the limited ability of a judge to look into a particular director's heart and mind. This is especially so when a special litigation committee chooses, as was the case here, to eschew any live witness testimony, a decision that is, of course, sensible lest special litigation committee termination motions turn into trials nearly as burdensome as the derivative suit the committee seeks to end. But with that sensible choice came an acceptance of the court's need to infer that the special litigation committee members are persons of typical professional sensibilities.

2. *The SLC Has Not Met Its Burden to Demonstrate the Absence of a Material Dispute of Fact About Its Independence*

Using the contextual approach I have described, I conclude that the SLC has not met its burden to show the absence of a material factual question about its independence. I find this to be the case because the ties among the SLC, the Trading Defendants, and Stanford are so substantial that they cause reasonable doubt about the SLC's ability to impartially consider whether the

Trading Defendants should face suit. The concern that arises from these ties can be stated fairly simply, focusing on defendants Boskin, Lucas, and Ellison in that order, and then collectively.

As SLC members, Grundfest and Garcia-Molina were already being asked to consider whether the company should level extremely serious accusations of wrongdoing against fellow board members. As to Boskin, both SLC members faced another layer of complexity: the determination of whether to have Oracle press insider trading claims against a fellow professor at their university. Even though Boskin was in a different academic department from either SLC member, it is reasonable to assume that the fact that Boskin was also on faculty would-to persons possessing typical sensibilities and institutional loyalty-be a matter of more than trivial concern. Universities are obviously places of at-times intense debate, but they also see themselves as communities. In fact, Stanford refers to itself as a "community of scholars." To accuse a fellow professor-whom one might see at the faculty club or at inter-disciplinary presentations of academic papers-of insider trading cannot be a small thing-even for the most callous of academics.

As to Boskin, Grundfest faced an even more complex challenge than Garcia-Molina. Boskin was a professor who had taught him and with whom he had maintained contact over the years. Their areas of academic interest intersected, putting Grundfest in contact if not directly with Boskin, then regularly with Boskin's colleagues. Moreover, although I am told by the SLC that the title of senior fellow at SIEPR is an honorary one, the fact remains that Grundfest willingly accepted it and was one of a select number of faculty who attained that status. And, they both just happened to also be steering committee members. Having these ties, Grundfest (I infer) would have more difficulty objectively determining whether Boskin engaged in improper insider trading than would a person who was not a fellow professor, had not been a student of Boskin, had not kept in touch with Boskin over the years, and who was not a senior fellow and steering committee member at SIEPR.

In so concluding, I necessarily draw on a general sense of human nature. It may be that Grundfest is a very special person who is capable of putting these kinds of things totally aside. But the SLC has not provided evidence that that is the case. In this respect, it is critical to note that I do not infer that Grundfest would be less likely to recommend suit against Boskin than someone without these ties. Human nature being what it is, it is entirely possible that Grundfest would in fact be tougher on Boskin than he would on someone with whom he did not have such connections. The inference I draw is subtly, but importantly, different. What I infer is that a person in Grundfest's position would find it difficult to assess Boskin's conduct without pondering his own association with Boskin and their mutual affiliations. Although these connections might produce bias in either a tougher or laxer direction, the key inference is that these connections would be on the mind of a person in Grundfest's position, putting him in the position of either causing serious legal action to be brought against a person with whom he shares several connections (an awkward thing) or not doing so (and risking being seen as having engaged in favoritism toward his old professor and SIEPR colleague).

The same concerns also exist as to Lucas. For Grundfest to vote to accuse Lucas of insider trading would require him to accuse SIEPR's Advisory Board Chair and major benefactor of serious wrongdoing-of conduct that violates federal securities laws. Such action would also require Grundfest to make charges against a man who recently donated $50,000 to Stanford Law School after Grundfest made a speech at his request.

And, for both Grundfest and Garcia-Molina, service on the SLC demanded that they consider whether an extremely generous and influential Stanford alumnus should be sued by Oracle for insider trading. Although they were not responsible for fundraising, as sophisticated professors they undoubtedly are aware of how important large contributors are to Stanford, and they share in the benefits that come from serving at a university with a rich endowment. A reasonable professor giving any thought to the matter would obviously consider the effect his decision might have on the University's relationship with Lucas, it being (one hopes) sensible to infer that a professor of reasonable collegiality and loyalty cares about the well-being of the institution he serves.

In so concluding, I give little weight to the SLC's argument that it was unaware of just how substantial Lucas's beneficence to Stanford has been. I do so for two key reasons. Initially, it undermines, rather than inspires, confidence that the SLC did not examine the Trading Defendants' ties to Stanford more closely in preparing its Report. The Report's failure to identify these ties is important because it is the SLC's burden to show independence. In forming the SLC, the Oracle board should have undertaken a thorough consideration of the facts bearing on the independence of the proposed SLC members from the key objects of the investigation.

The purported ignorance of the SLC members about all of Lucas's donations to Stanford is not helpful to them for another reason: there were too many visible manifestations of Lucas's status as a major contributor for me to conclude that Grundfest, at the very least, did not understand Lucas to be an extremely generous benefactor of Stanford. It is improbable that Grundfest was not aware that Lucas was the Chair of SIEPR's Advisory Board, and Grundfest must have known that the Donald L. Lucas Conference Center at SIEPR did not get named that way by coincidence. . . . Combined with the other obvious indicia of Lucas's large contributor status (including the $50,000 donation Lucas made to Stanford Law School to thank Grundfest for giving a speech) and Lucas's obviously keen interest in his alma mater, Grundfest would have had to be extremely insensitive to his own working environment not to have considered Lucas an extremely generous alumni benefactor of Stanford, and at SIEPR and the Law School in particular.

Garcia-Molina is in a somewhat better position to disclaim knowledge of how generous an alumnus Lucas had been. Even so, the scope of Lucas's activities and their easy discoverability gives me doubt that he did not know of the relative magnitude of Lucas's generosity to Stanford. Furthermore, Grundfest comprised half of the SLC and was its most active member. His non-independence is sufficient alone to require a denial of the SLC's motion.

In concluding that the facts regarding Lucas's relationship with Stanford are materially important, I must address a rather odd argument of the SLC's. The argument goes as follows. Stanford has an extremely large endowment. Lucas's contributions, while seemingly large, constitute a very small proportion of Stanford's endowment and annual donations. Therefore, Lucas could not be a materially important contributor to Stanford and the SLC's independence could not be compromised by that factor.

But missing from that syllogism is any acknowledgement of the role that Stanford's solicitude to benefactors like Lucas might play in the overall size of its endowment and campus facilities. Endowments and buildings grow one contribution at a time, and they do not grow by callous indifference to alumni who (personally and through family foundations) have participated in directing contributions of the size Lucas has. Buildings and conference centers are named as they are as a recognition of the high regard universities have for donors (or at least, must feign convincingly). The SLC asks me to believe that what universities like Stanford say in thank you letters and public ceremonies is not in reality true; that, in actuality, their contributors are not materially important to the health of those academic institutions. This is a proposition that the SLC has not convinced me is true, and that seems to contradict common experience.

Nor has the SLC convinced me that tenured faculty are indifferent to large contributors to their institutions, such that a tenured faculty member would not be worried about writing a report finding that a suit by the corporation should proceed against a large contributor and that there was credible evidence that he had engaged in illegal insider trading. The idea that faculty members would not be concerned that action of that kind might offend a large contributor who a university administrator or fellow faculty colleague (*e.g.,* Shoven at SIEPR) had taken the time to cultivate strikes me as implausible and as resting on an narrow-minded understanding of the way that collegiality works in institutional settings.

In view of the ties involving Boskin and Lucas alone, I would conclude that the SLC has failed to meet its burden on the independence question. The tantalizing facts about Ellison merely reinforce this conclusion. The SLC, of course, argues that Ellison is not a large benefactor of Stanford personally, that Stanford has demonstrated its independence of him by rejecting his child for admission, and that, in any event, the SLC was ignorant of any negotiations between Ellison and Stanford about a large contribution. For these reasons, the SLC says, its ability to act independently of Ellison is clear.

I find differently. The notion that anyone in Palo Alto can accuse Ellison of insider trading without harboring some fear of social awkwardness seems a stretch. That being said, I do not mean to imply that the mere fact that Ellison is worth tens of billions of dollars and is the key force behind a very important social institution in Silicon Valley disqualifies all persons who live there from being independent of him. Rather, it is merely an acknowledgement of the simple fact that accusing such a significant person in that community of such serious wrongdoing is no small thing. . . .

Of course, the SLC says these facts are meaningless because Stanford rejected Ellison's child for admission. I am not sure what to make of this fact, but it surely cannot bear the heavy weight the SLC gives it. The aftermath of denying Ellison's child admission might, after all, as likely manifest itself in a desire on the part of the Stanford community never to offend Ellison again, lest he permanently write off Stanford as a possible object of his charitable aims – as the sort of thing that acts as not one, but two strikes, leading the batter to choke up on the bat so as to be even more careful not to miss the next pitch. Suffice to say that after the rejection took place, it did not keep Ellison from making public statements in *Fortune* magazine on August 13, 2001 about his consideration of making a huge donation to Stanford, at the same time when the two SLC members were being courted to join the Oracle board.

As an alternative argument, the SLC contends that neither SLC member was aware of Ellison's relationship with Stanford until after the Report was completed. Thus, this relationship, in its various facets, could not have compromised their independence. Again, I find this argument from ignorance to be unavailing. An inquiry into Ellison's connections with Stanford should have been conducted before the SLC was finally formed and, at the very least, should have been undertaken in connection with the Report. In any event, given how public Ellison was about his possible donations it is difficult not to harbor troublesome doubt about whether the SLC members were conscious of the possibility that Ellison was pondering a large contribution to Stanford. In so concluding, I am not saying that the SLC members are being untruthful in saying that they did not know of the facts that have emerged, only that these facts were in very prominent journals at the time the SLC members were doing due diligence in aid of deciding whether to sign on as Oracle board members. The objective circumstances of Ellison's relations with Stanford therefore generate a reasonable suspicion that seasoned faculty members of some sophistication – including the two SLC members-would have viewed Ellison as an active and prized target for the University. The objective circumstances also require a finding that Ellison was already, through his personal Foundation and Oracle itself, a benefactor of Stanford.

Taken in isolation, the facts about Ellison might well not be enough to compromise the SLC's independence. But that is not the relevant inquiry. The pertinent question is whether, given *all* the facts, the SLC has met its independence burden. . . .

It seems to me that the connections outlined in this opinion would weigh on the mind of a reasonable special litigation committee member deciding whether to level the serious charge of insider trading against the Trading Defendants. As indicated before, this does not mean that the SLC would be less inclined to find such charges meritorious, only that the connections identified would be on the mind of the SLC members in a way that generates an unacceptable risk of bias. That is, these connections generate a reasonable doubt about the SLC's impartiality because they suggest that material considerations other than the best interests of Oracle could have influenced the SLC's inquiry and judgments.

. . . I make no finding about the subjective good faith of the SLC members, both of whom are distinguished academics at one of this nation's most prestigious institutions of higher learning. Nothing in this record leads me to conclude that either of the SLC members acted out of any conscious desire to favor the Trading Defendants or to do anything other than discharge their duties with fidelity. But that is not the purpose of the independence inquiry.

That inquiry recognizes that persons of integrity and reputation can be compromised in their ability to act without bias when they must make a decision adverse to others with whom they share material affiliations. To conclude that the Oracle SLC was not independent is not a conclusion that the two accomplished professors who comprise it are not persons of good faith and moral probity, it is solely to conclude that they were not situated to act with the required degree of impartiality. *Zapata* requires independence to ensure that stockholders do not have to rely upon special litigation committee members who must put aside personal considerations that are ordinarily influential in daily behavior in making the already difficult decision to accuse fellow directors of serious wrongdoing. . . .

Rather than form an SLC whose membership was free from bias-creating relationships, Oracle formed a committee fraught with them. As a result, the SLC has failed to meet its *Zapata* burden, and its motion to terminate must be denied. Because of this reality, I do not burden the reader with an examination of the other *Zapata* factors. In the absence of a finding that the SLC was independent, its subjective good faith and the reasonableness of its conclusions would not be sufficient to justify termination. Without confidence that the SLC was impartial, its findings do not provide the assurance our law requires for the dismissal of a derivative suit without a merits inquiry.

V. *Conclusion*

The SLC's motion to terminate is DENIED. IT IS SO ORDERED.

WORKBOOK

CHAPTER 9

FUNDAMENTAL TRANSACTIONS

CHAPTER 9 – EXERCISES:

---

(1) AMENDING THE ARTICLES REDUX:

Refer to the following sections in the Text to help you answer the questions below:

Text §9A-200

Facts:

The following summarizes the amendments to the articles of incorporation we analyzed in Exercise 10 of Chapter 5 in this workbook.

The corporation has three classes of stock:

Class A Common Stock

Class B (Non-Voting) Common Stock (no voting rights)

Preferred Stock (no voting rights)

The board proposes the following amendments to the articles of incorporation:

Reduce the dividend of the Preferred Stock

Increase the authorized shares of Class A Common Stock

Increase the authorized shares of Class B (Non-Voting) Common Stock

---

Please answering the following questions by applying the relevant statute provided below (which is based an earlier version of the RMBCA):

For each of the proposed amendments, which classes of stock have a right to vote?

For each of the proposed amendments, which classes of stock have appraisal rights?

Relevant statute:[7]

10-030 AMENDMENT BY BOARD OF DIRECTORS AND SHAREHOLDERS.

. . .

(5) Unless this chapter, the articles of incorporation, or the board of directors . . . requires a greater vote or a vote by voting groups, the amendment to be adopted shall be approved by:

(a) A majority of the votes entitled to be cast on the amendment by any voting group with respect to which the amendment would create dissenters' rights; and

(b) The votes required by 6A-250 and 6A-260* by every other voting group entitled to vote on the amendment.

**Editor's note: 6A-250 and 6A-260 require more shares voted in favor of the transaction than opposed.*

10-040 VOTING ON AMENDMENTS BY VOTING GROUPS.

(1) The holders of the outstanding shares of a class shall be entitled to vote as a separate voting group . . . on a proposed amendment if the amendment would:

(a) Increase or decrease the aggregate number of authorized shares of the class;

(b) Effect an exchange or reclassification of all or part of the shares of the class into shares of another class;

(c) Effect an exchange or reclassification, or create the right of exchange, of all or part of the shares of another class into shares of the class;

(d) Change the designation, rights, preferences, or limitations of all or part of the shares of the class;

(e) Change the shares of all or part of the class into a different number of shares of the same class;

(f) Create a new class of shares having rights or preferences with respect to distributions or to dissolution that are prior, superior, or substantially equal to the shares of the class;

(g) Increase the rights, preferences, or number of authorized shares of any class that, after giving effect to the amendment, have rights or preferences with respect to distributions or to dissolution that are prior, superior, or substantially equal to the shares of the class;

[7] Based on the Kentucky Business Corporations Act, K.R.S. §§271B.10-030, 271B.10-040, 271B.13-020.

(h) Limit or deny an existing preemptive right of all or part of the shares of the class; or

(i) Cancel or otherwise affect rights to distributions or dividends that have accumulated but not yet been declared on all or part of the shares of the class.

(2) If a proposed amendment would affect a series of a class of shares in one (1) or more of the ways described in subsection (1) of this section, the shares of that series shall be entitled to vote as a separate voting group on the proposed amendment.

(3) If a proposed amendment that entitles two (2) or more series of shares to vote as separate voting groups under this section would affect those two (2) or more series in the same or a substantially similar way, the shares of all the series so affected shall vote together as a single voting group on the proposed amendment.

(4) A class or series of shares is entitled to the voting rights granted by this section although the articles of incorporation provide that the shares are nonvoting shares.

13-020 RIGHT TO DISSENT.

(1) A shareholder shall be entitled to dissent from, and obtain payment of the fair value of his shares in the event of, any of the following corporate actions: . . .

(e) An amendment of the articles of incorporation that materially and adversely affects rights in respect of a dissenter's shares because it:

1. Alters or abolishes a preferential right of the shares to a distribution or in dissolution;

2. Creates, alters, or abolishes a right in respect of redemption, including a provision respecting a sinking fund for the redemption or repurchase of the shares;

3. Excludes or limits the right of the shares to vote on any matter other than a limitation by dilution through issuance of shares or other securities with similar voting rights; or

4. Reduces the number of shares owned by the shareholder to a fraction of a share, if the fractional share so created is to be acquired for cash [by the corporation] . . .

---

(2) BUSINESS COMBINATION 1:

Refer to the following provisions to answer the questions below:

RMBCA §§11.02(a)&(b) and 11.04(a),(b),(e)&(h) and 13.02(a)&(b)

For further help, please refer to the following sections in the Text:

Text §9A-401 et seq.

The board of directors of **X Inc.** and the board of directors of **Y Inc**. have agreed to a merger. In the transaction, **X Inc.** will be the surviving corporation.

The **shareholders of Y Inc.** will receive a combination of cash and X Inc. debt securities in the transaction.

The **shareholders of X Inc.** will receive nothing in the transaction.

Which shareholders have a right to vote in the transaction? What are the quorum and approval standards?

Which shareholders have appraisal rights? How do they perfect their appraisal rights?

---

(3) <u>BUSINESS COMBINATION 2:</u>

Refer to the following provisions to answer the questions below:

RMBCA §§11.02(a)&(b) and 11.04(a),(b),(e)&(h) and 13.02(a)&(b)

For further help, please refer to the following sections in the Text:

Text §9A-401 et seq.

The board of directors of **X Inc.** and the board of directors of **Y Inc**. have agreed to a merger. In the transaction, **X Inc.** will be the surviving corporation.

The **shareholders of Y Inc.** will receive X Inc. stock in the transaction.

The **shareholders of X Inc.** will receive a combination of cash and X Inc. debt securities in the transaction in exchange for their X Inc. stock.

Which shareholders have a right to vote in the transaction? What are the quorum and approval standards?

Which shareholders have appraisal rights? How do they perfect their appraisal rights?

---

(4) BUSINESS COMBINATION 3:

Refer to the following provisions to answer the questions below:

RMBCA §§11.02(a)&(b) and 11.04(a),(b),(e)&(h) and 13.02(a)&(b)

For further help, please refer to the following sections in the Text:

Text §9A-401 et seq.

The board of directors of **X Inc.** and the board of directors of **Y Inc**. have agreed to a merger. In the transaction, **X Inc.** will be the surviving corporation.

At the time the boards approved the merger, **X Inc.** had 150,000 shares of common stock authorized, with 100,000 shares issued and outstanding.

> The **shareholders of Y Inc.** will receive 21,000 shares of X Inc. stock in the transaction.
>
> The **shareholders of X Inc.** will receive nothing in the transaction.

Which shareholders have a right to vote in the transaction? What are the quorum and approval standards?

Which shareholders have appraisal rights? How do they perfect their appraisal rights?

---

(5) BUSINESS COMBINATION 4:

Refer to the following provisions to answer the questions below:

RMBCA §§11.02(a)&(b) and 11.04(a),(b),(e)&(h) and 13.02(a)&(b)

For further help, please refer to the following sections in the Text:

Text §9A-401 et seq.

The board of directors of **X Inc.** and the board of directors of **Y Inc**. have agreed to a merger. In the transaction, **X Inc.** will be the surviving corporation.

At the time the boards approved the merger, **X Inc.** had 150,000 shares of common stock authorized, with 100,000 shares issued and outstanding. It also had 100,000 shares of preferred stock authorized, with none outstanding.

> The **shareholders of Y Inc.** will receive 10,000 shares of X Inc. common stock in the transaction.

The **shareholders of X Inc.** will exchange their current 100,000 shares of X Inc. stock for 100,000 shares of X Inc.'s preferred stock.

Which shareholders have a right to vote in the transaction? What are the quorum and approval standards?

Which shareholders have appraisal rights? How do they perfect their appraisal rights?

---

(6) <u>BUSINESS COMBINATION 5:</u>

Refer to the following provisions to answer the questions below:

RMBCA §§11.02(a)&(b) and 11.04(a),(b),(e)&(h) and 13.02(a)&(b)

For further help, please refer to the following sections in the Text:

Text §9A-401 et seq.

The board of directors of **X Inc.** and the board of directors of **Y Inc**. have agreed to a merger. In the transaction, **X Inc.** will be the surviving corporation.

At the time the boards approved the merger, X Inc. had 200,000 shares of common stock authorized, with all 200,000 shares issued and outstanding.

The **shareholders of Y Inc.** will receive 10,000 shares of X Inc. stock in the transaction.

The **shareholders of X Inc.** will receive nothing in the transaction.

Which shareholders have a right to vote in the transaction? What are the quorum and approval standards?

Which shareholders have appraisal rights? How do they perfect their appraisal rights?

---

(7) <u>BUSINESS COMBINATION 6:</u>

Refer to the following provisions to answer the questions below:

RMBCA §§11.05 and 13.02(a)&(b)

For further help, please refer to the following sections in the Text:

Text §9A-403

A Corp owns 95% of the outstanding stock of **B Corp**. The other 5% of B Corp's stock is owned by various shareholders ("minority shareholders").

A Corp plans to merge B Corp into itself and cash out the B Corp minority shareholders at $10 per share.

Which board has a right to vote in the transaction? What are the quorum and approval standards?

Which shareholders have a right to vote in the transaction? What are the quorum and approval standards?

Which shareholders have appraisal rights? How do they perfect their appraisal rights?

Besides appraisal rights, are there any other protections for the minority shareholders of B Corp.?

---

(8) ACQUISITION PLANNING 1:

Refer to the following sections in the Text to help you answer the questions below:

Text §9A-404 et seq.

A Corp wants to acquire **Z Corp**. A Corp would like to keep Z Corp's business separate from A Corp's, so it wants **a structure where A Corp is the sole shareholder of Z Corp**.

Z Corp has 86 shareholders. Z Corp's controlling shareholder controls the Z Corp board and has 55% of the outstanding shares of Z Corp stock. The controlling shareholder strongly supports the transaction with A Corp. Most of the minority shareholders are also in favor of the transaction with A Corp.

Unfortunately, a number of minority shareholders, who hold somewhere between 5% to 20% of the total outstanding shares of Z Corp, will not sell their shares to A Corp under any circumstances. The shareholders of Z Corp do not have a shareholders agreement.

Please advise A Corp on its options.

---

(9) ACQUISITION PLANNING 2:

Refer to the following sections in the Text to help you answer the questions below:

Text §9A-800

Your client is the sole shareholder of a corporation. The client started out on a shoestring budget many years ago and has built a very successful business. She is now looking to sell the business, make lots of money, and retire to Hawaii.

One potential buyer is ready to buy the business. This buyer has sent a letter to your client. The letter is provided below.

Your client has several questions and comments about the letter:

> **Is the letter a contract? Will there be another written agreement?**
>
> **Why should she allow the other side to have access to confidential information?**
>
> **Will her business's confidential information and trade secrets be protected? If so, show her how the letter provides this protection.**
>
> **She is talking to two other potential buyers. If she receives a better offer from one of them, can she take that deal instead?**
>
> **Your client is starting to imagine her life after the sale of the business. She says: *"White sand beaches, here I come! . . . or maybe, I will start another business. I've done it before, I can do it again."***

Respond to your client's questions and comments.

The letter from the potential buyer begins on the next page

Dear [Seller]:

The purpose of this letter is to confirm our mutual intentions and to summarize the material terms of our proposed purchase of all of the outstanding capital stock of _______________ (the "Company") from you, the sole shareholder of the Company.

In this letter, we are the "Buyer" and you are the "Seller." The Buyer and the Seller are sometimes referred to as "Party", or collectively called the "Parties."

1. The Transaction and The Closing

The Seller would sell all of the outstanding capital stock of the Company to the Buyer for the Purchase Price described in Section 2, below

The closing of this transaction (the "Closing") would occur as soon as possible after securing governmental approvals required under applicable laws, if any, and Buyer's satisfactory completion of its due diligence review of the Company, including, without limitation the Company's financial, accounting, legal, and other records.

2. Purchase Price

The Purchase Price would be $8,000,000. At the Closing, the Buyer would pay the Purchase Price as follows:

- Buyer would pay $3,000,000 in cash to the Seller;
- Buyer would execute and deliver to Seller an unsecured, non-negotiable promissory note with a principal amount of $2,000,000, bearing interest at the rate of 5% per annum, maturing on the 5th anniversary of the Closing, and providing 20 equal quarterly payments of principal and accrued interest; and
- Buyer would deposit $3,000,000 with an escrow agent, to be held in escrow for at least four years to secure the performance of the Seller's obligations.

3. Employment and Noncompetition Agreements

At the Closing, the Company and the Seller would enter into a two-year employment agreement where the Seller would agree to continue to serve as the Company's Chief Executive Officer for a salary of $125,000 per year.

At the Closing, the Seller would also execute a two-year noncompetition agreement that will take effect when the Seller leaves the employ of the Company.

4. Definitive Agreement

The Parties intend to negotiate a definitive, written stock purchase agreement ("Definitive Agreement"), subject to Buyer's satisfactory completion of its due diligence review of the Company. In the Definitive Agreement, the Seller would make comprehensive representations, warranties and covenants, and provide indemnities and other protections for the benefit of the Buyer that are customary in a transaction of this size and nature.

The Buyer's counsel will be responsible for preparing the initial draft of the Definitive Agreement.

5. Expenses

The Buyer and the Seller will each be responsible for their respective costs and expenses incurred in connection with negotiating, preparing for, and consummating the contemplated transaction including, without limitation, expenses for legal and financial advisors and any broker's or finder's fees.

6. The Company's Operations

After signing this letter, the Seller shall ensure that the Company does not issue any further capital stock and that it operates its business in the ordinary course and refrains from any extraordinary transactions.

7. Exclusivity

From the date the Seller signs this letter until termination under Section 14, the Seller shall not, and shall ensure the Company and its agents will not, directly or indirectly, initiate, solicit, encourage, entertain, or accept any offer or proposal regarding the possible acquisition, by any person, of a material portion of the Company's capital stock, its assets or business, in whole or in part, directly or indirectly, through purchase, merger, consolidation, or otherwise (except for sales of inventory in the ordinary course of business), other than the transaction contemplated with Buyer under this letter.

Seller shall immediately notify the Buyer of any offer or proposal or any other related inquiry.

8. Break-Up Fee

The Seller shall pay the Buyer the sum $1,000,000 in the event the Seller

(a) breaches the exclusivity provisions of Section 7 or provides notice of termination under Section 14; and

(b) within 12 months after the date of such breach or notice of termination, Seller or Company signs a letter of intent or other agreement relating to the possible acquisition of a material portion of the Company's capital stock, its assets or its business, directly or indirectly, through purchase, merger, consolidation, or otherwise (except for sales of inventory in the ordinary course of business) and the transaction is ultimately consummated.

This fee is not the exclusive remedy for the Buyer under this letter. In the event of a breach by the Seller of any binding provisions of this letter, the Buyer will be free to pursue other legal or equitable remedies.

9. Buyer's Access to Company Information for Due Diligence Review

The Seller shall provide the Buyer full and free access to the Company, the Company's personnel, properties, contracts, accounting and financial records, and all other documents and data reasonably necessary for the Buyer to evaluate the purchase of the Company's capital stock.

The Parties shall cooperate to enable Buyer to complete due diligence review expeditiously.

10. Confidentiality

Other than for the use of evaluating the transaction contemplated in this letter, the Buyer shall not disclose or use any of the Company's Confidential Information (defined below) that is furnished to the Buyer by the Seller, the Company, or their respective agents, <u>provided, however</u> that the Buyer's obligations under this section do not apply to information that is:

A. already in the Buyer's possession at the time of disclosure;

B. part of the public domain, or later becomes part of the public domain, through no fault of the Buyer;

C. received from a third party having no obligations of confidentiality to the Seller or the Company;

D. independently developed by the Buyer; or

E. required by law to be disclosed, or necessary or appropriate in connection with legal proceedings.

Upon the written request of the Seller, the Buyer will promptly return or destroy any Confidential Information in its possession.

"Confidential Information" means any information marked "confidential" or identified in writing as confidential by the Seller promptly following its disclosure.

11. Public Announcement and Disclosure

Except as required by law, neither Buyer nor the Seller may, without the prior written approval of the other, make any announcement of the proposed transaction contemplated by this letter prior to the execution of the Definitive Agreement.

The Buyer and the Seller shall each direct their respective agents not to make, directly or indirectly, any public comment, statement, or communication with respect to, or otherwise disclose or permit the disclosure of the existence of discussions regarding the possible transaction between the Buyer and the Seller under this letter.

If a Party is required by law to make any such announcement or disclosure of the possible transaction, it shall first provide to the other the content of the proposed disclosure, the reasons that such disclosure is required by law, and the time and place that the disclosure will be made.

12. Entire Agreement

The binding provisions of this letter constitute the entire agreement between the Parties, and supersede all prior oral or written agreements, understandings, representations and warranties, and courses of conduct and dealing between the Parties on the subject matter hereof. Except as otherwise provided in this letter, the binding provisions may be amended or modified only by a writing executed by the Parties.

13. Governing Law

This letter shall be governed by the substantive laws of the State of___ without regard to conflict of law principles.

14. Non-Binding and Binding Provisions

This letter is an expression of interest only and is not intended to be legally binding, except with respect to Sections 5 through 15, inclusive, which are the legally binding obligations of the Parties.

15. Termination and Survival

Either Party may terminate the binding provisions of this letter, with or without cause, at any time, with written notice. The binding provisions of this letter automatically terminate at the earlier of 60 days after the Buyer has signed this letter or when either Party provides the other with written notice of termination.

The termination of the binding provisions will not affect the liability of a Party for breach of any of the binding provisions prior to the termination.

The binding obligations of the following sections will survive termination: Sections 5, 7, 8, 10, 12, 13, 14, and 15.

If you are in agreement with the terms of this letter, please sign and return one copy of this letter agreement.

Very truly yours,

BUYER

Date:

Signature of Seller: ______________________________ Date:

(10) ACQUISITION PLANNING 3:

Refer to the following sections in the Text to help you answer the questions below:

Text §9A-800

You represent **Acme Acquisitions Inc.**

Acme wants to acquire **Target Corp.** Acme has signed a letter of intent with Target's controlling shareholder. The terms of the letter of intent were flexible regarding the exact legal structure of the acquisition, but the parties intend for Acme to acquire 100% of Target.

During due diligence, you discover that Target Corp, has borrowed $100 million from Bank. In your review of the loan agreement between Target Corp and Bank, you find the following relevant provisions:

> . . .
>
> **Section 4 – Borrower's Covenants:**
>
> **4.01** For as long Borrower has not paid in full any amount payable under this Loan Agreement the Borrower shall not . . .
>
> (a) Undertake any merger or consolidation, (b) liquidate, wind-up or dissolve itself, (c) sell, or convey, transfer, assign, or otherwise dispose of substantially all of its assets in one transaction or in a series of transactions, voluntarily or involuntarily, or (d) acquire all or substantially all of the assets constituting a business, division, branch or other unit of operation of any Person.
>
> . . .
>
> **Section 5 – Default:**
>
> **5.01** Each of the following events is deemed an Event of Default without regard to whether the occurrence of the event is voluntary, involuntary, or caused by a legal requirement or operation of law:
>
> (a) the Borrower fails to pay principal, any interest, or any fee or other amount payable under this Loan Agreement when due and further fails to remedy the failure to pay for a period of 30 calendar days;
>
> (b) any representation, warranty, certification or other statement of fact made by Borrower in connection with this Loan Agreement proves to have been false or misleading in any material respect as of the date made,
>
> (c) the Borrower fails to perform or observe any covenant, term, condition or agreement contained in Section 4;

(d) the Borrower is subject to any case, proceeding or other action or order, whether voluntary or involuntary, (i) to adjudicate it as bankrupt or insolvent, (ii) for reorganization, arrangement, adjustment, winding-up, liquidation, dissolution, composition or other relief with respect to it or its debts, (iii) for appointment of a receiver, trustee, custodian, conservator or other similar official for it or for all or any substantial part of its assets, or (iv) with respect to general assignment for the benefit of its creditors; or

(e) any Change of Control occurs.

A **Change of Control** occurs when (a) any Person or group of Persons, other than the Majority Shareholder, becomes the beneficial owner, directly or indirectly, of more than 50% of the outstanding Equity Interests of the Borrower; or (b) during any consecutive two-year period, individuals who at the beginning of such period constituted the board of directors of the Borrower cease for any reason to constitute a majority of the Board of Directors of the Borrower then in office.

. . .

Default on the loan would result in all future principal and interest payments becoming due immediately, with hefty pre-payment penalties. Acme, Target's board, and Target's controlling shareholder agree that a default under the loan agreement with Bank would make Acme's acquisition of Target much more expensive.

What does this clause mean for the acquisition? Is there any way to structure the acquisition of avoid a default under the loan agreement without negotiating with Bank?

---

(11) ACQUISITION PLANNING 4:

Refer to the following sections in the Text to help you answer the questions below:

Text §9A-800

In a definitive Stock Purchase Agreement, the selling shareholder ("Seller") will make various statements to the buyer. These statements are called "**representations and warranties**." Normally, the selling shareholder will make comprehensive representations and warranties about the business, operations, and financial condition of the company, but only when the selling shareholder is the controlling shareholder.

If any of the selling shareholder's representations is not true, the buyer may rescind the contract. If the selling shareholder breaches a warranty, the buyer may sue for money damages. In other words, because each of selling shareholder's statements is both a representations and a warranty, buyer can rescind the contract, sue for damages, or both if the statement is untrue. Often the agreement will clearly provide the remedy for a breach of representations and warranties.

Representations and warranties shift the risk of the subject of the statement from the buyer to the selling shareholder. For example, if the selling shareholder states that the company is properly incorporated, and it turns out to be untrue, buyer is protected and selling shareholder is liable. If the selling shareholder states that the company has no liability under environmental laws, and it turns out to be untrue, buyer is protected and selling shareholder is liable.

If the transaction contemplated is a statutory merger, the target company (and the controlling shareholder, if any) would make comprehensive representations and warranties in the definitive merger agreement about the business, operations, and financial condition of the target company.

Read the representations and warranties of the selling shareholder. These are only a few examples of the numerous representations and warranties a selling shareholder might make in a Stock Purchase Agreement.

Where would it be appropriate to "soften" the representations and warranties by adding the following language:

> "to Seller's knowledge"
>
> "material"
>
> "in all material respects"
>
> "which would reasonably be expected to have a material adverse effect on the Company"
>
> "which individually or in the aggregate are reasonably likely to have a material adverse effect on the Company.

SECTION 3: REPRESENTATIONS AND WARRANTIES OF SELLER:

The Seller makes the following representation and warranties:

Organization. The Company is a corporation duly organized, validly existing and in good standing under the laws of the State of ______. The Company has all requisite corporate power and authority to carry on its business as presently conducted and as proposed to be conducted, and is qualified to do business in every jurisdiction that requires qualification.

Authority. The Seller has the full right, power, and authority to enter into and to carry out the transactions contemplated in this Agreement and each agreement, document, and instrument to be executed and delivered by the Seller pursuant to this Agreement. No waiver or consent of any person is required in connection with the execution, delivery, and performance by the Seller of this Agreement and each agreement, document, and instrument to be executed and delivered by the Seller pursuant to this Agreement.

Capitalization. The Company's authorized capital stock consists solely of ________ shares of common stock, of which ________ shares are issued and outstanding, and ________ authorized shares of preferred stock, of which ________ shares are issued and outstanding. Seller owns of record and beneficially all issued and outstanding shares of Company's common stock. There are no outstanding options, warrants, rights, commitments, or agreements of any kind for the issuance or sale of, or outstanding securities convertible into, any additional shares of capital stock of any class of the Company, and there are no voting trusts, voting agreements, proxies, or other agreements, instruments, or undertakings with respect to the voting of any Company stock to which the Seller, the Company or any of its shareholders is a party. There are no outstanding dividends, whether current or accumulated, due or payable on any of the capital stock of the Company.

Financial Statements. The Company's financial statements, attached as Schedule ___, fairly present the financial condition and operating results of the Company for the periods covered, and have been prepared in accordance with generally accepted accounting principles and practices. Except as set forth in the financial statements, the Company has no material liabilities or obligations, contingent or otherwise, other than (i) liabilities incurred in the ordinary course of business subsequent to the date of this Agreement; (ii) obligations under contracts and commitments incurred in the ordinary course of business; and (iii) liabilities and obligations of a type or nature not required under generally accepted accounting principles and practices to be reflected in the financial statements.

Title to Properties; Liens; Condition of Properties. The Company owns the equipment, furniture, fixtures, improvements, and personal property set forth in Schedule ___, attached. The Company has good title to all of such assets and none of the assets of the Company is subject to any mortgage, pledge, lien, conditional sales agreement, security interest, encumbrance, or other charge except as specifically reflected in Schedule ___.

All equipment owned or leased by the Company is in good repair and in working order, except for ordinary wear and tear.

Taxes. There are no federal, state, county, local or foreign taxes due and payable by the Company that have not been timely paid. There are no accrued and unpaid federal, state, county, local or foreign taxes of the Company that are due, whether or not assessed or disputed. There have been no examinations or audits of any tax returns or reports by any applicable federal, state, local or foreign governmental agency. The Company has properly and timely filed all federal, state, county, local and foreign tax returns required to have been filed by it and there are no waivers of applicable statutes of limitations in effect with respect to taxes for any year. All such tax returns were correct and complete in all respects.

Intellectual Property. All domestic and foreign patents, patent applications, copyrighted works, copyright applications, and registrations, trade names, trademarks and service marks, registered trademarks, and trademark applications, registered service marks and service mark applications which are used by, owned by or licensed to the Company (collectively, the "Intellectual Property") are listed in Schedule ___.

No other person has an interest in, or right to use, or license to use, or the right to license others to use the Intellectual Property.

There is no infringement of any of the Intellectual Property by others, nor is any of the Intellectual Property subject to any outstanding order, decree, judgment, stipulation, settlement, lien, charge, encumbrance, or attachment.

No claim or demand has been made and no proceeding has been filed or is threatened to be filed charging the Company with infringement of any patent, trade name, trademark, service mark, or copyright.

There are no royalties, fees, or other payments payable by or on behalf of the Company to any person with respect to any of the Intellectual Property.

Material Contracts. Except for contracts, commitments, plans, agreements and licenses listed in Schedule ____, the Company is not a party to or bound by any written or oral contract which calls for any of the following: (a) delivery of any goods or services at a cumulative value in excess of $_______ per year, or which obligates the contracting party for a fixed term; (b) loans, credit, financing agreements, promissory notes, or other evidences of indebtedness (including all agreements for any commitments for future loans, credit or financing), or any other material contract, commitment, or arrangements of any kind; or (c) any guaranty.

Litigation. There are no lawsuits, actions or administrative, arbitration or other proceedings or governmental investigations pending or threatened against or relating to the Company or the Company's properties or business. The Company has not entered into or been subject to any consent decree, compliance order, or administrative order with respect to any property owned, operated, leased, or used by the Company. The Company has not received any request for information, notice, demand letter, administrative inquiry, or formal or informal complaint or claim with respect to any property owned, operated, leased, or used by the Company or any facilities or operations thereon.

There are no existing or threatened product liability, warranty, or other similar claims, or any facts upon which a claim of such nature could be based, against the Company for services or products which are defective or fail to meet any service or product warranties.

Compliance with Laws. The Company is not in violation of any laws, rules, or regulations that apply to the conduct of its business or to any facilities or property owned, leased, operated, or used by the Company. There has never been any citation, fine, or penalty imposed, asserted, or threatened against the Company under any foreign, federal, state, local, or other law or regulation relating to employment, immigration, occupational safety, zoning, or environmental matters, and there are no current circumstances that will result in the imposition or assertion of such a citation, fine, or penalty.

---

(12) DISSOLUTION:

Refer to the following provisions to answer the questions below:

RMBCA §§14.05, 14.06, 14.07

For further help, please refer to the following sections in the Text:

Text §§9A-300, 9A-500

A Corp wants to acquire T Corp. T Corp. manufactures and sells medical devices. Its main product is a metal replacement knee-joint.

The two boards decide that the acquisition should take the form of an asset purchase because T Corp has potential contingent liabilities for the medical devices it has manufactured and sold. These potential liabilities are difficult to predict and quantify and would make pricing the transaction problematic unless the parties excluded them from the acquisition. A Corp will purchase T Corp's assets, but will not assume any of its liabilities.

In the transaction, T Corp sold all of its assets to A Corp. In exchange, A Corp. received 10,000,000 shares of A Corp. common stock.

After the transaction with A Corp had been completed, T Corp began the process of dissolving, liquidating its assets, and distributing the 10,000,000 shares of A Corp stock to the T Corp shareholders. T Corp has 100,000 shareholders, none of whom holds more than 0.5% of T Corp's outstanding stock.

T Corp has some known creditors.

How should T Corp deal with these known creditors?

There might be other persons with claims against T Corp that T Corp is unaware of.

How should T Corp deal with these potential claims?

Five years after the dissolution and liquidation of T Corp, it has become clear that their metal knee joints are defective.

Please discuss who will bear the liability for the defective metal knee joints T Corp. sold before its sale of assets and dissolution? (assume the statute of limitations for the warranty claims and products liability claims have not expired)

---

(13) HOSTILE TAKEOVER:

Refer to the following sections in the Text to help you answer the questions below:

Text §9A-404(d)

Company X and Target Co. are both public companies.

Company X approached the board of directors of Target Co., proposing a merger between the two companies where Company X would be the surviving corporation.

Target's board rejected the proposal. In response, Company X made a tender offer for a majority of the common stock of Target Co. for $42 per share. For the four months immediately preceding the tender offer, Target Co.'s common stock had been trading at price between $35 and $45 per share. In the week immediately preceding the tender offer, Target Co.'s common stock had been trading at price between $37 and $40 per share.

In response to the tender offer, Target Co.'s board amended the bylaws to allow the annual shareholders meeting to occur earlier than in previous years. The board also passed a resolution to convene the annual shareholders meeting in 14 days. Notice of the annual meeting was provided to shareholders within the prescribed statutory time.

Why would the board respond to the tender offer by calling for an early annual meeting?

Can the board do this?

WORKBOOK

CHAPTER 10

PROTECTING CREDITORS

CHAPTER 10 – EXERCISES:

---

(1) THE BALANCE SHEET:

Refer to the following sections in the Text to help you answer the questions below:

Text §10A-201 et seq.

When the company acquired the factory building, how much did it cost?

What is the book value of the company's equipment? What is the relationship between book value and fair market value?

If the fair market value of the company's land is $300,000, how would that appear on the balance sheet?

The company signs a long-term contract that it expects will be very profitable. Its shareholders are very happy. Does this contract appear on the balance sheet?

The company has used a full month of utilities, but has not yet paid for them. Where would this appear on the balance sheet?

The company enters into a contract to purchase goods, but has not yet paid or received the goods? Would this be a liability on the balance sheet?

If an investor invested $20,000 cash in exchange for shares in the company, where would this amount appear on the balance sheet? Hint: two places

If a company made a profit last year and did not distribute it to the shareholders, where would this profit appear on the balance sheet?

See balance sheet on next page

BALANCE SHEET for XYZ Inc. – Dec. 31, 20xx:

ASSETS:	
Current assets:	
Cash	217,500
Accounts receivable	71,000
Raw materials inventory	1,700
Finished goods inventory	27,000
Prepaid utilities	600
Total current assets:	317,800
Land, plant & equipment:	
Land	120,000
Factory	40,000
Less depreciation	6,000
Factory equipment	20,000
Less depreciation	3,719
Total land, plant & equipment:	170,281
TOTAL ASSETS:	**488,081**

LIABILITIES:	
Current liabilities:	
Accounts payable	20,000
Rent payable	600
Utilities payable	1,200
Wages payable	5,800
Income tax payable	44,070
Property tax payable	2,100
Total current liabilities:	73,770
Non-current liabilities:	
Loan payable	8,971
Total non-current liabilities:	8,971
TOTAL LIABILITIES:	**82,741**
OWNERS' EQUITY	
Capital (700 shares, par value $1)	700
Additional paid-in capital	220,300
Retained earnings	184,340
TOTAL OWNERS' EQUITY:	**405,340**
TOTAL LIABILITIES & OWNERS EQUITY:	**488,081**

(2) THE DIVIDEND 1:

Refer to the following sections in the Text to help you answer the questions below:

Text §10A-200 et seq.

Answer the questions in this exercise based on the **balance sheet of XYZ Inc.** provided in Exercise 1, above, and the **income statement of XYZ Inc.** provided immediately below:

INCOME STATEMENT for XYZ Inc. – Jan. 1 to Dec. 31, 20xx:

Revenue:	527,000
Costs of goods sold:	352,000
Gross profit	175,000
Overhead expenses:	
Rent Expense	7,200
Wages	34,000
Depreciation	2,125
Interest expense	1,200
Total overhead:	44,525
Loss on sale of equipment	(1,500)
INCOME BEFORE TAXES:	128,975
Income taxes:	45,141
NET INCOME:	**83,834**

(a) What is the maximum dividend the company could issue under the **earned surplus test**?

(b) What is the maximum dividend the company could issue under the **capital surplus test**?

(c) If the balance sheet showed no capital surplus and no earned surplus, what would be the maximum dividend the company could issue under the **nimble dividend test**?

(d) If the company were in a jurisdiction that used an **insolvency test** similar to RMBCA §6.40, what numbers on the financial statements would the CFO and accountants examine to help them determine the dividend the company could issue?

---

(3) <u>THE DIVIDEND 2:</u>

Refer to the following provisions to answer the questions below:

RMBCA §2.02(b)(4)

For further help, please refer to the following sections in the Text:

Text §10A-203

The company placed the following in provision in its article of incorporation:

> The directors will not be personally liable to the corporation for any unlawful distributions approved by the board.

Is this provision valid?

---

(4) <u>CONTRACTUAL PROTECTION OF CREDITORS:</u>

Refer to the following sections in the Text to help you answer the questions below:

Text §10A-102

Explain why Lender would want each of these covenants? How do they protect Lender?

Why would Borrower want the various exceptions that are in some of the covenants?

Why would Lender allow Borrower to have those exceptions?

Article 4: Borrower's Affirmative Covenants

For as long Borrower has not paid in full any amount payable under this Loan Agreement, the Borrower shall, and shall cause each of its Subsidiaries, to:

A. Preserve and maintain in full force its corporate or organizational existence and take all reasonable action to maintain all qualifications, licenses, rights, privileges and franchises necessary or desirable in the normal conduct of its business, except to the extent that failure to do so would not reasonably be expected to have a Material Adverse Effect.

B. Maintain and preserve in good working order and condition all of its property that is necessary or useful for its business, except for ordinary wear and tear.

C. Maintain insurance with respect to its property and business in amounts and covering risks that are consistent with similar companies engaged in the same or a similar business.

D. Comply with all obligations under its various contracts except to the extent where failure to comply would not individually or in the aggregate reasonably be expected to have a Material Adverse Effect.

E. Comply with all legal requirements applicable to its business except where failure to comply would not individually or in the aggregate reasonably be expected to have a Material Adverse Effect.

F. Permit Lender, or its agents, to visit and inspect any of its properties to examine its books and records and to discuss its business operations and financial condition with its officers, and employees, and its independent public accountants.

Article 5: Borrower's Negative Covenants

For as long Borrower has not paid in full any amount payable under this Loan Agreement, the Borrower shall not, and shall not cause or allow each of its Subsidiaries, to:

A. Enter into any business, directly or indirectly, except for those businesses the Borrower and its Subsidiaries are engaged in as of the date of this Loan Agreement and businesses that are reasonably related to the businesses the Borrower and its Subsidiaries are engaged in as of the date of this Loan Agreement.

B. Create, incur, or otherwise become liable with respect to any Debt, except (i) trade payables, accounts payable, and accrued expenses incurred in the ordinary course of business and not due more than 90 days after the date on which each was created, and (ii) Debt incurred to finance the acquisition, construction or improvement of fixed or capital assets; provided, however that the Debt incurred does not exceed the purchase price or the construction costs of the asset being financed.

C. Become a general partner in any general or limited partnership or joint venture.

D. (i) Undertake any merger or consolidation, (ii) liquidate, wind-up or dissolve itself, (iii) sell, convey, transfer, assign, or otherwise dispose of substantially all of its assets and Properties in one transaction or in a series of transactions, voluntarily or involuntarily, or (iv) acquire all or substantially all of the assets constituting a business, division, branch or other unit of operation of any Person.

E. Dispose of any of its property, whether now owned or later acquired, to any Person, except (i) the sale or disposition of machinery and equipment no longer used or useful in the business; (ii) the disposition of obsolete or worn-out property in the ordinary course of business; or (iii) the sale of inventory in the ordinary course of business.

F. Declare or pay any dividend on, make any payment on account of, or set apart assets or accounts for the purchase, redemption, defeasance, retirement or other acquisition of any Equity Interests of the Borrower or any of their respective Subsidiaries, or make any other distribution with respect to any Equity Interest, either directly or indirectly, whether in cash or property or in obligations.

G. Enter into or be a party to any transaction including any purchase, sale, lease or exchange of property, the rendering of any service or the payment of any management, advisory or similar fees, with any director, officer, Control Person, or other Related Person unless such transaction is in the ordinary course of business and on fair and reasonable terms that Borrower could have obtained in a comparable transaction and on an arm's length basis from an unrelated Person.

---

(5) INSOLVENCY:

Refer to the following sections in the Text to help you answer the questions below:

Text Chapter 6, §6A-210(c)

XYZ Corp. is insolvent. The board of directors is considering two different projects. The board can only invest in one project.

Project A: An investment of $1 million dollars. A 70% chance of an investment return of 25%.

Project B: An investment of $1 million dollars. A 97% chance of an investment return of 10%.

Which project should the board take?

Assuming the above estimates are accurate and can be proven, do the board's fiduciary duties require it to take one opportunity over the other?

---

(6) PIERCING THE LIMITED LIABILITY VEIL 1:

Refer to the following sections in the Text to help you answer the questions below:

Text §§10C-200, 10A-300 et seq.

Explain the purpose of the following provision from RULLCA § 304:

> (b) The failure of a limited liability company to observe any particular formalities relating to the exercise of its powers or management of its activities is not a ground for imposing liability on the members or managers for the debts, obligations, or other liabilities of the company.

---

(7) PIERCING THE LIMITED LIABILITY VEIL 2:

Refer to the following sections in the Text to help you answer the questions below:

Text §10A-300 et seq.

Please read the facts of ***Kinney Shoe Corp. v. Polan*** and provide your analysis predicting whether the court would pierce the corporate veil.

Kinney Shoe Corp. v. Polan

939 F.2d 209 (1991)

Plaintiff-appellant Kinney Shoe Corporation ("Kinney") brought this action in the United States District Court for the Southern District of West Virginia against Lincoln M. Polan ("Polan") seeking to recover money owed on a sublease between Kinney and Industrial Realty Company ("Industrial"). Polan is the sole shareholder of Industrial. The district court found that Polan was not personally liable on the lease between Kinney and Industrial. . . .

. . . In 1984 Polan formed two corporations, Industrial and Polan Industries, Inc., for the purpose of re-establishing an industrial manufacturing business. The certificate of incorporation for Polan Industries, Inc. was issued by the West Virginia Secretary of State in November 1984. The following month the certificate of incorporation for Industrial was issued. Polan was the owner of both corporations. Although certificates of incorporation were issued, no organizational meetings were held, and no officers were elected.

In November 1984 Polan and Kinney began negotiating the sublease of a building in which Kinney held a leasehold interest. The building was owned by the Cabell County Commission and financed by industrial revenue bonds issued in 1968 to induce Kinney to locate a manufacturing plant in Huntington, West Virginia. Under the terms of the lease, Kinney was legally obligated to make payments on the bonds on a semi-annual basis through January 1, 1993, at which time it had the right to purchase the property. Kinney had ceased using the building as a manufacturing plant in June 1983.

The term of the sublease from Kinney to Industrial commenced in December 1984, even though the written lease was not signed by the parties until April 5, 1985. On April 15, 1985, Industrial subleased part of the building to Polan Industries for fifty percent of the rental amount due Kinney. Polan signed both subleases on behalf of the respective companies.

Other than the sublease with Kinney, Industrial had no assets, no income and no bank account. Industrial issued no stock certificates because nothing was ever paid in to this corporation. Industrial's only income was from its sublease to Polan Industries, Inc. The first rental payment to Kinney was made out of Polan's personal funds, and no further payments were made by Polan or by Polan Industries, Inc. to either Industrial or to Kinney.

Kinney filed suit against Industrial for unpaid rent and obtained a judgment in the amount of $166,400.00 on June 19, 1987. A writ of possession was issued, but because Polan Industries, Inc. had filed for bankruptcy, Kinney did not gain possession for six months. Kinney leased the building until it was sold on September 1, 1988. Kinney then filed this action against Polan individually to collect the amount owed by Industrial to Kinney. Since the amount to which Kinney is entitled is undisputed, the only issue is whether Kinney can pierce the corporate veil and hold Polan personally liable.

The district court held that Kinney had assumed the risk of Industrial's undercapitalization and was not entitled to pierce the corporate veil. . . .

It is undisputed that Industrial . . . had no paid in capital. Polan had put nothing into this corporation, and it did not observe any corporate formalities. . . .

In this case, Polan bought no stock, made no capital contribution, kept no minutes, and elected no officers for Industrial. . . .

---

(8) PIERCING THE LIMITED LIABILITY VEIL 3:

Refer to the following sections in the Text to help you answer the questions below:

Text §10A-300 et seq.

Please read the facts of ***Sea-Land v. Pepper Source*** and provide your analysis predicting whether the court would pierce the corporate veil.

Sea-Land Services Inc. v. Pepper Source
941 F.2d 519 (1991)

This spicy case finds its origin in several shipments of Jamaican sweet peppers. Appellee Sea–Land Services, Inc. ("Sea–Land"), an ocean carrier, shipped the peppers on behalf of The Pepper Source ("PS"), one of the appellants here. PS then stiffed Sea–Land on the freight bill, which was rather substantial. Sea–Land filed a federal diversity action for the money t was owed. On December 2, 1987, the district court entered a default judgment in favor of Sea–Land and against PS in the amount of $86,767.70. But PS was nowhere to be found; it had been "dissolved" in mid–1987 for failure to pay the annual state franchise tax. Worse yet for Sea–Land, even had it not been dissolved, PS apparently had no assets. With the well empty, Sea–Land could not recover its judgment against PS. Hence the instant lawsuit.

In June 1988, Sea–Land brought this action against Gerald J. Marchese and five business entities he owns: PS, Caribe Crown, Inc., Jamar Corp., Salescaster Distributors, Inc., and Marchese Fegan Associates. Marchese also was named individually. Sea–Land sought by this suit to pierce PS's corporate veil and render Marchese personally liable for the judgment owed to Sea–Land, and then "reverse pierce" Marchese's other corporations so that they, too, would be on the hook for the $87,000. Thus, Sea–Land alleged in its complaint that all of these corporations "are alter egos of each other and hide behind the veils of alleged separate corporate existence for the purpose of defrauding plaintiff and other creditors." . . . . Not only are the corporations alter egos of each other, alleged Sea–Land, but also they are alter egos of Marchese, who should be held individually liable for the judgment because he created and manipulated these corporations and their assets for his own personal uses. . . . (Hot on the heels of the filing of Sea–Land's complaint, PS took the necessary steps to be reinstated as a corporation in Illinois.)

In early 1989, Sea–Land filed an amended complaint adding Tie–Net International, Inc., as a defendant. Unlike the other corporate defendants, Tie–Net is not owned solely by Marchese: he holds half of the stock, and an individual named George Andre owns the other half. Sea–Land alleged that, despite this shared ownership, Tie–Net is but another alter ego of Marchese and the other corporate defendants, and thus it also should be held liable for the judgment against PS. . . .

. . . Marchese is the sole shareholder of PS, Caribe Crown, Jamar, and Salescaster. He is one of the two shareholders of Tie–Net. Except for Tie–Net, none of the corporations ever held a single corporate meeting. (At the handful of Tie–Net meetings held by Marchese and Andre, no minutes were taken.) During his deposition, Marchese did not remember any of these corporations ever passing articles of incorporation, bylaws, or other agreements. As for physical facilities, Marchese runs all of these corporations (including Tie–Net) out of the same, single office, with the same phone line, the same expense accounts, and the like. And how he does "run" the expense accounts! When he fancies to, Marchese "borrows" substantial sums of money from these corporations—interest free, of course. The corporations also "borrow" money from each other when need be, which left at least PS completely out of capital when the Sea–Land bills came due. What's more, Marchese has used the bank accounts of these corporations to pay all kinds of personal expenses, including alimony and child support payments to his ex-wife, education expenses for his children, maintenance of his personal automobiles, health care for his pet—the list goes on and on. Marchese did not even have a personal bank account! . . .

And Tie–Net is just as much a part of this as the other corporations. On appeal, Marchese makes much of the fact that he shares ownership of Tie–Net, and that Sea–Land has not been able to find an example of funds flowing from PS to Tie–Net to the detriment of Sea–Land and PS's other creditors. . . . The record reveals that . . . Marchese . . . "borrowed" over $30,000 from Tie–Net; money and "loans" flowed freely between Tie–Net and the other corporations; and Marchese charged up various personal expenses (including $460 for a picture of himself with President Bush) on Tie–Net's credit card. . . .

WORKBOOK

APPENDIX A

ACCOUNTING PRIMER

BALANCE SHEET OF XYZ CORP.
December 31, 20XX

Assets:	
Cash:	50,000
Accounts receivable:	2,000
Pre-paid expenses:	1,500
Inventory:	7,000
Equipment:	30,000
Less depreciation:	5,500
Building:	105,000
Less depreciation:	20,000
Land:	60,000
TOTAL ASSETS:	**230,000**
Liabilities:	
Accounts payable:	3,000
Rent payable:	4,000
Wages payable:	8,000
Advance payments:	2,000
Bank loan:	57,000
TOTAL LIABILITIES:	74,000
Owners' Equity:	
Capital:	1,000
Additional paid-in capital	99,000
Retained earnings:	56,000
TOTAL OWNER'S EQUITY:	156,000
TOTAL LIABILITIES AND OWNERS EQUITY:	**230,000**

INCOME STATEMENT OF XYZ CORP.
January 1 – December 31, 20XX

Revenues:	345,000
Costs of goods sold:	143,000
Gross profit (loss):	202,000
Other expenses:	
Wages:	102,000
Utilities:	9,500
Depreciation	7,000
Rent	52,000
Advertising	1,000
Interest on bank loan	3,000
Other gains (losses):	(1,500)
Income (loss) before income tax:	26,000
Income tax:	5,000
NET INCOME (LOSS):	**21,000**

CASH FLOW STATEMENT OF XYZ CORP.
January 1 – December 31, 20XX

Cash flow from operating activities:	
Cash from customers:	349,000
Cash used for operations:	310,000
Net cash from operations:	39,000
Cash flow from investing activities:	
Cash from investing:	1,000
Cash used for investing:	4,500
Net cash from investing:	(3,500)
Cash flow from financing activities:	
Cash from financing:	10,000
Cash used for financing:	6,000
Net cash from financing:	4,000
Net increase in cash:	39,500
Cash at beginning of period:	10,500
Cash at end of period:	50,000

APPENDIX A – EXERCISES:

---

(1) THE BALANCE SHEET:

Please refer to the balance sheet of XYZ Corp., above. Answer the following questions:

(A) What is the book value (i.e., balance sheet value) of the company's building? What is the market value of the building? (See Text §§A-102(d). A-102(f), A-204(a) for help).

(B) How much has the company's equipment depreciated since the company acquired the equipment? (See Text §§A-102(f), A-201, A-204(a) for help).

(C) How much money do customers owe the company? (See Text §§A-102(d), A-201, A-204(a) for help).

(D) How much money does the company owe suppliers? (See Text §§A-102(g), A-201, A-204(a) for help).

(E) What is the remaining principal on the bank loan? (See Text §§A-102(g), A-201, A-204(a) for help).

(F) How much money have the owners invested in the company over the years? (See Text §§A-201, A-204(a) for help).

(G) Where is the balance sheet's representation of the residual claim? What is the dollar number? (See Text §§A-102(h), A-201, A-204(a) for help).

(H) Where is the balance sheet's representation of the fixed claim? What is the dollar number? (See Text §§A-102(g), A-201, A-204(a) for help).

(I) The company entered into a contract with a customer. The customer promised to buy $500 worth of products from the company. Currently, the company has not yet delivered the products to the customer and the customer has not yet paid. Would this $500 contract appear on the balance sheet at this time? If so, under what item(s)? (See Text §§A-102(d), A-201, A-204(a) for help).

(J) The company entered into a contract with a customer. The customer promised to buy $100 worth of products from the company and immediately paid the $100 in cash to the company. Currently, the company has not yet delivered the products to the customer. Would this $100 transaction appear on the balance sheet at this time? If so, under what item(s)? (See Text §§A-102(d), A-201, A-204(a) for help).

(K) The company entered into a contract to purchase raw materials from a supplier for $700. The supplier has already delivered the raw materials to the company. The company has not yet paid. Would this $700 transaction appear on the balance sheet at this time? If so, under what item(s)? (See Text §§A-102(g), A-201, A-204(a) for help).

(L) The company entered into a contract to purchase raw materials from a supplier for $1,200. The company has made a $600 down payment. The supplier has not yet delivered the raw materials to the company. Would this $600 transaction appear on the balance sheet at this time? If so, under what item(s)? (See Text §§A-102(g), A-201, A-204(a) for help).

(M) The company borrows $10,000 dollars from the bank. The company has signed the loan agreement and the bank has transferred the money to the company's account. Would this $10,000 transaction appear on the balance sheet at this time? If so, under what item(s)? (See Text §§A-102(g), A-201, A-204(a) for help).

---

(2) <u>THE INCOME STATEMENT:</u>

Please refer to the income statement of XYZ Corp., above. Answer the following questions:

(A) Assume the company is a merchandiser of shoes. It purchases shoes from suppliers and re-sells them to customers. The company sold shoes to customers – total selling price was $345,000 – during the year. How much did it cost for the company to acquire the shoes it sold? (See Text §§A-102(e), A-202, A-204(b) for help).

(B) Near the end of the year, the company sold a $200 pair of shoes to a customer, who agreed to pay next year. The customer took the shoes home. Is this $200 sale included in the revenue on the income statement? (See Text §§A-102(a), A-202, A-204(b) for help).

The company purchased these shoes from a supplier for $120. Is the $120 included in the cost of goods sold on the income statement? (See Text §§A-202, A-204(b) for help).

(C) Near the end of the year, a customer made a down payment of $50 for a pair of shoes priced at $150. The company promised put the shoes to the side and deliver them next year when the customer finished paying. Is either the $50 or $150 included in the revenue on the income statement? (See Text §§A-102(a), A-202, A-204(b) for help).

(3) <u>THE CASH FLOW STATEMENT:</u>

Please refer to the cash flow statement of XYZ Corp., above. Answer the following questions:

(A) Does the cash flow statement tell us the following: how much cash the company received from goods the company delivered to customers during the period the cash flow statement covers? (See Text §§A-203, A-204(c) for help).

(B) Assuming the company did not take out any loans during the year, what does the $10,000 under "Cash from financing" represent? (See Text §§A-203, A-204(c) for help).

(C) The company sold some old equipment for $1,000. Where is this transaction reflected on the cash flow statement? When it sold the equipment, the book value of the equipment (i.e., cost of acquisition less depreciation) was $2,500. Would the $1,500 loss appear on the cash flow statement? (See Text §§A-203, A-204(c) for help).

(4) HOW THE FINANCIAL STATEMENTS MOVE TOGETHER:

These problems are more advanced. Try your best.

Please refer to the financial statements of XYZ Corp., above.

Imagine you are the comptroller for XYZ Corp. You have prepared the company's financial statements as presented above. At the last minute, one of your bookkeepers claims to have found records of transactions that were not included in the financial statements you just completed

Your job is to incorporate the transactions into the three financial statements by changing all the numbers that need to be changed. You do not need to change the various subtotals and totals, as long as you understand that they will change if you make revisions to any of the other numbers.

(A) Bookkeeper: "We forgot to include one credit sale that occurred at the end of the year. We sold a pair of shoes to a customer for $200 on 30 days credit. Because the sale happened near the end of the year, the customer had not yet paid at the year's end.

The records show that we acquired those shoes from the supplier for $100 cash. We also forgot to record that transaction"

(B) Bookkeeper: "Oops, my bad. Did I say that we made a credit sale for $200 [in A, immediately above]. Actually, I just found the proper records. It was a cash sale for $200."

(C) Bookkeeper: "We forgot to include a transaction with a new investor during the year. We issued 1,000 shares to Ms. Investor in exchange for $10,000."

CPSIA information can be obtained
at www.ICGtesting.com
Printed in the USA
LVOW09s1359150817
545097LV00011B/186/P

9 781600 422836